C000111111

A NEW THEORY FOR AMERICAN POETRY

A New Theory for American Poetry

Democracy, the Environment, and the Future of Imagination

ANGUS FLETCHER

Harvard University Press
Cambridge, Massachusetts, and London, England · 2004

Printed in the United States of America

Library of Congress Cataloging-in-Publication Data
Fletcher, Angus, 1930–
A new theory for American poetry : democracy, the environonment, and the future of imagination / Angus Fletcher.
p. cm.
Includes bibliographical references and index.
1. American poetry—History and criticism—Theory, etc. 2. Whitman, Walt, 1819–1892—Influence. 3. Clare, John, 1793–1964—Influence. 4. Environmental protection in literature. 5. Ashbery, John—Influence. 6. Democracy in literature. 7. Ecology in literature. 8. Nature in literature. 9. Imagination. I. Title.

PS303.F58 2003
811.009—dc21
2003056645

To my dear wife, Michelle

Acknowledgments

My work on environmental poetics and on John Clare was greatly helped by a Senior Fellowship from the National Endowment for the Humanities, awarded in 1995, and I wish to record my thanks for this support. In 2001, Michael Warner invited me to lecture on Whitman at the English Institute, and his timely invitation provided the nucleus of this book, my chapter "The Whitman Phrase." Over the years various colleagues have been a particular source of inspiration, chief among them John Hollander and Harold Bloom. On forays in the West I have learned much from Harry Berger, Jr. (University of California at Santa Cruz) and James Crutchfield (Santa Fe Institute). At my home institution, Joan Richardson of the CUNY Graduate School has unfailingly shared her ideas and her pragmatic support, and I am especially pleased to thank her.

Other friends have variously enlightened and encouraged me over the years: Paul Bray, Kenneth Gross, Susan Kelly, Jerome Mazzaro, Mitchell Meltzer, Derek Miller, David Rooney, Gordon Teskey, my brother Peter Fletcher. I am deeply indebted to all these professors of good cheer. This acknowledgment allows me to record an important moment in my earlier studies of the environment. One afternoon my oldest brother, Donald, a newspaper journalist, showed me the operations of a small ecosystem in the woods bordering his Connecticut home; this demonstration, which gave him serious pleasure, left a powerful impression on me. I miss him now, thinking that had he lived, he would have appreciated the strivings of this book.

Marie-Ross Logan, the distinguished editor of *Annals of Scholarship,* has particularly helped me in my studies of the poetry of John Ashbery, and I am most grateful to the *Arizona Quarterly* and my hosts at the University of Arizona, especially Edgar Dryden and Suresh Ravel, for asking me to speak about Ashbery at the annual Colloquium on American Literature. An early version of Ch. 12 appeared in *Murmur,* 2, no. 1 (1998).

The poems of John Clare quoted in their entirety, *The Mouse's Nest, School Boys in Winter, Autumn, and Salters Tree,* are reproduced with permission of Curtis Brown Ltd., London on behalf of Eric Robinson. Copyright Eric Robinson, 1984 and 1989. I am grateful to Mr. J. D. McClatchy and to The Literary Estate of James Merrill at Washington University for permission to quote from "Scripts for the Pageant" (1980). To John Hollander and to the publisher, Alfred Knopf Inc., I am grateful for permission to quote "A Theory of Waves" in its entirety, from Hollander, *Selected Poetry* (1993). To John Ashbery I extend my warmest thanks for permission to quote excerpts from a number of his poems, drawn from a number of his books. Quotations from *Flow Chart,* copyright © 1991 by John Ashbery, are reprinted by permission of Georges Borchardt, Inc. The poem "From cocoon forth a butterfly" is reprinted by permission of the publishers and the Trustees of Amherst College from *The Poems of Emily Dickinson,* Ralph W. Franklin, ed., Cambridge, Mass.: The Belknap Press of Harvard University Press, copyright © 1988 by the President and Fellows of Harvard College. Copyright © 1951, 1955, 1979 by the President and Fellows of Harvard College. "Papyrus" (a four-word fragment) by Ezra Pound, from *Personae,* copyright © 1926 by Ezra

Pound, is used by permission of New Directions Publishing Corporation.

Encouragement of a particularly critical and practical kind came to me from the Dactyl Foundation of New York and from its directors, Victoria Alexander and Neil Grayson, and to them I owe a very special debt of gratitude. Throughout the various stages of the writing of this book, Lindsay Waters has, as before with a previous book, made my task not only intellectually demanding but more entertaining than I would have thought possible. It would be hard to say how much I owe to his friendship, his intellectual challenge, and his practical advice. My editor, Anita Safran, has once again saved me from a range of stylistic and formal slip-ups, and I am delighted to acknowledge her skill, and her patience. Finally, I want to thank my wife, Michelle, who in so many ways has contributed to the writing of this book, not least conceptually. My dedication of this book expresses only a small part of my gratitude.

Contents

A NEW THEORY FOR AMERICAN POETRY

Introduction

"I greet you at the beginning of a great career, which yet must have had a long foreground somewhere, for such a start." The letter, to Walt Whitman, was dated July 21, 1855. Ever since Emerson wrote this famous greeting and prophetic commendation on the appearance of *Leaves of Grass,* Americans have known that they had a truly revolutionary poetic voice, from which there could be no turning back. Whitman's practice revolutionizing American poetry always discovered, hence revealed, an almost animal wildness, barbaric (to use Whitman's word) when compared with European models or antecedents. Understandably, his later imitators have frequently produced failed simulacra, and the Emersonian lesson remained a hard one, for he saw that our literature could not be officially Romantic. His early lectures declaring our poetic independence could only propose a culture moving away from European tradition, and when *Leaves of Grass* broke radically with earlier models, it broke also with High Romanticism. After 1855, the task of growing into poetic freedom became our long and still unfinished journey outward, to which this book dedicates its own adventure.

To be sure, important critics have held that the spirit of Romantic poetry still informs our thoughts, recycling the Revolution. Think only of Hart Crane and Wallace Stevens with their followers in the twentieth century, and this view seems irresistible! Nevertheless, I believe the Romantic claim obscures an artistic problem—in truth there is a deeper, a more truly underlying strain of English poetry that both precedes and grounds English Romanticism and later subtends for us what Emerson called the transcendental and the extraordinary in our American poetic vision. This earlier strain we might understand as the *beginning* of American genius. Our pragmatic tendencies (always in strife with religious beliefs, with irrational pseudo-scientific dogmas) underlie an essentially pragmatist American literature, swerving away from the Romantic tradition, drawing back to an alternative poetics, which in the eighteenth century was called "descriptive poetry."

While common sense might suggest there is something unpoetic about descriptions, which are tied to representing facts and factual conditions, one basic principle of my approach is that if the poet is able to transfigure the facts and express this transfiguration without losing their perceived quality, the poetry will always retain a measure of transcendental value. By means of an unprecedented descriptive technique, Whitman gave Americans and the world the model for an authentic voice. Unlike many in power today, he took seriously the notion of the public trust. Thinking simultaneously of both environment and democracy, he was to say that he wanted "a readjustment of the whole theory and nature of poetry."[1]

Most critics of Whitman's art have noted his lifelong involvement with spiritual transcendence, and yet his transcendental powers derive from an inspired, highly elliptical pragmatism. This characteristically American philosophic method concerns the doing of things and the taking of actions, unlike poetry, which concerns a making of verbal artifacts. Doing (*praxis*) and making (*poesis*) are not the same, although one of our great critics, Kenneth Burke, often thought in rhetorical terms when he spoke of "symbolic action." The mere mention of pragmatism, with its secondary Jamesian emphasis on belief, raises philosophic issues which here lead to a question: how shall we deal with the apparent ordinariness, the factual simplicity or complexity of descriptive accounts? Surely they almost want *not* to be inspired. In one sense, this whole book seeks to illuminate this artistic problem. In fact, although description might seem antithetical to poetic imagination, we will find it is as close to electricity and lightning as poetry needs to be. Poetry can describe in ways that are extremely powerful, although, like all artistic styles, this one has an attendant risk—it may suck the poet down into prosy unmusical chatter, poetic only according to its label. Instead, the poetry I celebrate is alive with a strong tension between verse and prose, as it is alive with unexpected, often extravagant personal response, reminding us that with a truly expressive literature the reader is experiencing the immense resources of language itself. In discursive prose of all kinds this wealth is manifest in the power of words to represent the inflections of the natural and the human world, and especially of our thoughts, theories, and evaluations of that world. Such representing powers are nowhere more evident than in the fields of science and philosophy, although scientists who use mathematics as what Galileo called the "language of science" always question the idealizing or qualitative tendencies of philosophic language. If we turn to poetry, we may equally question both the powers and the constraints operating upon poetry when it seeks to represent the world around us.

Since this study intends a broad cultural relevance, it may be asked, why focus on poetry rather than the prose discourse of environment? My claim is that while the literature of prose naturalism is extremely rich and culturally influential—consider Thoreau or Darwin—poetry takes environmentalist concerns to a higher level, at least in one respect. Unlike most prose discourse, poetry expresses close personal involvements, and hence pertains to the way we humans respond, on our own, to environmental matters.

This poetic emphasis on the "Person" (Walt Whitman's name for the individual citizen) is furthermore a peculiarly American problem, in that while we seek democratic groupings and articulations, we as a people are dedicated to valuing the individual citizen possessing rights and obligations. An art like poetry that enhances the presence of the individual is bound to be central in showing how we should understand our environmental rights and obligations. The issue then is this, what is my own response to my surrounding? If, as I believe, such questions are now more than ever essential to furthering a general cultural benefit, there is every reason to examine our most intense personal expressions alongside the norms of scientific discourse, whether in prose or mathematical form.

Furthermore, if Whitman is correct in thinking that poetry is elemental for democracy, then it follows that on the cultural plane the intensifying art of poetic expression must for us always remain a compelling, if not best-selling, political problem. This art gives voice to the unbreakable link between nature and humanity, since poetry, our imaginative making, seems to participate in nature. There is no more striking index to the nature of poetic language, as distinct from discursive language, than the fact that poetry seems unable to exert its expressive and representing powers without using naturalistic terms. What we usually call poetic imagery tends to be derived from myriad fundamental images of nature, such as the rising moon or setting sun, rushing rivers, wind-blown branches of trees, and all the distinctive movements and appearances of animals. We are nature's fabulists, and it seems that no poet can write strongly without recourse to natural imagery. Typically, for American poetry one imaginative excursion takes the poet into the Wild, or, closer to home, to that "civil wilderness" Emily Dickinson discovered in her own back yard.

Both exegesis and evaluation of Romantic poetry have emphasized the poet's role as voiced consciousness, in this dynamic relation between nature and our species, but the present study takes almost the opposite view, while never denying our human need for transcendental and extraordinary flights of the imagination. It could be argued that a substratum of naturalistic study and description is determining for the Romantics, but remains often obscured by clouds of glory, whereas American poetry meets a new scale of *things,* a larger scale. The Americans are somehow troubled by the fact that Nature is simply bigger than we are, so that by artificial means we must acquire the same magnitude. Given these contrasts, my concern has been to promote the determining role of nature, even when poets have transcendental goals. Indeed, I would hold that the most factual of relations to nature give rise to a new form of the transcendental, namely the gnomic expression of immanent transcendence. John Burroughs, the naturalist, remarked once that among the eminent poets of our language, those most friendly to science were Emerson and Whitman. The former especially was aroused by the science of physics. The bold realism of science, with its willingness to change positions, inspires the truly original American poets, nor does this delight prevent them from larger philosophic speculations. It is as if in this way the Americans were able to start over and to reject the burdensome theological historicity of Puritanism, treating the vast land mass as if it were a disordered laboratory. In turn, the tragedy of this wild, aggressive, natural exploitation led the best of our poets, like Whitman himself, to cultivate a visionary reserve, masking fervor beneath the gnomic phrase.

Nothing could be stranger than our best poetry, thus the argument of the ensuing pages demonstrates some quite unexpected fundamental properties of Whitman's revolution, while showing how they contribute to his famed acquisition of voice, his lyrical expression of new perceptual experiences. Beneath the formal division of the book into fourteen chapters, there are six main parts to the theory. We begin with the *concept of horizon,* which implies the immediate boundary to any environment. Next, the argument turns to the broad question of *the poet's way of being in the world,* when this world is defined as an ecological surrounding. Then, concentrating on Whitman, my central chapters develop a dynamic theory of *poetry as environmental form.* A fourth main division of the theory shows *the power of underlying rhythms* in this unique poetry. A fifth section of the whole account is devoted to the exemplary work of John Ashbery, treating him as a philosopher of *the poetry of becoming.* Finally, in sixth place I show how a *theory of coherence* yields the value-system of the bonding of literature and environment. In these various senses, then, the theory may be understood to proceed according to a six-fold sequence of connected chapters, of which the cardinal one is the sixth, "The Whitman Phrase," where I show how the poet's radical use of the suspended grammatical phrase gives rise to large and utterly unprecedented poetic forms. With this formal invention, even more extreme than Longfellow's obsessive use of the formulas of ancient Scandinavian poetry, Whitman implemented his own call for prophetically reimagining American poetry. In 1871, as we shall see, he authorized his own practice by saying that our democracy implied an artistic revolution: "there must imperatively come a readjustment of the whole theory and nature of poetry." In this he followed Emerson's piece-by-piece technique of composing lyric essays. Most important, the phrase is used as a democratic device, but to grasp how this method can have such political force, we need to rethink a part of literary history, radiating outwards into various general questions about poetic form. Above all, at all points this book began with reflections on Whitman.

Fourteen Doors Opening Outward

The whole consists of fourteen chapters that will hopefully resemble William James's house, of which his sister Alice recalled him saying: "It's the most delightful house you ever saw; it has fourteen doors, all opening outwards."

Here the first door opens out on the concept of imaginative horizon, which it derives anecdotally from an episode in the life of the peasant poet, John Clare, who lived in English fen country during the early nineteenth century.[2] Horizon is critical to this study, because it indicates the shape of a meeting ground between imaginative and perceptual vision. This is the question elicited in Keats's sonnet, "On First Looking Into Chapman's Homer," where an actual horizon is juxtaposed to the imaginative limit of a wild romantic surmise. Despite common interests in nature, the poets I deal with, unlike Keats, tend to focus on actual horizons and only secondarily on surmised boundaries of thought. They remain sharply conscious of the extended real world, whose materiality tempers the Romantic surmise. For poets like Clare, Whitman, and Ashbery horizon is a guide to natural constraints, necessary to any critical reading of the surrounding natural environment.

Chapter 2 introduces the idea of poetic description, perceived initially as a Presocratic response to whole manifolds in nature. Without being caught up in quasi-religious ideas of the End, the Purpose, the *telos* of nature, this early scientific philosophy sees things in large holistic terms. The Presocratics were wont to say such things as "All is fire," "All is water," or indeed that all is one element or other, thereby insisting on the priority of a holistic response to Nature. The sense of encircling natural manifold leads to a poetic principle whereby the poem is always searching for methods of containment, such as the heroic couplet in Augustan English verse. The fate of description then is a search for simultaneous perception of the surrounding circle of our material being, disciplined by the need to show free play within this circle of contending forces.

Chapter 3 defines description as such, showing its relation to the familiar, that with which we are acquainted. It also shows that if the poet is to describe Nature, then Nature must pose for the depiction. A new question arises when any natural scene so tumbles about in wildness that the poem must try for the improbably picturesque effect of describing the nondescript. This paradox gets more detailed treatment in Chapter 4, where I introduce the special relation between John Ashbery and John Clare, departing from Ashbery's Norton Lecture on his predecessor. Ashbery showed how Clare discovered his unique vision and poetic art simply by making his virtually chaotic rounds as naturalist, wandering without any predetermined plan or design to follow a Platonic order in nature. A contrast is drawn between the high transcendentalism and epistemological questionings of Wordsworth and the direct, Presocratic, immanent, naturalist metaphysics of Clare. The former leads to sublime aesthetics, the latter to a method of animated descriptive precision.

If this second poetic art is not Romantic, if it too needs a matching intensity of expression, the argument requires that a new sort of knowledge, a poetic wisdom, emerge from the complex process of visionary description. This is the topic in Chapter 5, where *diurnal knowledge* is the awareness of the daily, quotidian round of life, to be distinguished from the news of each day as chronicled by the journalist. Unlike the poet, the journalist—who today uses the cant expression "at the end of the day" which has nothing to do with day's endings—writes of each single day in fact to ensure that each day's news disappears into oblivion as fast as possible. Diurnal knowledge connects to the major traditional extension of diurnal time, namely, the myth and fact of the changing seasons, often rendered as an undated yearly calendar. In the modern terms of Complexity Theory, the myth of the eternal return is represented as a continuous emergence of order from any chaotic beginning.

Chapter 6 develops the temporality and grammar of expressing such emergent orders, but it also relates Whitman's revolutionary poetic discoveries by connecting him to the rapid changes we often call "Jacksonian democracy." With Jackson's presidency a new American leveling occurs, inherently opposed to the hierarchical political tendencies envisioned by the Founding Fathers. By means of the phrase, which is inherently a democratizing unit of language, this new poetic art permits a pragmatic vision of the natural and social environment. The democratic paradox, *e pluribus unum,* is a challenge even to Whitman, as he urges the eagle of liberty to soar! Some scholars, including the hermetic Harold Bloom and the Derridean Tenney Nathanson, have found Whitman to be less the poet of democracy than he always claimed; instead, their Whitman aims chiefly to project his own rare selfhood, "the me myself." From my perspective, such views narrow or constrain Whitman's authentic quest, which I take to be the central issue for democracy: how are self and community to interact with each other? Pursuing this quest, accepting the ambiguities of his own sexuality, Whitman invented poetic forms that honor a more egalitarian democracy, while these forms reveal poetic methods of intensifying, not dulling our experience.

So extreme in method is this new art, quite unlike the traditional mastery of a Longfellow or Bryant, that we discover in the view of Chapter 7 how environmental sensitivity demands its own new genre of poetry. This I am calling the *environment-poem,* a genre where the poet neither writes *about* the surrounding world, thematizing it, nor analytically represents that world, but actually shapes the poem to *be* an Emersonian or esemplastic circle. Deeply influenced by Emerson, in Whitman's case, these environment-poems aspire to surround the reader, such that to read them is to have an experience much like suddenly recognizing that one actually has an environment, instead of not perceiving the surround at all.

Chapter 8 shows how Whitman develops not only an iconography of the wave and of wave forms, but uses this symbolism to structure the undulant forms of virtually all his poems in *Leaves of Grass.* All poetry seeks verbal intensifiers. Here the intensity chiefly arises, scholars have shown, from the extreme prominence given to the present participial phrase-unit. From antecedent literary models such as the prose-poetry of Ossian, the Whitman rhapsody, perpetually liminal, acquires a Thoreauvian wildness.[3]

Chapter 9 moves the argument deeper into grammar, by showing that if Whitman (and other poets genuinely like him) are to achieve their natural vibrancy, they have to adopt the middle voice, where the expression deliberately evades the polarities of active and passive and builds on an implicit *interest* of the speaker in whatever he or she says, without falling prey to a language of gross activity or passivity. Instead, this poetry voices neutral awareness, an initial acceptance of the fact of a surrounding. The expression censors no such fact, and hence remains free to produce a deeper criticism. The middle voice speaks for a continuous, ever changing reciprocity between nature and humankind. Grammatically, the middle voice expresses participation.

Chapters 10, 11, and 12 carry this Whitman poetic forward into our own time, with an extended discussion of the work of John Ashbery. Chapter 10 analyzes this poet's work in relation to the ancient philosophic question of the being and becoming of things. This perspective leads to the question: how does the poet of becoming achieve animated description if not by using metonymy, the locating figure, as opposed to metaphor, the classifying figure? The chapter accounts for Ashbery's important relation to Boris Pasternak, by means of metonymic interpretations given by the linguist Roman Jakobson.

Chapter 11 shifts to a different theoretical angle, and shows how the new science of Complexity Theory illuminates Ashbery's poetic practice. This theory broaches the problem of adaptive systems—living systems, we might say—and therefore gives a picture of living networks that advances upon the organic theorems of Romantic aesthetics. Familiar ecological examples of a complex system are the weather or the turbulence of a stream of water flowing in the wild, and their apparent relation to chaos is what readers have long noticed about form in Whitman's poems, and more recently, with Ashbery. This chapter explains wherein resides the shaping of meditation for an Ashbery poem, taking it to be paradigmatic for our time.

To show how such structures of change support the extensions of Ashbery's long poem *Flow Chart,* Chapter 12 introduces the relation of form to *scale,* which has also always been a central issue for ecological science. Here the wavy lines of meditation in *Flow Chart* gather into an emergent closure by means of Ashbery's virtuoso double sestina. This poem within the poem is all the more remarkable because its form stands classically opposed to the free flow of prose-poetry the poem has mainly been using. The double sestina checks the flow of the poet's charted year and leaves the reader knowing that diurnal knowledge, generated through the course of an autobiographical poem, is scaled to produce a new kind of slightly skewed annual completeness.

Chapter 13 brings together the strands of all the previous steps in the argument of form for this type of art. My conclusion is that the great American poetry, like other fundamental orders of thought, is subject to an inward dialectical questioning of opposites, whether to seek completeness or consistency. The celebrated *proof* or Incompleteness Theorem of Kurt Gödel provides one basis for this account, and its idea is shown to model the way a true environment-poem holds together. The choice for the poet is like the mathematician's choice; either the poem is complete, or consistent, but it cannot be both of these. The complete, or as I would say, the coherent environment-poem is necessarily inconsistent at some point, and for this reason it coheres. "Cohere" was one of Whitman's favorite terms for what he was attempting, and this penultimate chapter shows how the coherence he sought goes all the way back, in its presentation of natural strife, to the ancient poem of the earth, Hesiod's *Works and Days.* Hesiod is a critical point of origin, furthermore, because he establishes the poetry of space as opposed to place—a basic requirement of the later Georgic tradition. Whenever pointed place gives way to the more profound idea of extended space, the chorographic vision underlies the genre of the environment-poem, a genre where orders of society and nature are shown coming together as an aggregate of complex adaptations, which in their nature deny the claims of raw power. Such unnatural claims perforce rely on games of unacceptable ignorance and environmental stupefaction. Coherence in this context is then to be associated with the "coherence theory of truth" whereby, when things and relationships hang together, they possess conviction and hence demand assent, as distinct from the opposed, exceedingly powerful theory which defines truth as accuracy and adequacy in representation.[4] The latter I associate here with a rigid adherence to consistency, a *logos* ideally without missteps or exceptions. The Whitman idea of adherence and coherence was clearly intended to permit a social role for endless anomalies, if not misfits. A varied system of coherence allowing inconsistency (he called it "contradiction") thus became his ideal.

Concluding the six-fold sequence, Chapter 14 shows mainly through the example of Whitman's poem, "Sparkles from the Wheel," how a description without place, as Wallace Stevens might have said, is able to express the life of an environing space, a self-organizing chorography. The environment-poem bridges the gap between the opaque thingness of nature lying "out there," and the philosophical and scientific access we gain by developing terms, formulas, explanations, and theories of the order and meaning hidden within that opaque nature.[5] Furthermore, the strong message of this poetry, if it needed one, would be that a good society must become a self-organizing system, without too much top-down control. The Whitman poem exquisitely limns this thought, in that it shows how humans gather where there is a harmonious ensemble of artificial and natural elements.

Theory and the Environmental Imperative

Looking back over this summary account, I experience the cold empty spaces of real literary theory; one has to live with vast stretches of particular omission. Not only are there many poets I would wish to discuss, such as the Elizabeth Bishop of instantaneous scale-changes, but also prose authors, such as Virginia Woolf in her novel, *The Waves.* The whole question of the passage between inward and outward forms, between genre and attitude, must languish, deprived of a sufficient encyclopedia. Theory is condemned to play the sorcerer's apprentice, sweeping good things away forever. Theory sadly must mainly omit one's favorites. It would be more congenial to speak richly and exactly in the poet's dialect, commenting upon artistic aim and manner, as defined by the endless variety each artist in principle makes possible. Yet without theory as I try to practice it, imitating the sciences, it will be impossible to discover what underlies that variety. At their best, our poets give us images and figures of the strangeness of our "new" world. They show how old it is, and in what respects. They lift us free of misplaced allegorical thematizing, which in its ritual aspect produces anesthesia. They tell us who and what we are, and where and how we inhabit our space. Because theory permits us to allow a few poets to stand for many others of similar grace and accomplishment, whose spirits abound between the lines of the argument, such theorizing provides conceptual space in which we can locate many authors whose work we cannot, for accidental reasons, consider at length in the course of building our theoretical architecture. Here, among contemporaries, I analyze only John Ashbery, yet tacitly I have many other names in mind at the very same moment.

This critical essay will be seen to draw upon various scientific analogies and approaches, most notably ecological science and the question of scale. One broad ecological conclusion may here suffice to indicate my concern for that science. Looking back on his important book, *The End of Nature* (1990), Bill McKibben observed that he and other ecologists were discovering three ominous things about human behavior in advanced Western societies: that "we tell time badly," that "our sense of scale is awry," and thirdly, that our more-is-better obsession with "positive" numbers prevents us from seeing that we have ruptured our link with Nature.[6] We dream of the Wild, but our consumerist behavior militates against our dream. Even the Environmental Protection Agency in one report stated that its investigations and results, requiring intelligent response, "are also inherently limited by our imaginations." We seem as societies to lack what poetry teaches, namely, the capacity to *imagine* what may or might happen.

A convergence between science and art now occurs. Since literature and the humanities are the training ground for educating the imagination, we have every reason to look closely at the most intense expression of a fully aware long-term environmental understanding. Thousands of pages of discursive writing have been dedicated to discussion of environmental change, and this work has what we might call extensional force. Yet one hazard of such discourse is that it must thematize its subject, removing the individual response from center stage. The individual response to natural conditions gets swallowed up in the facts and figures of the science or the activist argument. By contrast, the poetry I am singling out for study is exactly the expression that looks for an awareness of what naturally surrounds us. McKibben's three errors—Bacon might have called them "idols"—are positively reversed in the poetry under consideration, for this art shows dramatically how we need to understand the time-frames, scale-differences, and the cardinal role of numbers in the political and social worlds and more largely in the environment. Only a poetry that resists its own transcendental impulses, as I show the environment-poem resists them, will usefully address the most serious conditions of our time along with numerous global changes. A more extensive treatment would allow me to show that many conflicts today considered political are actually *environmental* conflicts, which need to be treated as such. The single word "oil" should alert us to this geopolitical fact. Literature and politics always have an uneasy relationship. Thus poetry, especially lyric verse, focuses larger issues onto limited screens and hence intensifies social issues to the point where individual writers and readers can begin, as individuals, to think these matters through according to their own personal lights. Only by stressing this individual perspective will the aggregate social ensemble, adopting Whitman's phrase, reach a more deeply felt involvement with our world and its future.

I

Clare's Horizon

One day, when he was a small boy, John Clare went looking for the horizon. Throughout his life as poet, and this included his enforced dream-life when he was placed in an insane asylum, he never ceased this journey. Pursuing the horizon without interruption inevitably prohibits *landfall, harbor, home,* unless one radically redefines these ends to include their own contracted horizons. Landfall is the sailor's term for reaching a destination, which necessarily interrupts the impossible search for any final edge of what surrounds us. The horizon, however, marks the idea of end as purpose, as a magnetic pull drawing ever forward our wish for "immanent transcendence," as Husserl paradoxically named the mixing of inward and outward apprehension.[1] This may seem like an unfounded otherworldly dream, but Emerson thought it real enough in his "Circles," where the fluid and volatile universe asks us to respond in this double way: "The eye is the first circle; the horizon which it forms is the second; and throughout nature this primary figure is repeated without end."[2] The horizon thus formed is of course a primary figure in two senses. It cuts a line between our animate selves and what we see in the distance, physically; but given its mental and theoretical force, horizon also cuts a further line between our physical world and what we see beyond it in a visionary sense. There is perhaps no final horizon of our ideas, although within the sphere of our senses there is that narrower perceptual horizon toward which our senses carry our thoughts like an invisible cargo of selfhood. If finally this ineffable cargo never reaches port, it fails because space at last becomes a modality of time, as Clare's three great sonnets on a winter flood once showed in one wild scene.[3]

Rushing madly toward the unbounded, beyond the known, the untamed flood is no longer a placid river of time.

> —On roars the flood—all restless to be free
> Like trouble wandering to eternity

As we shall see throughout this book, horizon may or may not imply transcendent dimensions of thought, but at least for the poets I am considering, horizon always implies description. John Clare's own autobiographical words best indicate the source of this mutual relationship between self, horizon, and description.[4]

> I loved this solitary disposition from a boy and felt a curosity to wander about spots where I had never been before I remember one incident of this feeling when I was very young it cost my parents some anxiety it was in summer and I started off in the morning to get rotten sticks from the woods but I had a feeling to wander about the fields and I indulged it. I had often seen the large heath call'd Emmonsales stretching its yellow furze from my eye into unknown solitudes when I went with the mere openers and my curosity urged me to steal an oppertunity to explore it that morning I had imagin'd that the worlds end was at the edge of the orison and that a days journey was able to find it

We might think that young Clare was engaged here in what he called "pursuits after happiness," the chase after "astonishment," to use another Clare word, as if he had already imagined his horizon to be the defining limit for the poetry he wrote. It is perhaps more appealing simply to think that the joy of searching for the horizon is the delight of discovery in its extremest form, in its limiting idea of the ultimate boundary of our real and imaginary knowledge. As a child, Leo Tolstoy too would "whirl around to see if he could catch sight of the nothingness" in just such a quest. In his massive biography of Solzhenitsyn, D. M. Thomas mentions Tolstoy's childhood experimentation with ontology along with similar experiments Solzhenitsyn had tried.[5] For the two novelists such childish adventures appear connected with what Thomas calls a "mastery of strategy and large-scale movement of forces." No doubt the onset of the reality principle, which suppresses primary and secondary narcissism, leads to a weakened interest in the mere being of horizons, or emptiness, or the nothing, or even things whose Being is believed to pre-exist their material existence. As child and man Clare made many ontological experiments in Tolstoy's vein, but few grownups can make this journey, except as an artful intimation of immortality. For Clare, though, the lifespan always collapsed into *single* moments of immanent transcendence; he was always walking toward the horizon, which maybe he learned to do early, from his flat fenland home.

> so I went on with my heart full of hopes pleasures and discoverys expecting when I got to the brink of the world that I coud look down like looking into a large pit and see into its secrets the same as I believd I coud see heaven by looking into the water so I eagerly wandered on and rambled among the furze the whole day till I got out of my knowledge when the very wild flowers and birds seemd to forget me and I imagind they were the inhabitants of new countrys the very sun seemd to be a new one and shining in a different quarter of the sky still I felt no fear my wonder seeking happiness had no room for it I was finding new wonders

> every minute and was walking in a new world often wondering to my self that I had not found the end of the old one the sky still touched the ground in the distance as usual and my childish wisdoms was puzzled in perplexitys

Clare's horizon defines a conundrum: what can be the enclosing space that does not enclose? Horizon promises neither beginning nor end, but only the growing awareness that by describing a circle one has reached beyond the idea of either beginning or concluding. Philosophers ancient and medieval, for example, Nicholas of Cusa, had long wondered about the nature and extent of the cosmos, reaching well into the modern period of scientific telescopic observation in its most recent developments. When Clare spoke of the new world and the old one, what kind of explorer was he? We can say that as a small boy walking the heath, he was doubly in touch with that felt human universe of which a fragment of Empedocles speaks: "the earth that envelops us, the body." One recalls embodied childhood. Escaping over and under stone walls and fences, one knew the mingled thrill and fear and strangeness of trying to cheat the too short day of its diurnal limit. Clare was later to recall this fear, discovering in every encounter uncanny powers whose apprehension was to haunt him for the rest of his life. In this he resembles other Romantics, yet his quest differs.

> night crept on before I had time to fancy the morning was bye the white moth had begun to flutter beneath the bushes the black snail was out upon the grass and the frog was leaping across the rabbit tracks on his evening journeys and the little mice was nimbling about and twittering their little earpiercing song with the hedge cricket whispering the hour of waking spirits was at hand when I knew not which way to turn but chance put me in the right track and when I got into my own fields I did not know them everything

> seemd so different the church peeping over the woods coud hardly reconcile me

As Joseph Conrad once wrote, "a Landfall may be good or bad." This particular landfall for the child was significantly ominous, reminding us that in country life the untoward is uncanny, because the voyager on land as upon the sea can hope to encompass the earth with one particular spot of home beckoning to the eye, but there is always danger, and approaching a harbor is the trickiest navigation of all. Landfall, to be successful, requires a clear eye and a clear atmosphere. Perhaps because Clare's native terrain was so flat and featureless, he seems the voyager for whom Conrad's dictum is appropriate: "From land to land is the most concise definition of a ship's earthly fate."[6] On the occasion of Clare's journey to the horizon, landfall and nightfall came together in one dark moment.

> when I got home I found my parents in the greatest distress and half the vill[a]ge about hunting me one of the wood men in the woods had been killed by the fall of a tree and it servd to strengthen their terrors that some similar accident had befallen myself as they often leave the oaks half cut down till the bark men can come up to pill them which if a wind happens to rise fall down unexpected

The essence of description seems to be that for its poets the objects described are empirically delimited, emotionally powerful sources of the uncanny. Even happiness is like this. Clare would say, "I used to be fondly attached to spots about the fields," and these spots he would forever revisit. Each revisiting meant a renewal of the familiar in a new light, so that finally he could base descriptions of the unfamiliar and its receding horizon against his intimate knowledge of places to which he was fondly attached. "I never unriddled the mystery," he once reminisced about another search for fact. In this sense he was precisely unlike a tourist, the paying traveler one suspects of not much liking his own home, hence given to the alienation of touring, unless, of course, like a fanatical nomad, he makes wandering without home the chief aim of life. Again Conrad comes to mind; *The Mirror of the Sea* recurs constantly to the sailor's home on land.

The art of poetry has many ways of constraining linguistic flux and holding context at bay, and within these limiting constraints the horizon marks an outer limit of hopes, fears, and dreams. This is sometimes a hard business, calling the ship to reach the impossible edge of a dull, leaden shadow line, as in Conrad's great story. In Clare's perhaps unwitting pun, horizon is the orison of a prayer to nature. Continually changing its inscription of the full reach of what we can see, horizon fails of geometric elegance, remaining subject to all the changes of wind and weather and of changing terrain. Horizon is a function of all the obstacles to an observer's line of sight, and hence only on the ocean or on great open plains does it appear to be an absolute geometrical limit. But even then it is always only a phenomenon of beckoning promise, reminding us that we are encircled by our own ignorance, even as we are protected by the circle of our tentative knowing. Finally, horizon carries us outside of ourselves, yet keeps our feet on the ground. Conrad has a monitory role to play here, because his Captain McWhirr or Captain Giles, among so many others including the young "Conrad" of *The Shadow Line,* constantly demonstrate that despite all fears we can keep our feet on the ground, even when we are literally at sea. This knowledge leaves us free or at least somewhat more free to deal with the way things are. Besides recognizing the truths hidden in the long annals of natural history and natural science, we can recognize another truth, that poets seem quite unable to express what counts most for humans without invoking the merest things of nature and nature's various appearances. When I speak in later pages of description, I am speaking about this almost genetic connection between poetry and natural fact.

2

The Argument of Form

When the journey to the outer bounds of perception inspires poetic art, it generates a method rarely formalized as a convention in our own recent literature. Yet such a method and its literary genres were well known in earlier times, especially during the eighteenth century, and in English at least going back to Michael Drayton's massive poetic survey of his country and its rivers and its history and its heroes, the *Poly-Olbion.* Robert Arnold Aubin's thoroughly amusing monograph, coming from a happier time of mere learnedness, *Topographical Poetry in XVIII-Century England* (1936), gives us a *catalogue raisonné* of a massive, regular, and finally stultifying output.[1] In 1793, reviewing Wordsworth's *Descriptive Sketches: Taken during a Pedestrian Tour in the Alps,* the *Monthly Review* was bored to death: "More descriptive poetry! Have we not yet enough? Must eternal changes be rung on uplands and lowlands, nodding forests, and brooding clouds, and cells, and dells, and dingles? Yes; more, and yet more: so it is decreed." Throughout the period the influence of painting on description was strong and reciprocal, largely because James Thomson's descriptive poem *The Seasons* (1726–30) cast a wide literary spell over the visual arts. Yet we recognize that walking to the horizon could place the poet in touch with almost anything he passed, and all such phenomena might chaotically call out for their place in the poem, thus subverting the tight forms of classic European poetry.

At this juncture a question of literary history and theory arises, to suggest that almost all the accepted recent criticism of Romantic poetry has mistaken its own ground, nor will it be possible for students of Romantic epiphanies (located most famously in Wordsworth's "spots of time") to claim that they are simply going beyond the meaning of the tired outburst in the *Monthly Review.* The point may be stated sharply, but I think correctly: when Romantic poetry turned to its involvement with nature, it committed itself to deepening, analyzing, but generally idealizing a practice which the study of nature makes virtually unavoidable, namely, the description of the natural scene. No matter how differently and with what stylistic variety individual poets approached the task of description—and the contrast between Wordsworth and John Clare or Wordsworth and Coleridge shows how various the styles could be—the fundamentals of confronting nature remain paramount, and they determine the poetry toward its base, the accounting of elements present in the scene before the poet's gaze. This whole book is an attempt to show the environmental and poetic logic of this claim. By failing to grasp the role of description as the grounding strategy of the Romantic impulse, criticism has been forced into its overestimation of the problems of authorial consciousness and creativity. Such criticism has always been able to lean on the Coleridgean theory of imagination, as presented in the *Biographia Literaria* and elsewhere, but it has never dealt seriously with the problem enunciated in the *Lyrical Ballads* and its famed Preface (with later additions), that is, the role of the common in poetry, as distinct from the commonplace. Marxist approaches involve different but related issues, such as the class struggle, the power of capital investment, the conditions of work, the plight of the proletariat, and so on. But Marxist criticism is not really interested in poetry. Its concern is to advance active change in social conditions, so that when Oliver Goldsmith attacks callous disregard of poverty, in *The Deserted Village* and elsewhere,[2] such an awareness is one thing for a Marxist, and another for a theorist of poetry such as myself. We may both be interested in these conditions of poverty, but each from a different angle.

Understanding *the common* as a function of poetic form and language—the subject of Wordsworth's Preface to the *Lyrical Ballads*—requires an ecologically detailed accounting for its expression, which is only one of many reasons why a criticism that fails to recognize the descriptive tradition and its influx into the Romantic cannot possibly succeed in thinking through the Platonism of Romantic vision. To pursue the metacritical discussion, however, would be the subject of a book other than the one I have written, although the theorist should see that it hardly needs writing, once he or she grasps the role of environment as what is *around,* as what is *surrounding* the poet's seeing eye. Here the wisdom of the late Isaiah Berlin is much to be esteemed: "we must learn to exaggerate," he said, if we are to shake the accepted ideas of any large cultural construction.[3] Criticism may have suffered the inevitable consequences of its own snobbism, having discovered a respectable way to talk about the Romantic, namely, as High Romanticism. This elevated vision is most difficult to restrain, given the role of the sublime during the period, but at the very least it needs to be moderated and analyzed from the perspective of Low Romanticism.

Description, at first sight, has no internal principle of organization, neither narrative nor dramatic nor lyrical, but follows the scene observed. In theory, other ways to find it would do, but walking on a "pedestrian tour" was the most convenient approach to the experience, as walking allowed more detailed notice of the changing scene, which journals like those of Dorothy Wordsworth and especially Coleridge at once reveal. This kind of chronicling aims almost to be obsequious.

When we think of the stylistic transition from *Paradise Lost* to *The Prelude,* we recognize a large transformation of the norms of the English grand style. Milton's blank verse is musical in polyphonic Renaissance style; Wordsworth deliberately takes the aerial lift out of the medium, and instead settles its rhythm upon walking. If there is one pragmatic preparation for his larger poetic career, it must be his practice of the outdoor excursion. This was always made on foot, he and his sister Dorothy vigorously clambering about on the damp hillsides of the Lake Country, an activity paralleled on roads and pathways during the 1791 continental walking tour. Walking, prose, and verse come together.

In American natural history, the greatest walker and perhaps the greatest poet among prose writers is not Emerson, nor perhaps even William Bartram in Florida, but Thoreau. In 1980, Robert Sattelmeyer collected essays in which Thoreau focused exactly on his method of discovery, "A Walk to Wachusett," "A Winter Walk," and the very important "Walking."[4] In "Autumnal Hints" he states the principles of what I shall be calling description: "Objects are concealed from our view, not so much because they are out of the course of our visual ray as because we do not bring our minds and eyes to bear on them; for there is no power to see in the eye itself, any more than in any other jelly. *We do not realize how far and widely, or how near and narrowly, we are to look.*" This sense of the mind of the observer is supported, furthermore, by his view that "the greater part of the phenomena of Nature are for this reason concealed from us all our lives. The gardener sees only the gardener's garden. Here, too, as in political economy, the supply answers the need." Always the ecologist, Thoreau says in a lecture on huckleberries that there is nothing trivial in all this small-scale precision with its minute details, as some had said, but rather it provides for the naturalist what Milton had called "intellectual food," the exact phrase Thoreau quotes. In another collection Laurence Stapleton edited a series of Thoreau's journal entries from 1851 under the heading "Walking by Night." Stapleton's purpose was to show how Thoreau connected his walking with his writing: "a writer, a man writing, is the scribe of all nature; he is the corn and the grass and the atmosphere writing."[5] Thoreau is the exemplary case, although preceded in even more extreme solitude by John Clare, another great walker. Thoreau's profession of surveyor required him to walk, and surveying may be understood to be a scientific version of description, but the key to the method, for poetical purposes, is the quiet or even the complete solitude of the walker. In this sense the walker, the rambler, the explorer, has a kind of love affair with perception itself. Walking in the woods changes one's sense of sound, and the lightest footfall signals the nature of the earth.

Description, then, is not the highly structured social account of manmade society or technologically patterned engineering. To describe is to see whatever disarray surrounds the sensating and even sensual walker, since the receding horizon alone controls the quest. The walker is one kind of archetypal observer, and his example leads us to examine the role of the attendant poetic forms that express this particular mode of ambulatory observation. The questions are basic; they would be immediately understood by the earliest philosophers, whose physical studies do not occur in the laboratory. Their observations would not be mediated by instruments, but in a sense may be called "direct." The issues for poetics in our field pertain to differing degrees of obliquity, mediation, and empirical interest, in a climate of great art that often aspired to transcendental freedom of thought. It follows then that if we are to fully experience any poetry that describes, we must ask fundamental questions about *poetic* form, which in turn lead to questions about the idea of form itself, pursued *in the argument of form* that goes all the way back to ancient Greek philosophy.[6]

The Remarriage of Argument and Imagination

Plato had argued in *The Republic* that the polis should crown the poets with garlands and send them on their way, on the grounds that poetry is a delusive art, dealing pleasurably in phantasms or secondary images of a world which is itself a kind of dream. For the philosopher the Ideas constituted the ultimately unchanging shapes underlying all truth.[7] The Platonic attack on poetry reduces to this: once you have thought of a triangle, you cannot remove the idea of it from your thought, and you cannot find it perfectly in nature. The triangle remains an imperishable exactness, if only within the mind. Even supposing that in curved space the plane triangle has to bend like the fragment of a broken Indian pot, it still remains a bent triangle, an unchangeable Form persisting in the midst of change and hence resisting change.

In contemplating such profound human inventions as Plato's Theory of Ideas, we need to move as freely as possible, while still appreciating the questions philosophy has raised, around those epochal discoveries and their equally epochal development over the centuries. If we do so, we find an argument, never settled but only deferred, between Plato's mathematical intuition that his Ideas are "eternal" and the poets' belief that whatever undergoes change (and indeed change itself) yields the only true idea. To hold such a belief means to accept paradox or to fly into a decidedly unplatonic view of things. For it is contradictory or at least paradoxical to hold that change can embody any "eternal" given. Hence it has often been asked: what is the fixed notion of the unfixed, and could that truly be an Idea? This hard question is precisely what the poets have always perceived in their own (partially Aristotelian) way, by regarding form as immanent and by expressing this immanence through metaphor.[8] The poet plays in a field of sensuous delivery, treating poetic forms as approximations of an accepting vision of change, a changefulness that with poetry does not threaten ideal orders of being.

Despite all the authority of philosophy, descending in "a series of footnotes to Plato," there is no doubt that if mathematics had not become (long before Galileo so named it) the "language of science," there would be no difficulty in seeing that the poets also have an argument. Poets indeed create the argument of form, bringing us always back to a Presocratic vision of reality. If a Theory of Ideas leads thinkers to a geometric account, to a belief that mathematics ideally always separates the One from the Many, it must lead also to a schematic view of our world. It schematizes to reduce the many-sided multiplicity of phenomena to a purified and much smaller number of principles, concepts, theories, and laws—the Ideas. Without such reductive thinking we would have no science. Even the most complex scientific work, as in high-energy physics, depends upon reductive geometric notions such as parity, spin, symmetry, and the like. Science acts as if it could escape the pleasure principle. Like religion, it aims at evading death, which it tries to manage by reducing the frightening variety of natural forces threatening a single-minded stability. William James found such an impulse to reduce underlying most of the varieties of religious experience, which suggests why, psychologically at least, science and technology can easily become a religion. Yet the primacy of *the One,* the Great Idea producing the Ultimate Theory, need not tyrannize all thinking, for there is an alternative tradition. John Hollander, having observed the essential importance of Stanley Cavell to literary theory, describes the way philosophy begins, and, by implication, the way philosophical arguments may need to be remarried to poetic imagination. "One crosses the brink of common sense into philosophy by desiring, wondering, framing the wonder in questions, asking the questions, and asking what the consequences of various sorts of answering might be. One crosses the brink of literalness into poetry by desiring, remembering desire, noticing, fixing on something, and wondering what to make of it."[9]

Poet as Presocratic

In our present discussion the Ideas powerfully work to *prescribe* the outlines of significant things, whereas in a Presocratic view, which lives more directly in a world of immediate responses to the cosmos and to the immediate environment, an opposite effect occurs. Here form and idea are felt to lose their absolute stasis, so the art of saying and expressing the Logos reverses its direction: instead of prescribing the forms of the world's multiplicity, the poet as Presocratic insists on *describing* the world. He or she is mimetic in this sense, and, not always content to *hold* that things participate in ideas, appears often to affirm that ideas participate in things. Ideas then would be subordinate to things. The error, if there is one, with this last sentence is that it does not ask "when are ideas subordinate to things?" a question leading to the deeper meaning of description. For description is the expressive mode that works *in time,* as poets seek to speak *in time.* Poets cannot accept the ideality of Plato's timeless formulations, because these would abrogate death, change, and our becoming undistinguished atoms of momentary existence. Poets confront death, they celebrate life, and hence are forced into an imaginative method of refusing final truths and prescriptions. Even the allegorical poets seek this method, as we learn from Dante (Auerbach called him the poet of the real world) or Spenser, whose wild mythmaking always undermines the schematized prescriptions of allegorical "morals" and "messages." In describing, poets never begin by saying: this is how the world must or should be. Rather, they say: this is what we see and sense in this world. Would it were a better world, but we must begin with whatever it is, however full of change it is, which explains why we begin at the phenomenal level of sense and perception and wonderment. Networked ideas must not prescribe what is taken to belong to nature, or we shall lose what is poetically significant, since poetry is always a meditation on human time.

The One is of course another name for what most people loosely and uncritically call God. That fact alone is sufficient to alienate the poet who, if he or she does not precisely rival a divine creative power, is alerted by the mere condition of art and craft to understand that the One, to be a sort of Godhead, must cease to be a term or sign. But then Godhead seems to abolish the possibility of its own ceasing to be. The poet of change generally stays more alert than the average person to C. S. Peirce's semiotic domain, to an aesthetic continuum that enters our thinking in an appreciation of our human play of signs. Thus for the poet the One must fall, becoming simply the supreme omnisignificant sign—the hypersign—working along with a myriad apparently lesser signs. Above all, the poet prevents any hypersign or "god-term" from arrogating rulership. Some ideas and their names may control larger conceptions than others, but there is in poetry an abiding upper limit of movement toward a transcendent level of power masquerading as a mode of ultimate fixed Being. It was to preserve this openness that led Wallace Stevens to read Darwin and to think like a Presocratic, or an Ovidian seer, when he said of poetry at highest pitch, "it must change." By contrast, the idea of God inevitably undermines the poem's life in the moment. If Thales chooses water, and Heraclitus fire, these elements engage in rivalry with each other as equally natural entities. By contrast, absolutes brook no rivals. Given nature's variety, there is always an argument for the literary advantages of polytheism, as my friend, the late Kenneth Koch, liked to argue. Poetry, even in its neoclassic (say, Augustan English) hierarchical forms, seems to prefer a natural verbal merit system that would imply an egalitarian nobility. The mere eminence of metaphor and metamorphosis in poetic history tends to undermine absolute power. Poetic politics wants to choose within a wide field of semiotic choices. Since Plato and his philosophic successors believe in the need for all-powerful "guardians"—the *archons*—they tend to refuse such drifts toward what we call democracy, which they would have questioned as a discouragement of nobility and stable government. After the lapse of many centuries, however, the Romantics promoted a more open vision and hence thought that poetry should derive from a more neutral nature, as opposed to any absolute godhead, or any other variety of the Platonic One. What is odd about Romantic thought is that simultaneously it promotes personal *arête* in the form of the noble individual.

The Fate of Description

The fate of description is usually tied to the history of topographic poems, celebrations like Sidney's *To Penshurst* (the classic "great house" poem) and Denham's *Cooper's Hill* (the classic "prospect" poem), which at heart always envision a *genius loci.* The trouble with a narrow emphasis upon topographic, as distinct from *chorographic* (the sort of poetry I shall be emphasizing later), is that topography defines scene much too narrowly. The topographic poem typically points to a *specific* place and its immediate prospects. The vista is provided by its outlook, usually an outlook from a high place. (This prospect poetry has been extensively discussed by students of the picturesque and the sublime.) The problem is that if you emphasize the topographic as traditionally understood, you neglect the broader notion of environment, and you lose track of the medium by which all visions of external reality must be presented to the reader. You lose track of description, even as you privilege one of its genres, the prospect poem.

Description in stories and poems has a history as long as literature itself, flourishing in oral as well as written and printed works. The presence and absence of the descriptive detail provides the nub of Auerbach's *Mimesis.* Description may not be the most intense response to our natural surroundings, but it is certainly the fullest, nor does it ever lack thoughtful purpose. Even so, criteria for true, or complete, or legitimate descriptions will vary widely, depending on historical periods and broader visionary aims, as Auerbach showed. What he called the "representation of reality" involves not only our perceptual and cognitive skills and devices (the moon seen through a telescope or seen by the naked eye), but at the same time as perceptual habits flourish or die away, our powers of description develop varying epistemic rules, to use Foucault's well-known formula. After the Renaissance, new rules call for increasing the detachment of observer from the observed, especially with the rise of taxonomic classification. In this new epistemic order, description itself was bound to seek new forms, those of a figural self-restraint in prose (so that a Sir Thomas Browne could no longer be seen as writing "scientific prose"), while in poetry the ancient art of rendering scenes and persons (as in Chaucer's *Prologue*) could begin to intensify its acceptances of fact and the pressure of fact. Generally, for both poetry and prose, metaphors were curtailed. Numbers and measurement can always be perceived to oppose verbal troping, if not the use of literal denotations in prose definitions. Metaphor is not exactly a mathematical instrument.

The *locus classicus* of this view, Bishop Thomas Sprat's *History of the Royal Society,* expresses the preference for the literal in terms which directly ally description with number. Writers were to "return back to the primitive purity and shortness, when men deliver'd so many *things* almost in an equal number of *words.*"[10] In his monumental and invaluable book on what he called "the art of discrimination," Ralph Cohen demonstrated to what lengths and depths the critics of the eighteenth century studied the problem raised by Sprat and others, namely, the ambiguous relation between the poetical and the descriptive, as these questions centered upon contemporary thought and upon Thomson's own evolving epical length in his extremely popular magnum opus, *The Seasons.*[11] Cohen followed up on his initial metacritical and historical study with *The Unfolding of The Seasons* (1970), a detailed account of the poem's complex development as vision and text. Thomson himself in later editions made changes of wording so as to suggest emotional or moral atmospheres rather than the cultural atmosphere of scientific observation. As he revised, he felt almost obliged to leave aside his interest in meteorology or Newtonian notions of the optics of light. A serious artistic question arose: could scientific statements and scientific styles provide the vivid and catching aesthetic powers of literary art? It was an issue to be decided finally only in practice, with poets like Wordsworth and John Clare at the end of the Enlightenment period, as to whether description could be at once both truthful and exciting. The enigma lay in the fact that description itself is an immensely broad category, as Cohen's first Thomson study showed, and the ancillary fact that description on some level probably has to amplify poetry (and prose) of all kinds and purposes. We can *describe* a bounded geometrical figure, and know what we have done, exactly. But beyond this mathematical notion there lie vast stretches of varying expression in ordinary language, and these are the central puzzle for understanding the shift into what we call High Romanticism. A new enlargement of scope seems to have been the main requirement in terms of artistic form—a shift most obvious when we note the enlargement of musical forms in the classical repertoire. Full-scale Romanticism seems to have required, paradoxically, an art of lyrical description. It required an extension and new amplitude of scales of utterance, which is perhaps easiest to see and hear in the Romantic symphony, where eventually we reach Wagner and Mahler. As Bishop Sprat implied, scientific literalism required a different economy—ideally brief and to the point—and we need to emphasize the poetic devices of order and rhythm which were at first available to utter poetry's descriptive equivalent of this brevity and point.

Couplets and Containments

The method of James Thomson, whose Miltonic rhythms herald the infusions of prose into Wordsworth's blank verse, would seem to establish a major connection between prose amplification and descriptive precision. The influence of Thomson is impressive in the Wordsworthian direction, but in a remarkable way the eighteenth-century descriptive tradition leans most heavily on a stylized minimal unit of descriptive accuracy, the rhymed couplet.

The technical modern problem of poetic description begins historically quite strangely to our ears, because with Drayton and Daniel and other late Elizabethans, the description of nature falls comfortably into heroic couplets. Such couplets imply a normalizing use of rhyme, which in these late times we may incorrectly imagine enforcing rigid or invariant thoughts, but to the trained ear the couplet is full of variety. Of course we tend to quote couplets—for example, from the second epistle of Pope's *Essay on Man,* lines 59–60—for their aphoristic clip,

> Two Principles in Human Nature reign;
> *Self-Love,* to urge; and *Reason,* to restrain,

but then we may forget that Pope strings his couplets together in whole paragraphs, his semicolon and comma being as frequent as his periods. Otherwise, of course, he could not have created his masterly (and intensely *visual*) translations of the Homeric epics, not to mention numerous more distinctly descriptive passages and whole poems like *Windsor Forest.*

Underneath the bipolar structure of the couplet there always lurks a desire to define, to enclose, to delimit. A bipolar symmetry between the two lines provides one essential component of enclosure; like any container, the couplet achieves its strength from the symmetry of its sides. Its tension permits a power of defining both edge and volume, for such is the consequential benefit of balance. Ordering by symmetry accounts for Pope's completely orthodox command that we should not "scan" God. Equally, it controls his elegance and point:

> True wit is Nature to advantage dress'd;
> What oft was thought but ne're so well express'd.

The dance of the couplet depends upon the pirouette, as if in its poetic form the couplet were describing a circle. It is tempting to speculate that the heroic couplet contracts discourse to its ultimate hermeneutic circle,[12] to our understanding that when Alexander Pope plays often on the theme of the part and the particle, he is poetically projecting Schleiermacher's vision of interpreting texts, namely, that within the hermeneutic circle we must understand the whole to understand the parts, and we must understand the parts to understand the whole. This seemingly text-bound interpretive notion, as developed later by Dilthey and others, is curiously significant when we consider that the descriptive poets and authors of the past were directly or indirectly writing about nature, which they perceived as whatever surrounds us.[13] The encircling horizon of nature parallels the circle of hermeneutic enclosure, suggesting that the latter derives from the former. When Emerson wrote his "Circles," he was following in the footsteps of his formal master, Montaigne, whose late essay on three kinds of society, commerce, or association, as the word is variously translated, centered upon the description of his library: "The shape of my library is round with only sufficient flat wall for my table and chair; as it curves about, it offers me at a glance all my books arranged in five rows of shelves all around."[14]

Framing the idea of this imaginative horizon differently may broaden our question in the correct fashion for poetry. The hermeneutic circle is the inevitable consequence of our being textually surrounded by the library, as we are environmentally surrounded by ecological conditions and Emerson's "circular wave of circumstance," where part and whole share a complementary relationship.

Commonly, critics define descriptive poetry in terms of its objects of description—the landscape, the domestic interior, articles of dress, manner and design, and so on. But already we must go deeper to the philosophy of the idea. Since ideas and form are lexically the same—*idea* being translated into the Latin *form*—it follows that the history of ideas is actually the history of forms, and these in turn belong as much to poets—who manipulate form, arguing against the Platonic absolute—as to the "theory of ideas," which by its nature must fixate and hypostatize each idea.

The philosopher forbids the argument of form; the poet revels in it. And the revelry is expressed by plays of poetic design, such that with heroic couplets, for example, any idea represented through them becomes *de facto* a truncated piece of dialectic argument, a brief epitomizing description of the main features of whatever is under observation. The art is inherently directed toward a mental horizon proposed by Dr. Johnson.[15]

> Let Observation with extensive view
> Survey Mankind from China to Peru.

The couplet form is the balanced, framed, symmetrically ordered, fundamental unit of description—the ideal snapshot. It pleases as symmetries often do. But poets came to see that its formal rhythmic balance could not generate adequate energy unless daimons or personifications were introduced, as with Johnson's couplet and throughout Augustan didactic and descriptive verse. The blank verse of *The Seasons* is an epic rejection of symmetry, harking back to Milton's baroque torsions. The comment Thomson's choice elicits is that description may require a more than usual contact with natural environments, since nature itself does not write in couplets, however much symmetry there is at the atomic and subatomic level. The rebuttal cuts in the opposite direction. Since Clare makes obvious contact with environment, and he uses couplets for the purpose, why should we assume that Miltonic blank verse better catches the weave of nature? Is not Wordsworth's walking rhythm a powerfully *natural* effect? True, Clare's sonnets in particular show how couplets could be made virtually to disappear, by means of an undoing containment of their sharp symmetries within the fourteen-line structure; Clare's rhymes seem often almost not to rhyme, even when perfectly consonant. They fit the disappearing looseness of drifting observation. Hence it is beginning to be clear that we need a broader sense of the aim of description in general, especially since there appears to be more than one way to achieve its encircling closure, its containments.

Distinguishing between nature as environmental fact, and nature as source of momentary inspiration, will lead to a new vision of the whole idea of description. Thence the technical poetic forms need not be limited to devices like the couplet or blank verse, although these have powerful links to the descriptive. A brief lyric by Robert Frost, "Snow Dust,"[16] is written in two quatrains of the simplest shape, and it shows how description may lead immediately into mood and its flux:

> The way a crow
> Shook down on me
> The dust of snow
> From a hemlock tree
>
> Has given my heart
> A change of mood
> And saved some part
> Of a day I had rued.

Overtones of an earlier poem of Housman ("On an athlete dying young") inflect the tone here, yet the source in the Frost poem for the force of "a day I had rued" is based on an initial description of a natural event, the sort of note we find everywhere in poets like Clare and Edward Thomas, or Hardy. Poetic forms and genres, therefore, are the flexible servants of description, never confined to any most efficient shape, such as the epistemically powerful heroic couplet. John Ashbery, we shall see, stretches the forms to exploit prose-poetry in the French manner. The genius of Enlightenment thought and action had allowed a gradual extension of mood in poetry, as the shift toward feeling (after the epochal

Sterne and Mackenzie and other sentimental fiction writers) permeated literature at large, including gothic descriptions that atmospherically drive the action of novels, stories, and poems, where now we come to expect actions motivated by ambience. I live in the High Desert, and many of the actions we take are entirely controlled and inspired by our climate. It was always thus, before air conditioning. It could be that the "man of feeling" and "the woman of sensibility" were always present, but had gone untreated in extreme form, because the control of climate and environment before the nineteenth century was simply too hard to imagine, hence the atmosphere was not capable of being romanticized. One is reminded of a remark about the Depression: "We were too poor to be mentally ill."

Descriptive arts working within the Romantic episteme invent atmospheres of all kinds, as if atmosphere and ambience were finally available concerns for the first time in the West. *On the surface* description appears an unromantic occupation. Rhapsody (for example, the rhapsodic passages in *Tintern Abbey*) seems to preclude descriptive precision. Nevertheless, there is still a strange way in which descriptions may arouse what we might call a paradoxical *nostalgia for the present,* and this provides a way of sensing the romantic in nature. On another plane, the history of description is peculiarly entangled with the history of personification. Throughout the eighteenth century personification engages in an ambiguous dance with two partners, allegory and dream. As soon as descriptive impulses strive for accuracy of record, personifications arise, like will-o'-the-wisps rising from the ground, to invest the material description with spiritual meanings, most powerfully those intimations of genius and threat, imagination and terror, the very ingredients of the sublime and picturesque. Every true occasion calls now for its attending spirit, and this will be personified. Such was the concern of Collins' *Ode on the Popular Superstitions of the Highlands of Scotland* (1749–50). In a secular context the post-Enlightenment poet has always to deal with the antithetical claims of fact and spirit, as if the genius of place were always at war with the facts of place. Much of the argument of this book therefore concerns the idea that only by understanding poetic environments can we understand the internal conflict between *daimon* and description.

This discursive instability is nowhere more prominent than in the British discussion of Platonism, as evidenced by Coleridge's vaguely esoteric interpretation of Kant as a partially Aristotelian *conceptionist* for whom ideas were regulative only. A true follower of Plato, by contrast, would be an *Ideist* and, given this polarizing view, Kant could never lead the way into full ideality, so much was he dedicated to his scientific categories. In the *Biographia Literaria* the struggle to sort out a primary from a merely secondary imagination is a search for a vital principle adequate to creative powers of the highest kind, of a kind almost godlike in combinatory unifying force. The argument of form is deeply troubled in Coleridge's own poetry, ranging from folk mystery in *Christabel* and the *Rime of the Ancient Mariner* to philosophic abstractions governing his formal odes, so that we find him being inspired by differing philosophical concerns to adopt differing poetic forms. The pressure of philosophy is perhaps most acute in the drive to create the famed "conversation poems," which in fact mark an early phase of a new sort of descriptive poetry, neither classic nor Romantic. David Newsome, a master of this material, claims for Romantic Platonism that "it is an attempt to transcend the bounds of understanding by exploring the realms of the infinite."[17] By rejecting a materialist, Lockean and Newtonian theory of knowledge, the successors to Blake and Coleridge turned to the primitive and to mythic mysteries, and thence to an indeterminate passion for the "beyond," the transcendent. In so doing they had to reject or negotiate a new zone of transaction within the foundations of poetry itself. The problem for the Romantics was this: could they fully accept the belief that change-filled, change-making poetic forms are the true forms of life, which had been essentially Aristotle's belief? In most cases the Romantics followed an easier, more neoclassically influenced path, namely, the substitution of the sublime and the picturesque, emblems of the transcendent, for the turbulent rendition of change itself. They hence preserved the eighteenth-century art of personification, the art of abstract nouns in capital letters. Newsome's Birkbeck Lectures, *Two Classes of Men: Platonism & English Romantic Thought,* along with E. D. Hirsch's *Wordsworth and Schelling* (1960) and other, more recent researches, make one thing clear, that a sublime Platonism could never fully escape its occultist, hermetic, Behmian background. Romantic poetry may well support the "alternative tradition" described by Anthony Nuttall in his gnostic studies of Milton and Blake, and certainly arguments advanced by Harold Bloom have always caught the vision and tone of spiritual struggle in these authors. My sense, however, is that by widening our notions of the metaphysical, we will find that High Romantic poetry is not the only poetic approach to questions of sublime transcendence. A passion for the infinite may inspire Romantic poetry, as Newsome says, but Romantic sublimities are only one version of the possible approach to higher mysteries.

Among the Neoplatonists, Plotinus had argued in his *Enneads* that the higher realities of the pure Idea are expressed by emanations from higher to lower levels, and therefore, as Stephen Halliwell has observed, Plotinus can equally go in the other direction. "Instead, he can reconfigure artistic mimesis in terms of something more than a correspondence to appearances, converting it into a movement upward in the direction of the formative principles, *logoi,* which lie behind the world of mere phenomena."[18] Throughout a descending and rising scale, the mimetic representation of nature can point either toward transcendental meanings or to the present, changing, phenomenal world that surrounds us. Mimesis thus retains a kind of vertical mobility, never necessarily rejecting the claims of the environment. In fact, by finding mystery in the ordinary, the descriptive endeavor explores the same deep questions of what we take to be real and what we understand to be our intuitions of the real as given by nature, while this exploration in turn leads us to wonder at higher things, if indeed "higher" is the right epithet for what Clare once called our "journey through this lower earth."

3

Description

Description appears to be the humblest of intelligent symbolic acts, yet, because it *is* so common, its possible range eludes us. Webster's, for example, says it is a discourse, or an example of discourse, which is "designed to give a mental image of a scene, person, emotional situation, etc." Immediately, this last etcetera grabs our attention; it is the key to our difficulty, since there may be an infinite number of characteristic features denoting any class, sort, or type of object to be described.

This imagined plethora of features leads to another aspect of description, its sense of tracing, traversing, scribing a path or track. Tracing is connected to the geometric, as when we speak of "describing" a circle, where outline seems to imply the logical aim of setting a limit. Indeed, the symbolic power to surround may be the crux of description in the modern context, for by describing sufficiently numerous traces, we always achieve reach, enclosure, as in a logical circle.

Imaginative literature leads away from the logos, however, and we notice throughout all narratives that "what happens" is often described discursively, so that the descriptive part is removed from lists, enumerations, and catalogues of formal content and shifted into a mode of active discovery. If one wants a description of a process, for example, one has to narrate changing states. Consequently, most novels, when they are avoiding represented dialogues, are engaged in the representation of events which are open to an escape from any "described" circle. This is the describing of a circle that virtually expands to contain ever further items in the story line.

If then, among central attributes of the descriptive, there is a power to place inventories in motion (if only as the result of adding up a sequence of discoveries), the descriptive implies an ever receding horizon. Or, we might say, horizon itself is the edge of the human circle, which philosophically considered is the hermeneutic circle. Narratologists like Gérard Genette leave no doubt that any mere description is likely to show at least some small touch of drama.[1] There are, however, different eras and kinds of intellectual pressure brought to bear upon any simple notion of descriptive accounting.

Acquaintance and Description

One such pressure appeared prominently in the early twentieth century, when Bertrand Russell developed his problematic "theory of descriptions"—a theory he later abandoned. Russell contrasted two kinds of knowledge, by "acquaintance" and by "description."[2] The former is direct, such as knowing sugar by sensory acquaintance with its sweetness, or a musical string note by sensing and perceiving the frequency at which the string is vibrating. This direct unmediated knowledge may also be extruded into a "descriptive" mode, as when the sweetness is registered within a theory of taste, or the musical vibrations are correlated to positions on a musical scale. One might think such descriptive extensions of immediate material acquaintance would be the only way knowledge can be abstract, but Russell held (with others) that one might be "directly" acquainted with highly abstract ideas, as in mathematics. Philosophers, including Russell himself, found there were logical difficulties with his theory, but at least from the layman's viewpoint it captures a profound and familiar human experience: the movement of mind into what seems its *natural* use of sense-data, namely a developing grasp of the field in which, broadly, our sense-data and our experience play a large role in the construction of our understanding of the world. We may always, almost nostalgically, want to return to the familiar, but we need, as it were, to leave home, to put our experience to work in and for a larger world, usually in and for social purposes. Altogether, Russell's "theory of descriptions" puts pressure upon the familiar, even upon the family from which one springs, where the most serious knowledge is so *un*descriptive that it can only be retrieved by psychoanalysis—or by poetry.

This second function equally puts imaginative pressure upon description the moment we leave prose and go to verse, where regular forms such as meter and rhyme seem to obstruct the descriptive purpose. Throughout poetic history descriptive passages abound, and in the eighteenth century become the center of the whole generic development of topographic verse. Nevertheless, if we hold that descriptions are always *of* something, that something is seen to exert a binding control over the forms and pieces of the description. The object of description commands its own descriptive treatment, so, for example, one would describe *brie* differently from a *bassoon.* That is, one's means of description would have to follow a rule given by the cheese, or the instrument. For this reason, in grammar "descriptive clauses" are designed to convey those rare and special and often seemingly inessential properties of objects when we try to evolve those objects for others. The descriptive is frequently less than tightly restrictive. One asks: well, how far do I need to go, to describe *brie?* Will a narrow definition separate bassoons from English horns? The role of description seems inherently unclear, as if its language-game needed room to breathe. This lack of clarity appears early in the West, where philosophy begins with the Presocratics, who, as W. K. C.

Guthrie remarks, "were much nearer than ourselves to the mythical, magical or proverbial origins of some of the principles which they accepted without question," leading us in turn to reject their protoscientific genius out of hand.[3] When Anaximander calls our cosmic origin "the unlimited," or Anaximenes identifies this *arche* with air, or Thales with water, and so on, they are all claiming that descriptions of the world and of the foundations of knowledge would have to begin from these elemental claims. But while theirs are inspired notions of environment, they remain primitive, far from subdividing knowledge into dimensions that could be counted and mathematized. It is the larger Presocratic interest in nature that inspires a modern understanding of description. Precisely the "mythical, magical and proverbial" residues are the link that strict modern science must deny, but which here, for poets, allows a bridge between their impressionistic art and the rigors of observation. The descriptive author is almost forced to avoid measurement, as satires on Wordsworth showed sharply enough, because measurement works against myth and the protoscientific.

Even so, by the time modern science has fully entered upon its epic story, analytic questions of limit, of scale, and quantity enter as atmospheric aspects of poetic descriptions. The tension between counting and sensing is increasingly tight, however, until, as we approach the Romantic period, description increasingly vexes the poets who want to ground their works in descriptive procedures, but need to mystify the domain of Russell's knowledge by acquaintance. Clare's exemplary acquaintance with deeply familiar things seems to High Romanticism too simple; their simples, like tiny surreal celandines, need to be raised up into a higher sphere. But Clare imagines the miracle of the simplest arrangements in nature:[4]

> We wondered at the spell
> That birds who served no prenticeship
> Could build their nests so well

& finding linnets moss was green
& finches chusing grey
& every finches nest alike
Our wits was all away . . .

This is the language of naive scientific astonishment, and it lacks the grand manner; on the other hand, it also lacks a kind of higher emptiness. Clare comes before the romantic impulse and does not desire the *heimlich* to be *unheimlich,* the familiar to be uncanny. Quite differently, High Romantic poetry grew out of a troubled meditation on Russell's two kinds of knowledge and sided with the more abstruse reaches of thought, pulling away from actuality.

Such matters are central to my own discussion of three poets, and throughout what follows we need to keep several relationships in mind.

I. What is, or might be, description in itself, as an epistemological procedure of encoding? This would be the Russellian concern.

II. What is the relation between description and the narrative rendering of action? This would occur if a poet recounted an exploration, or perhaps when things described are said to cause unexpected sequences of discovery. Problematic examples occur all through the history of the novel, mostly strangely in a fiction like *Moby Dick,* formally a type of narrated anatomy which is at last overcome by its own pressure toward myth, away from science.

III. What is the relation between description and expression? Here arises an almost paradoxical genre—the descriptive lyric, a genre Clare often practices.

IV. What is the relation between description and Enlightenment rationality? The question suggests that there can be such a thing as transcendental description. Examples appear not only in Emerson and Whitman, but perhaps more curiously in Carlyle. Flaubert's *Bouvard and Pécuchet* seems to be a satire on the desire to achieve this immiscible compound.

V. Finally, what is the formal, historical, and factual relationship between description and our knowledge of the environment? The earlier notion of "natural history" suggests that in its environmental origin this relation mixed fact and story, as it mixed our human history with the externals of the evolution of natural forms (in Darwin's manner).

It is mainly to address this fifth relationship that this book has been written, for numerous consequences flow from questioning the relation between description and environment. For example, in Shelley's "Ode to the West Wind," one can ask whether the "solid atmosphere" of the approaching storm (Section II) is to be understood simultaneously as an epithet for a mental event, and an impression of the darkness of the storm, the latter being an entirely natural phenomenon. Or, in Clare's sonnet "Written in November," is Clare's epithet "winnowing north winds" intended to convey the working of some natural harvester in a literal sense, or is this a biblical winnowing—in short how do we balance the claims of nature and belief in this sonnet, the rest of which is starkly realistic? Above all, we are led to a critical suspicion of a new kind, namely, whether the sheer materialism of the interest in nature manifested by Romantic poetry is not more important than questions about the Romantics' powerful projection of ideas. The issue then becomes, not the dialectic of nature and self—as many have thought—but the dialectic of natural fact and philosophical idea.

Description and Nature's Pose

Description is always *of* something, hence the object of the description maintains some control over the method being used. Recently, Harry Berger, Jr. has shown in great depth to what extent the "fictions of the pose" in Renaissance portraiture depend upon the prearrangement of the sitter's pose, as if it were clearly intended, in art, to guide the representation by an intermediate stage in which the represented object sets out to represent itself in a pose, even before the final depiction is produced by the artist.[5] This approach to the visual arts has its parallel in the descriptive arts of poetry, where the writer equally does not work within an entirely abstracted independence of the chosen landscape, a landscape that also has its "pose." The picturesque fundamentally implies a scene that is picture-like, hence deriving from the viewer's sense that a certain scene—an outdoor scene—"looks as if someone painted it." Wordsworth in particular always writes about his impressions as if he thought nature were posing for him. One does not imagine him deriving representations from a flat and undemonstrative sitter such as Clare's fenland. For good or ill, Clare never saw the Alps. Nor are the romantic Alps the fearful scene of John Donne's "Elegy," though for Wordsworth and Jones in their famed 1790 walking tour they might have been the scene of an attack by brigands.[6] But the Alps are beginning to be domesticated, their landscape assimilated to the familiar. We can see this development easily in classic European fiction, where the familiar and hence "improved" landscape of Switzerland and its quaint towns and villages belong finally to the Grand Tour. Even in twentieth-century fiction of an author like Hermann Hesse, this landscape, which possesses a highly ordered sublimity, finds its equivalent in the Hudson River Valley and similar views in the United States. The landscape indeed begins to pose

Consider a brief passage of conventional description in Hesse's *Peter Camenzind:* [7]

Our bags were sent ahead, we sat in a train carriage, the green fields and hills flitted past, Lake Urner, the Saint Gotthard pass, then the mountain hamlets and brooks and boulder-strewn slopes and snow-capped peaks of the Ticino, and then the first dark stone houses on the more gently sloped vineyards, and the journey full of expectation along the lakes and through the fertile plains of Lombardy toward the lively, noisy, strangely attractive yet repulsive Milan.

Calling this passage conventional is unexceptionable, since Hesse not only follows conventions of nineteenth-century novels; he also makes use of a style which could be found in guidebooks. Yet in either case of literary influence, the overriding pattern for the passage comes from the topography of southern Europe itself. This interaction between landscape and literature is yet one more instance of the interaction that occurs when art imitates nature, but we need always to recall the modern principle that nature also imitates art.

Anyone who has seen the mountains in Scotland will have experienced this peculiar interaction between nature and art. In *The Antiquary,* which begins one chapter with an epigraph from George Crabbe's descriptive poetry,[8] Scott presents for us "a mind employed in admiration of the romantic scene, or perhaps on some more agitating topic." This is the passage in question:

As Sir Arthur and Miss Wardour paced along, enjoying the pleasant footing afforded by the cool moist hard sand, Miss Wardour could not help observing that the last tide had risen considerably above the usual water-mark. Sir Arthur made the same observation, but without its occurring to either of them to be alarmed at the circumstance. The sun was now resting his huge disk upon the edge of the level ocean, and gilded the accumulation of towering clouds through which he had traveled the livelong day, and which now assembled

> on all sides, like misfortunes and disasters around a sinking empire and falling monarch. Still, however, his dying splendour gave a sombre magnificence to the massive congregation of vapours, forming out of their unsubstantial gloom the show of pyramids and towers, some touched with gold, some with purple, some with a hue of deep and dark red. The distant sea, stretched beneath this varied and gorgeous canopy, lay almost portentously still, reflecting back the dazzling and level beams of the descending luminary, and the splendid colouring of the clouds amidst which he was setting. Nearer to the beach, the tide rippled onward in waves of sparkling silver, that imperceptibly, yet rapidly, gained upon the sand.

There is no way for the reader of this passage to avoid its allusive literary quality. This quality is presented as a function of the landscape the passage represents, and indeed the idea of the passage is that the landscape, but not its verbal expression, is about to affect the inward and almost apocalyptic thoughts of Sir Arthur's daughter. We are left with a typical question about description: is the topos of the dying splendor of falling empire generating a very literary prose style, or is it the other way round? Is a descriptive style leading to new levels of awareness? There is probably no answer that will disentangle these two options, and they remain central not only to Romanticism, but also to the genre of description that leads into Romanticism—since description in fact is the most important necessary preliminary to Romantic aesthetics.

The force of our unanswerable question appears in the fact that European Romanticism as represented in this passage from Sir Walter Scott, a Romanticism Walt Whitman knew from his own reading, seems always to combine two opposed impulses. On the one hand, the archetypal romantic scene displays a wild and disordered *accumulation.* But, on the other hand, the scene is entirely ordered and circumscribed as a sublime idea. In this second aspect, the scene lends itself to orderly description, much as the train journey in Hesse lent itself. Nothing in a general way could be farther from the situation confronting American authors, for whom a disorder enters descriptive relationships precisely because of the unprecedentedly large scale of the terrain to be described. This scale in turn influences the disorderly way in which, despite urban and suburban development, Americans have made use of scale itself.

Whatever appears stylistically in Romantic prose appears with poetry as well. Prose simply makes it easier for us to see that wildness is the primary topos of the topographic, and it is a pleasurable wildness, whose tone lingers in American efforts to preserve ecological balances in our own time. The pleasure of fear is a sublime hallmark, betokening a passion for aesthetic ambivalence. This art always draws a fine line between the ineffable and the indescribable.

Describing the Nondescript

In fact American literature and art go further; they are intensely involved in describing the nondescript. The genius of Abstract Expressionism in the United States is precisely that this artistic style permits the rendering of the nondescript. In short, we need a major artistic category of the nondescript. This sense of landscape and setting might be paralleled in parts of eastern Russia, in the steppes (I myself saw such scenes in the Ukraine, in the sixties) but hardly discovers open, unbounded disarray in the older, more densely settled European states. Clearly, one aim of descriptive glamour and gothic mysteries in verbally drawn landscapes was to permit the novel to use actual settings whose gothic disarray was in fact organized so as to provide fictional effects, as if *the real* could formalize the wildness of the imagined. When nature intrudes upon description, as if it were a demiurgic author who insists on being sublime, the reader is led to adopt a new and quite skeptical view of description. In the middle range of a Kantian Beautiful, natural scenes are controlled as far as possible, achieving an aesthetic neutrality. But as a general and more comfortably available wild nature becomes a favored artistic subject, the pose of nature eases into something like what we understand by gothic effects in novels, and this gothic excess marks descriptions of human bodies, faces, dress, gestures, stance, and physical expression. The neoclassic ordering of a landscape by Claude Lorrain is counterpoised by the wildness of a Turner, or a Caspar David Friedrich, or by their American counterparts.[9] Finally, since it is clear that the eye sees too much in the landscape, artists discover that the local is at least knowable. Here a nondescript excess makes for a controllable plethora, a situation nowhere more evident than with American art and literature.

The problem of locality is intense for American literature, where we associate it with the "regional." Our scale of terrain is simply enormous, much of it not even occupied by humans. In this book, I have been wishing to distinguish between the locus and the *chora,*[10] between the point and its surrounding space, largely because my main focus is upon Whitman and Ashbery, with whom it is helpful to distinguish place from space. This distinction is required for understanding our politics as well as our geography. In America, it could be argued, democracy is significant only insofar as it occupies space. As a political system, American democracy tends to undermine the sense of place, a point made frequently by Tocqueville. Place is not space.

When Emerson imagined the combination of place and space, he identified it as a play of circles which could bend, collide with each other, deform each other, and finally reform. In his essays Emerson plays back and forth between ideas of place and space, in order to favor the latter. He gives to natural American disorder—in a dark moment his *Journal* calls it "miscellaneousness"—the benefit of being contained in a circle of American space, which his sparkling geometry describes. He specifically wanted to go beyond the ordered taxonomic system and layout of the Jardin des Plantes, as these have been so well described in the Emersonian context by Lee Rust Brown.[11]

As we try to decipher an essay like Emerson's "Circles," we realize that the paradox of descriptive poetry is that it simultaneously both *is* and *is about* a way of picturing nature. Staying within the conventions of the art, we see that the descriptive employs one traditional term for poetic figuration, topos. As the poet continues to employ topoi to render his subjects imaginatively, his images and turns of phrase finally join ordinary language; they become commonplaces. Therefore, to use the topos (place in rhetoric) figuratively for the topos (place in nature) is to want the mirror to reflect itself. The description then is intended to describe itself. My sense is that personification plays a central role in visionary poems, especially in descriptive vision, because poets are attempting to break the cycle of self-reflection. The daimons of personification speak for a horizon beyond the scene described and the passage describing. The daimons belong to a higher order of perspective, and with poets like Clare, their presence is enfolded into the language and scene that his descriptive poetry is mobilizing. Unlike some of his favorite poets such as James Thomson, Clare is delighted by the nondescript because he sees into the mystery of its merely existing. He discovers diurnal knowledge, as I shall be calling it. A naive philosopher, fascinated by the mere fact that something can be, he is never deterred by what might appear to others a triviality in ordinary things. His poetry is a lesson in the paradox of the nondescript, since in describing the nondescript, he reaches out to some of the most teasing questions we may propose in relation to Being.

This book is not a study of Clare's remarkable poems, only one tenth of which did he ever see into print. The general point can be made, however, that among students of the environment he displays the two most necessary gifts, precise observation and a sense of scale. He does not, for example, write a memorable poem on a single bird, let us say the skylark or the nightingale, and then pass on the Vale of Wherever. He writes many poems on birds, many on other creatures, many on trees and grasses and nests and hedges and heath—in short, his work, as displayed in his first published volume, the *Poems Descriptive of Rural Life and Scenery* (1820) and in the next three volumes and then in the vast unpublished body of other poems, amounts to a full description of his home country and what (we have seen) he called "my knowledge," so varied and extensive and detailed that it amounts to the representation of the environment a scientist would be happy to have written down. The Tibbles, who are honored as Clare's major early editors and biographers in the twentieth century, convey this range merely by noting what Clare and his editor John Taylor (Keats's editor, too) decided to include: forty descriptive and narrative poems, twelve songs and ballads, and twenty-one sonnets, no doubt all of them influenced by prior literary models, for already Clare was a tireless reader and assimilator.[12] (He was proud never to have been a plagiarist, he wrote to a friend.) But what is striking in the book and in the other bodies of Clare poems is not just the precision of imagery and naturalistic record, and more important the yearning for exactitude which seems to have come naturally to him, but equally the fact that he sees what for humans in fact constitutes an environment. He wrote his sonnets, especially, in the form of poetic notes, often sitting on the ground to write his thoughts down—and his later *Northborough Sonnets* are an almost mesmerizing exercise in camera work.[13] He registers sounds and sights as the modern lens catches the dispersed flux of city minutiae.

Furthermore, the songs and ballads he included in *Poems Descriptive* are not simply examples of his early skill in song writing, but more important, they array before us a manifold of known cultural practices. Songs and ballads provided the chief symbolic wonder and delight for the peasantry with whom he lived—they all knew the power of song, of an evening, and at work in the fields. Clare's father, Parker Clare, was known to have more than a hundred songs he could sing at a moment's notice. Robert Burns inserts similar aspects of rural life in his famed "Cotter's Saturday Night," published in 1786, but there is no need to adduce confirming examples. The issue is one of scale, the scale in which refined details of observation are to become parts and particles of a larger order of things. Song is a main index of that larger scene, and hence is intuitively placed centrally in the rural life, and its description. When, as Clare scholars have often said, the abiding feeling of his chorographic poems is one of loss—the loss of an older world—the full range of what is lost has to be a component of the manifold expression. Range itself, the extending *chora* of the scene, makes all the smaller pieces in the scene significant. The idea or ideal aspect of this *chora,* which we take over from Plato's late *Timaeus,* is an embracing and gathering concept, which privileges space rather than the pointed occasion of place.

In Clare's fenland and across America place is the space of the nondescript, whose paradoxical mode of description can only emerge when the poet "observes" the uncanny. Democratic poetry runs a risk: how to avoid being carted about in Dr. Williams's red wheelbarrow. So often, as strong readers know, our American poetry hardly deserves the name; it is bad prose, neither here nor there. But if uncanny, the poem's common apprehensions will resonate, as the familiar is rendered deeply unfamiliar, the *heimlich* made *unheimlich*. This description implies no fall into the banal, even as it seeks to contain multitudes. With gnomic precision, the poetry wrought by the poets I praise aspires to a new mode beyond either the sublime or the picturesque, such that its descriptions are always strictly uncanny; they penetrate the familiar wall all the way to its secret unfamiliar side, passing through the mirror into a gnomic transcendency, where they discover their more subtle relation to the scale of things.

4

Ashbery's Clare

The poet John Ashbery spoke about genius and excellence in his Norton Lectures at Harvard, the first of which he called "Grey openings where the light looks through," a line from one of his favorite poets, John Clare, the subject of the first lecture.[1] Ashbery admits to being influenced by certifiably major authors such as Auden, Stevens and Mandelstam, Marianne Moore and Elizabeth Bishop, but his lecture on Clare was one of six on other, more peripheral authors who function for him as "jump starts"—poets "one reads habitually in order to get started." Clare is the first of the six.

Clare flourished, if that is not too ironic a word, during the 1820s, was a land-laboring peasant, often desperately poor, even though he slowly accumulated a fairly large library. He ended his life abandoned for some twenty years, enduring endless melancholy days and nights in a lunatic asylum only a few miles from his birthplace.[2] Having succeeded in London literary life for a few years, maybe really only for two years, he disappeared from sight, as the fashion for his kind of poetry changed. Then there is Ashbery, the art critic, the *habitan* and *literatus* of New York, the distinguished and well-known poet—they seem completely unlike, at first glance. Yet their affinities run deep, revealing some of the most important connections between mind and art.

Catalytic friends, as one might name the other five jump starters—Thomas Lovell Beddoes, Raymond Roussel, John Wheelwright, Laura Riding, and David Schubert—are, among various things, a mirror in which their devotee reads his own lineaments. Of Clare's long poem "The Village Minstrel" and of his Northborough sonnets, Ashbery says: "These are rare instances of perfection in a poet whose habit, one might even say whose strength, is imperfection."[3] This could be a note on Ashbery himself, signs of a deeper brotherhood. On Clare's *The Shepherd's Calendar,* Ashbery writes: "It takes a special kind of reader to appreciate it for what it is: a distillation of the natural world with all its beauty and pointlessness, its salient and boring features preserved intact."[4] Detail-dreaming is an odd sort of almost autistic mentality, and Ashbery is aware that as Clare's madness increased, he might have come to resemble Nerval in rustic disarray, imagining at least one more wife than he had. But, if madness produced austere sublimity in Clare's last lyrics (the ones Bloom so admires), these and earlier poems had a descriptive purpose, and out of that poetic they typically produce "spar-like fragments of great and enigmatic beauty," such as the quatrain from which the first Norton Lecture draws its title:

> The elm trees heavy foliage meets the eye
> Propt in dark masses on the evening sky.
> The lighter ash but half obstructs the view,
> Leaving grey openings where the light looks through.

The spare and the occult merge here, as Ashbery is quick to see, and he associates the vision with a kind of uncontrolled disframing of scene, as if the right way to read Clare were to stress the role of chance as the controller of his poetic forms. Arthur Symons had written: "He begins anywhere and stops anywhere"[5] and Ashbery counterposes the Symons insight against what might seem, on casual inspection, to be a contrary view strongly stated by

Robert Graves, who speaks of a "most unusual faculty of knowing exactly how and when to end a poem." This seems to involve a deliberate use of chance. Ashbery writes: "Clare often starts up for no reason, like a beetle thrashing around in a weed patch, and stops as suddenly." The beetle image gives a perfect sketch of Clare's antennae picking up nature's signals, but in the manner of an oblique, ever-shifting reflector. The portrait of the two poets and their casual mode of discourse might well be the portrait of fraternal twins.

If this understanding of Clare sees him "capturing the rhythms of nature, its vagaries and messiness," the poetry amounts to a "nakedness of vision" we associate with more modern poets who descend, one way or another, from the time of Whitman and Dickinson. Such poets like to begin *in medias res,* for as Ashbery says of Clare, "if you suddenly burst into tears, that will seem to him another natural phenomenon, like the rain or the squeal of a badger," since these natural phenomena, including human behavior, seem to possess no inherently centralizing midpoint. The poet obeys a law of continuously shifting center—not abandoning the idea of center *per se,* as with some deconstructionists, but rather allowing a general denial of privilege to permit a paramount role to perception itself. Inherently, of course, perception operates without any sense of privilege; conversely, "selective perception" makes a mockery of perception's neutrality. For a neutral poetics, to be is indeed to be perceived, and my guess is that without ever having read Bishop Berkeley, Clare would have understood and shared his main ontological notion. When the badger is caught and killed, the poet adopts no dominant "higher" stance from which he judges or prejudges the value or seriousness of the event. Instead, in a narrative that commonly would cry out for ironic comment on the cruelty of man—the attitude abounding in Burns—Clare notes with almost mild surprise that badgers croak when they die, and life goes on.

Whatever else it is, this poetry is for Ashbery a model of "seeing things," and in this he agrees with Seamus Heaney's estimate of Clare. The uncanny effect of such art is that there is no spectacular *unheimlich* seeking to interfere with perceptual powers, nothing on a gothic plane, although Clare does possess his own special uncanniness based on his idea that what we simply see, in all its immediacy, without plays of consciousness, is uncanny in the sense that its mere being is a wonder of nature. Comparing Clare with Constable's landscapes, Ashbery astutely observes: "the point is that there is no point." There is no grand, egotistically sublime Wordsworthian vision, no prophetic announcement up to which, on more than one occasion, the poem might portentously advance with alpine steps. Clare has his own subtle Presocratic version of the hidden meanings of nature, which are perfectly hidden on the surface, like a quail resting on a bed of grayish grass and twigs. Presenting the scarcely known Thomas Lovell Beddoes in his second Norton Lecture, Ashbery builds a powerful contrast of styles and aims by quoting a touchstone sonnet of Clare's, the "Mouse's Nest."[6] Commentary on the sonnet reveals it to be a masterpiece of the unplanned, the casual, the intensely and precisely observed: "Here is Clare on his rounds again, telling us what he has just seen but neglecting to mention why he thinks it ought to interest us or even him." This old female mouse, a mere natural mother, her babies clinging desperately to her teats, is exactly the opposite of Robert Burns's famed "wee, sleekit, cowerin', timorous beastie," a personifying creature endowed with every social significance a liberal mind might give to it. Clare has given us a creature who is nature's ancient child, whose children are nature's ancient timeless progeny. They are (we must understand) simply *there,* significant by virtue of their raw naked existence. They have a genealogy anonymously present (and now accounted for) within an environment which is quite beyond something as trivial as meaning. Clare resides in the interim before commentary, such that he refuses the interpretive impulse as much as possible.

"Mouse's Nest"

I found a ball of grass among the hay
And proged it as I passed and went away
And when I looked I fancied something stirred
And turned agen and hoped to catch the bird
When out an old mouse bolted in the wheat
With all her young ones hanging at her teats
She looked so odd and so grotesque to me
I ran and wondered what the thing could be
And pushed the knapweed bunches where I stood
When the mouse hurried from the crawling brood
The young ones squeaked and when I went away
She found her nest again among the hay
The water oer the pebbles scarce could run
And broad old cesspools glittered in the sun.

Despite all its sense of the suddenly strange, this sonnet remains oddly neutral. Even the grotesque appearance of the old mother mouse is noted solely for its being a fact within the narrative moment. Odd and grotesque is what she "looked," in the moment of surprise, a moment more the poet's than the creature's. Clare registers an odd discomfort, despite his negative capability, whereas the mouse, who is unshaken, simply runs back to her nest. In a Wordsworth poem the sense of the odd would have led to moral thoughts on the human failure in natural piety. With Clare the observation is hardly intended to comment upon the miserable condition of the animal, but instead leads us to think about the limits of the poet's perceptual powers. Writing on imagery in Wordsworth and Yeats, Paul de Man praised Wordsworth's effect of vagueness in representing the landscape, for this vagueness conjures up an inward-turning reflective thinking.[7] The horizon for Wordsworth is *diffused* by design, or as de Man says, "nor should the sky be cloudless [as it might be in a cloudless noonday

Mediterranean landscape]; in that case the eye would be irresistibly drawn upward, whereas the clouds force it to turn inward, from an open to an enclosed space," which we may call the space of self-involved reflection. With poets more clearly dedicated to description, by contrast, like Clare and Ashbery (not to mention Whitman), horizon remains a sharply present concept because all the local detail of the description is designed to show just how far toward the horizon the perimeter of the environment extends. Strictly speaking, this extension is radial, by which I mean that the perceived perimeter of sense-perception—the poet's world perceived to the horizon—is conveyed as scope or "landscape" radiating outward from the observation point. In the art of painting, Claude Lorrain's landscapes formalize this view to the horizon, while the later landscapes of Constable, Turner, and other masters of what Turner called "indistinctness" place observation in the midst of its surround, so that the artist in a new way appears to be part of what he is observing and depicting.[8] Staying in the middle of the scene, he enters into his own picture, not above or beyond it. One might expect this to occur strongly when a High Romantic like Wordsworth diffuses the horizon. But almost in reaction, Wordsworth blocks the effect of his thoughts moving into an actualized landscape of mind, because he immediately idealizes his thoughts, tying them to high abstractions, to his grand ideas, all of which are worded as concepts with capital letters, all of which are above and beyond the middle of perceptual experience. Indeed, Wordsworth's strength of abstract philosophical conception may work well for him precisely because it undermines his more limited strength of natural observation. It is not an accident that Wordsworth depended upon his sister Dorothy to learn how to observe, though not to formulate his grand ideas, a reliance one sees, for example, in the sonnet "Composed after a Journey across the Hamilton Hills, Yorkshire," taken verbatim from Dorothy's Notebook.[9] Leaning on the word "after" makes little difference to the argument here, since we discover from Coleridge's notebooks just how hard it was for these poets to organize their thoughts on the proper role of description in the inward-leaning poems they wanted to write, since they also wished to represent actual common life along with aspects of visionary, touring Romanticism. In all these changes the problem was almost ideological, for nature had become the new and mysterious recourse for imaginative refreshment.

Ashbery's Clare is an intimate friend to his muse and to musing, and they share a fascination with the ordinariness of nature, a nature deprived of its capital N. Unlike other great Romantics, Clare is never addicted to the allegorical consequences of the sublime and the picturesque, rather he takes the natural and nature as categories of the self-evident. Like Ashbery, Clare prefers to describe a scene rather than build it into a rhapsody on Platonic themes, and in this pursuit both poets enhance the primacy of perception over any other mental category, a preference which becomes extraordinarily rich with interleaved commentaries upon these perceptions, frequently in casual asides. Clare inspires Ashbery by recalling our simplest natural and social world, whose ultimate facts of being give to the poet the horizon of poetic inspiration—"the grass below, above, the vaulted sky"—those final surroundings upon which as mortal beings we can make no final judgment.

There is a singularly important early prose-poem in *The Double Dream of Spring,* "For John Clare," that catches the connection between the two poets with marked poignancy.[10] The poem begins: "Kind of empty in the way it sees everything, the earth gets to its feet and salutes the sky." The poem goes on to tell us how it is almost impossible to hold in our mind's eye the multiple pictorial truth of all we so readily perceive, so quickly does our perception resolve into an excess of detail. We are of many minds, an odder situation than one might think, since it would follow, at least from the Parmenidean principle that "thinking and being are one,"[11] that our many minds imply many worlds all at once existing everywhere. The irony is of course that as the poem colloquially says, "there ought to be room for more things, for a spreading out, like. Being immersed in the details of rock and field and slope—letting them come to you for once, and then meeting them halfway would be so much easier—if they took an ingenuous pride in being in one's blood. Alas, we perceive them if at all as those things that were meant to be put aside—costumes of the supporting actors or voice trilling at the end of a narrow enclosed street. You can do nothing with them. Not even offer to pay." The incorrect reading of this poem would hold that the poem is saying nothing much matters, but Ashbery and Clare believe the exact opposite: everything, including the smallest thing, matters too much. Don't even offer to pay for it! One can see that in advanced civilizations, where efficiency is prized, the hyperactive ensemble subversively threatens both science and society. Our two poets are observing that we are surrounded always by too much, such that our fate, much as Conrad envisioned it, is always to be immersed.

The poetics arising in this situation, and the task before the poet, will be to discover a language for this immersion in excess, a language capable of expressing the common fact of being perpetually overwhelmed. On a sublime plane, poetry would say our problem is oceanic, and we recall Freud's *Future of an Illusion* when he casts doubt on the religious acceptance of the oceanic metaphor. For the difficulty encountered by any full environmental intelligence is that it perceives massively complex issues, all of them infinitely detailed, minute, and seemingly pointless or trivial, as if one tried to imagine all the seaweed in the Sargasso Sea, or those oceans of plankton devoured by whales, or the virtual infinity of other facts Melville discovered in the whaling business. Science fiction constructs empty utopias and dystopias and then fills them up in more or less entertaining odysseys. Humanizing the risky and heroic adventures of Ulysses was a peculiar concern of James Joyce, perhaps deriving from his Thomist training. As a master of language, in any case, he discovered that language itself would be severely stressed if it were to express masses of detail without anesthetizing us. His more rigid (less Irish?) Romantic predecessors, such as Wordsworth or Shelley, inflated their use of high abstractions with the express purpose of maintaining hierarchical levels in order to contain the plethora of the overfilled space of nature. But that hierarchical method severely limited the will to explore environments from which it started.

Clare and Ashbery take a different view as they contemplate nature. "For John Clare" gives us some idea of this different vision: "it is possible that finally, like coming to the end of a long, barely perceptible rise, there is mutual cohesion and interaction. The whole scene is fixed in your mind, the music all present, as though you could see each note as well as hear it. I say this because there is an uneasiness in things just now. Waiting for something to be over before you are forced to notice it." Such a vision of earth and sky is neither sublime nor picturesque. Instead, the tone is quiet, as if coming from deep description, and, although Ashbery is painfully aware that Clare's so-called madness brought upon the poet "a long desolation, ending in death," the larger truth could be expressed in words he quoted here from an essay written by Edward Thomas: "words never consent to correspond exactly to any object unless, like scientific terms, they are first killed. Hence the curious life of words in the hands of those who love all life so well that they do not kill even the slender words but let them play on; and such are poets." Thought here is distinct from language, and while Clare was a naïve natural scientist, as poet he was a vitalist.

Edward Thomas's own poems comprise a twentieth-century gloss on Clare,[12] and we are not surprised to learn that the sentences Ashbery quotes come precisely from a Thomas essay on John Clare. Underlying the poetry itself and all strong responses to it, whether by Heaney,[13] or Ashbery, or Edward Thomas, or whoever, we begin to see that Clare is to be valued above all for his sense and exploration of *ground.* The term means earth—where lightning finds one dissipative home for its deadly force and beauty, or ground in another sense, when the hunted animal "goes to ground." These are the "earth to earth" from which we come, to which we adhere. Such ground is never an unexamined given, claiming without skepticism to be original, to be immemorial, to be archetypal and natural. In this context Clare is important: he shows us the *experienced* ground, from which, unlike Wordsworth, he never runs. Clare inherits the clichés of his age, and like a good song writer, he uses them; simultaneously, he stands free of any uncritical, obsessive, usually resentful desire to get rid of foundations, even at those frequent moments when he attacks tyranny and greed. His innate capacity for philosophy leaves him thinking of more fundamental questions such as his Heraclitean fascination with universal, ever onrushing flux, "like trouble rushing to eternity."

The Peculiar Function of Wordsworth's Genius

Wordsworth does various things differently from Clare, such as, without allowing his trick to be seen, hasting and sliding onward as if he were "covering" the trip or the impressive moment. He is impatient, while pretending to be leisurely and on holiday. Hence he will focus powerfully on an inscription, because this gives him permission to dwell on the scene marked by the written text, especially if that text has an unknown author or donor. His big ideas are mobilized to authorize the vision. As with all the Romantics in their different ways, this mobilization is physical as much as mental. We learn from Kenneth Johnston's biography that when Wordsworth and his corpulent, cheerful friend Jones walked through France and Switzerland in 1790, "their pace was indeed extraordinary. Through the summer, covering 2000 miles on foot, they averaged nearly 30 miles a day, mostly on foot, including many days in difficult mountainous terrain." It has been calculated that their total mileage, including some boat travel on rivers, came to over 3,000 miles in three months. This was not walking;

it was running. As Johnston says, since the two young men spent two nights in the same place on only four occasions, they evinced (and clearly this was Wordsworth's plan) "an almost obsessive determination to crowd as many sensations as possible into the time available."[14] There is no other way to describe the 1790 tour except as a tour, and its athletic pair as avid tourists. Otherwise the adventure is merely absurd, which it cannot be. Yet for the experience to bear the magnificent fruit it always later on did bear, some sort of compensatory compositional device would be required. It is poetically important to grasp that Wordsworth's version of Miltonic cadence is designed to brake an unnaturally impatient briskness of gait. On the face of it, he seems not to have liked or understood the natural scene, though he could admire it. In this regard the contrast with Dorothy is always revealing. Robert Graves joked that Wordsworth was up too early in the morning to learn much about nature.[15] On the other hand, he remains a masterful picture-maker, a master of the highest picturesque. His mind proposes a relentless hike toward higher visions; those Alps and Lake Country heights are the perfect scene for his climb toward the Truth, and these in turn beckon forward into unpredictably varying vistas. To achieve this kind of variety, this distance from nature, one finds no better scene than the mountains of an old country like Switzerland, as anyone who has climbed would know, the summit always rising one ridge higher than one ever expected, so that finally there is something as unreal as it is exhilarating about reaching the summit itself. The descent is always a kind of climb, often the trickiest, most fatiguing, most dangerous aspect of this wavy search for more noble vistas.

Quite homebound by nature and less obviously ambitious to achieve an imperious outlook on life, Clare is not looking for surprises; he just finds them, without going much of anywhere, by just making his rounds, as Ashbery put it.

It is hard to imagine two poets of such deeply different characters: Wordsworth always active and brisk even in his repose, Clare leisurely, when at all possible. Clare pays attention; Wordsworth pays homage. Clare had experienced the danger, pain, and monotony of physical labor, whereas Wordsworth could only think and write about the meaning of such labor with a kind of learned radical sympathy. Their poems are correspondingly dissimilar, the one seeing or intuiting as if for the first time in history, a thought residing in some fact before him, in the thing he simply has the fortune to perceive, sense, feel, recognize, the other always driving towards the big idea. Essentially Wordsworth wants everything important to seem new, and only in that sense new born. Clare, who could perceive natural phenomena with a precision unknown to his great compeer, was far beyond novelty, as the best scientists are beyond novelty, however much Nobel Prizes seem to canonize the scientific quest for the new. For Clare the unknown is what clearly is the most and best known. This leads him to a very different sort of description than is known to Wordsworth and to a finer, more subtle metaphysics. This is not to say that the future Poet Laureate is not a superior poetic genius, but simply that his powers are gained at the expense of a crudity of spiritual rapture. All things being equal, which they never are, Clare was evidently the more sensitive poet. Less public in ambition and quite untrained by origin and status and education, he was never able to construct the larger poetic forms with Wordsworthian or Byronic success, nor to deploy the larger rhythms whose *meaning* he more perfectly understood than Wordsworth. He could never have invented *The Prelude,* even if he had been allowed to live a decent life for the quarter century he lived in hell, his two asylums. Of course he lacks Wordsworth's stride. He dallies; he thinks sensual pleasure is a good thing. This makes him important for readers today, readers surviving the modern and postmodern world of dubious system, homesteading in dubious suburbs.

If Wordsworth differs from Clare in being more *recognizably* speculative, this means he belongs with orthodox Platonizing philosophy. When he announces sublime vistas of High Romantic dream, he is allowing himself to think his way into his ideas—besides hurriedly advancing on foot toward them, he is discovering their logic of development. There is nothing the matter with this, so long as the future Poet Laureate has his eye on public recognition. Clare, by contrast, does not fear wasting time, since he perceives that *here* is a matter of "eternity," *here* a matter of freedom, *here* of friendship, *here* of superior cheer, which is the heart of the chorographic instinct, an instinct Wordsworth seems to have needed to learn, mostly from his sister. For Clare the present moment is nature's and it provides the experience and sensation and idea all at once, which satisfies and is enough, as it would have been for a Presocratic philosopher. Clare finds the *uncanny* everywhere, in the simplest things. It sounds like name-calling, but one has to say that by comparison Wordsworth is virtually an eco-tourist, prospecting for higher laws.[16] Here, in poems chosen at random, is Clare searching for the immanent transcendence:[17]

School Boys in Winter

The school boys still their morning rambles take
To neighbouring village school with playing speed
Loitering with pastimes leisure till they quake
Oft looking up the wild geese droves to heed
Watching the letters which their journeys make
Or plucking awes on which the field fares feed
& hips & sloes—& on each shallow lake
Making glib slides were they like shadows go
Till some fresh pastimes in their minds awake
& off they start anew & hasty blow
Their numbd & clumpsing fingures till they glow
Then races with their shadows wildly run
That stride hugh jiants oer the shining snow
In the pale splendour of the winter sun

Or, in another sonnet which I take from Robinson and Powell's edition, "unimproved" by the standardizing of spelling and grammar which would have been imposed had either of the two sonnets been included in *The Village Minstrel.*

Autumn

Summer is gone & all the merry noise
Of busy harvest in its labouring glee
The shouts of toil the laughs of gleaning boys
Sweeing at dinner hours on willow tree
The cracking whip the scraps of homely song
Sung by the boys that drive the loaded wain
The noise of geese that haste & hiss along
For corn that litters in the narrow lane
Torn from the wagon by the hedge row trees
Tinkles of wetting scythes amid the grain
The bark of dogs stretched at their panting ease
Watching the stouk were mornings dinner lay
All these have past & silence at her ease
Dreams autumns mellancholly life away

These are not the usual poems of the Romantic period, but they are standard Clare, and they have that uncanny power of depiction he brings to the familiar Romantic scenes of childhood and seasonal change. In the first sonnet we learn what shadows really are, and in the second, we learn an inner meaning of Shakespeare's phrase, "such stuff as dreams are made on." If one is to understand the genuine ground of Romantic vision, one has to begin here with Clare and with his lesser descriptive brothers and sisters. In them winter is actually cold, the autumn bleak and ominous, the summer warm and festive. They present us with humans as a species that knows these things, before higher thoughts ensue.

A native groundling, Clare is furthermore to be distinguished from Keats, the late analyst of sentiment, who based his great Odes on redactions of natural scenery, as in "To Autumn." Keats wrote to their publisher, John Taylor, that Clare needed to pay more attention to "sentiment" and less to his enumerations of country knowledge.[18] But, as John Ashbery says, Clare was writing "dispatches from the front"—"I found the poems in the fields / And only wrote them down."

"Resting his scraps of paper on his outdoor desk, an old crushed felt hat, a laborer's hat of all weathers, the resulting *plein-air* effect is similar," says Ashbery, "to the studies of John Constable, Clare's exact contemporary . . . Clare is constantly wandering, in his circumscribed domain, but there is not much to see; the land is flat and fenny and devoid of 'prospects.'" If there are few Claudian prospects, as we have learned from the central work of John Barrell, there is equally no directed sense that "all this is leading up to something"—a vision of higher harmony, of sublime excitation and terror, of transcendently *structured* union with higher powers.[19] Instead, as we keep saying, in agreement with recent Clare scholars who have done so much to clarify his stance, Clare is not like other nature lovers. By concentrating on the last Blakean lyrics, Harold Bloom made a final troubling judgment when he classed Clare as a lesser Wordsworth. The most that could be said is that Clare is a powerful Low Romantic.

A clouded critical vision would necessarily derive from our failing to recognize the temporal extension of ground. Since ground in a poetic sense is known only by acquaintance with the passing of a day, Ashbery's Clare, his valuation and use of Clare, are important in bringing us back to this awareness.

Clare also gives Ashbery a technical model. George Deacon insists and shows that Clare was "the first serious English collector of local folk materials."[20] This claim may not be strictly true—

consider the older county histories, earlier antiquarianism, and the loosely folkloric character of Percy's *Reliques,* or some of Burns's collecting—but among major poets Clare is unusual in being seriously "hands on," radically influenced by his collecting (note his rejection of his editor's attempts to standardize his grammar, diction, idiom, and style). In discovering and publishing Clare's folksong collection, Deacon establishes the more telling aspect of the poet's researches. As Clare "jotted down tunes, songs, dance instructions and the details of local customs," he nourished his own song, and above all a ruthlessly authentic local and regional poetic craft. In David Schubert's "Short Essay on Poetry," with which Ashbery concludes the Norton Lectures, Schubert spoke of "the music of the vowel and consonant . . . the happy-go-lucky echo of time itself." If the final Schubertian allusion in these Lectures is to *Tristram Shandy,* it will only remind us that literature, in giving us a melodic fragment of life—a wisp of disappearing song—is also, as such, dependent upon that earth whose footing is the digression. Sterne says digressions are the sunshine, and in their light we learn to wander through an indeterminate daily labyrinthine existence whose intricate maze is paralleled, as Wittgenstein said in his *Philosophical Investigations,* by the "labyrinth" of language.[21]

The problem is then, not how we shall avoid privilege and superior position, but how shall these be prevented from exerting tyrannical force? More than one side to this question, hence more than one answer, will occur to us. For the poets I am considering the questions refer primarily to a choice: how shall we resist the labyrinthine character of a world that is being increasingly observed and described? The role of the sublime in particular concerns an attempt to dominate and prevent digression, because the sublime preserves and enhances privilege. The task of poets like Wordsworth—though in the eminence of poems like "Michael," "The Solitary Reaper," or "Tintern Abbey," not to mention his longer poems, he stands almost alone—was paradoxically to deploy and resist the sublime at the same time. He sees the defect of the sublime turning into allegorical banality and reminds us that if we are to heed the instruction of nature—Shakespeare's nature—we will have to question the sublime, to question allegory, to question transcendental emptiness when it occurs in the guise of the Idea. Modern philosophy, for example with Wittgenstein, may see nothing good in the Transcendental, but humans seem to want intercourse with the Ideal and the Idea. Certainly we make perpetual use of ideas as concepts, such that our prime need is to remain skeptical of their stereotypic misuses, as when Clare rejected the pieties foisted on him by his patrons, Miss Emmerson and Lord Radstock, to whom he admitted he owed so much in his literary struggles. We recognize the Idea; we employ it; we need not be its slave according to some fantasized all-powerful perfection whose sovereignty is firmly based on its not existing or being anywhere in the world. Maybe Clare made too much trouble around the house, and that way ended up being cast off from his treasured home and world. Some said he was obviously an extremely intelligent man, indeed one of the most intelligent men they had ever met. Maybe, though, he was at heart a gypsy, too much of a local wanderer. There is no evidence that any members of his immediate family ever visited him during the long years of his incarceration at the Northborough Asylum. Yet despite his own prose writings, including the natural history writings edited by Margaret Grainger,[22] we know too little about his perceiving mind, as mind, or about his mental troubles, and hence we know too little of his intercourse with others, including especially his own family. What we see mainly is an immense solitude filled out by excess of mental activity. Dozens of the poems express a literary loneliness, to use John Sitter's phrase, but the difficult events of Clare's literary disappointments and of his clearly troubled family life altogether conspired to keep him from writing a full-scale autobiography, although we have fragments of such a project. Clare scholars look forward to Jonathan Bate's forthcoming biography, but in the meantime we remember that close to the end of his life, weary Clare wrote simply to the unknown stranger, "I do not know who you are." In one of his last great asylum poems he wrote, "I only know I am."

Clare was always searching for a primordial language, because he studied an environment few if anyone before him had ever described. He lived the folklore George Deacon has helped to recover, as he lived his ornithology, which experts still value. It may seem odd, but Ashbery is equally folkloric, sharing the same strange mixture of the utterly common and the densely sophisticated. Significantly, both Ashbery and Clare are more sensitive and locally precise than Wordsworth, I think because they have a more delicate metaphysic, a subtler response to natural surroundings. Or perhaps we should simply say: they actually work with and in the world of which Wordsworth said that, at least as far as cities were concerned, it is too much with us, a world to be rejected. He was certainly a prophet. By comparison Clare and Ashbery are more troubled to discover human limits in the face of the excessive world that preexists the urban and the political. In fact they are simply more interested in a real world, as it is called. Coming from a different philosophy, they are poets of immersion. Strangely, though so much less grand, seemingly less prophetic, they have a more intimate relation to the universe.

5

Diurnal Knowledge

If we accept that Ashbery's Clare is an imaginative and partly imaginary relation between two minds, between two visitations of a poetic gift, then it must be asked how Clare might belong in the same Ashberian universe as Thomas Lovell Beddoes—that grotesquely eloquent and decadent scion of the line of the Jacobean dramatists Cyril Tourneur and John Webster. Yet Clare and Beddoes unite those opposed sides in Ashbery's art: weary passion for the quotidian and relentless pursuit of style. They share Ashbery's obsession with the day, or perhaps we should say, with the succession of days. Clare wrote as if each day's farm labor was another poem's work, as if to know the old "common lands" and to know the pre-enclosure agrarian life of old Northamptonshire was to know that each day provided a separate journey, that (without patently being Christian) the pilgrim's progress was always the experience of a single day following another and another and another, until the full season was accomplished. In this sense Clare is peculiarly akin to a journalist, but with no axe to grind, even when he expresses his rage against the masters of enclosure and captains of modern industrial agriculture and the foolish moral politeness of his patrons.

Meanwhile my fundamental association of Clare with Whitman and Ashbery is based on a complex response to writing of and for each day, a writing distinct from any debased, decadent version of what A. C. Bradley called "half-educated journalism."[1] In a sense all journalism must look to the news of the day, so that in this domain each day is a source of its own novelty, not its own nature. Questions of coherence always bedevil journalism, in that it is often neither possible nor desirable for journalists to see or state what causes are driving the ephemeral flux of daily happenings as they simply follow one another without apparent structural sequence. Evidently, Clare, Whitman, and Ashbery all write poetry as if it were a revelatory or metaphysical journalism. Surely this writing of the day, this symbolic turning of the earth, veers away from the sublime, with different purposes and a less "permanent" idea of the written. Much then depends upon the definition of the day. While there is no easy way to ground poetry in common human lives, as Wordsworth and Coleridge discovered, Clare's writing of the day somehow detaches from the perpetual search for "what's new." Novelty is a troubling value for poetry, since it plays such a large role in Enlightenment thought. In the twentieth century Whitehead grounded his philosophy of process on novelty as a creative function, but a thinker as unlike Whitehead as Dr. Johnson had early been almost addicted to a demand for novelty. Nevertheless, it remains unclear how novelty plays a part in events that repeat their forms from day to day.

David Bergman reminds us that Ashbery "has credited journalism for altering his writing methods."[2] Having to grind out copy, "rain or shine," whether for the Paris *Tribune* or *ARTnews,* meant that a creative model, based on the *journalier,* could carry over into poetry. The poet could sit down with a poem to write, as he might review an event (an exhibition) in the art world. The pressure on poetry, for Ashbery and Whitman at least, would be to legitimate description. Clever description may beguile the reader. Jeremy Strick of *Newsday* is quoted on the cover of *Reported Sightings:* "Ashbery describes beautifully, but his description also functions as inquiry or retelling: in describing an image, he recounts the process of its making and the concerns that guided its maker." Of course, these are descriptions of artworks, that is, descriptions of works that may themselves be descriptions. In one of his more story-like chronicles, Ashbery tells us, quite literally, with journalistic notes of succeeding days and dates, how Jean Hélion paints a picture. Here description is, perforce, a type of journalism. Each description in some sense marks the day of its composition, but only journalism puts a date on it.

Journeying suns and moons provide a time system akin to that of the anecdote, but in general the anecdote betokens random casual research—Herodotean *historia*—an inquiry into and reporting of events significant but disconnected from the flow of the river of diurnally marked time. Journalism may diverge or decline into amusing anecdote, so that we might call anecdote an interpretive—Ashbery once suggested it was an exegetical device—"historicism" (Meinecke's *historismus*), a type of historical writing which relentlessly thematizes the actual flux of events in past time. This was exactly what Proust, as opposed to the Tolstoy of *War and Peace,* refused to do. Yet even these two great novelists could not resist deferring their *theoretical* passages on the nature of historical time until the latter pages of their novels, as if there were an intuitive poetic understanding that life and the theory of history are not the same thing at all.

The question arising from these and similar considerations is, finally, what kind of knowledge do we acquire on a daily basis, and then, for poets, what visionary version of this knowledge does poetry project when based or grounded upon the diurnal? It will be cyclical knowledge, that is, knowledge of the sun's presence and absence, creating a daily round, giving earth its vital energy. This will be knowledge of waking and not waking, and at its edges it will deal with transitions between those states. Diurnal knowledge will slide imprecisely into larger analogies to effects of the earth's rotation. This knowledge will be so intimately linked to waves and cycles that it will often appear to be shapeless, since modernity often identifies *shape* with progression, with moving distinctly from earlier to later. This was Montaigne's concern in his essay "Du repentir," on repenting earlier errors, since he perceived that early and late are fused into a cyclical movement of actual life which is so lacking in forward thrust that, instead of progression, we should speak of living as a state of "natural drunkenness." The radical repetition of one moment in the next is the source of our life in nature, but we thereby are born to accept an indistinct, imprecise, wavy existence. As we intently look back into our past, we meet ourselves as if not detached from the imperious present that provides the temporal grounding of our retrospection. Our past sticks with us, no matter how hard we shove it away from the scene of our present moment. Obversely, the present seems equally to stick to the past. The problem with Bishop Berkeley's *esse est percipere* is that we must locate the time frame of perceptions, which are significant only in time, while Being (unlike existence) is touched by the eternal.

Such a picture of human time, ever passing, never surpassing, is bound to lead into a special poetics, which we are calling descriptive, from which the High Romantics seek a measure of escape. They would triumph over cyclical natural fact by imagining higher laws; we stare in wonder at their effusions and at Shelley's last chilling fragment. If, however, we follow Russell's contested distinction between the two sorts of knowledge deriving from acquaintance and from description, we find strength in the former, which is grounded in a direct, non-inferential contacting of immediate reality. We know this as we *know* our own shoes by being intimately acquainted with their look, their feel, their effect on gait. But a description of them would require us to say something defining about them, something of a general nature that would relate "my own shoes" to sets of truths, ideas, even principles of the shoe, which could escape the private acquaintance from which not only my own pair, but all shoes, would get their knowable existence. We go from my shoes to shoes in general, to footwear, maybe to the *schuh an sich.* Some famous paintings of boots have in fact raised this Hegelian question of concrete universals, whose philosophic thrust animates so much of eighteenth-century descriptive poetry, and latterly exercised Martin Heidegger and the art historian and philosopher Meyer Shapiro. This genre seeks to sustain the intimate value of acquaintance (most often with natural phenomena), while at the same time projecting such knowledge out into a more generally shareable descriptive episteme. What we lose in tactile familiarity, we gain in extended communication.

Such also is the function of a poetics of diurnal knowledge. By aligning this knowledge with knowledge by acquaintance, we get clear about what matters most in the discussion of poets like Clare, Whitman, and Ashbery. We need to rescue poetry from an uncritical belief (very strong among academic ideologues, both left and right) that literature is covertly an arm of ideological affirmation. Concerns with clarifying such beliefs and their antipoetic results occupy much of Jonathan Bate's work, where the artist is shown to ask and to answer the questions: "What, then, are the politics of our relationship to nature?"[3] Is pastoral a reactionary genre? Was Sidney's *Arcadia* the hypocritical evasion of a family land grab, as Raymond Williams suggested? Does the modern scholar, who very likely grew up in a modern city, know more about shepherds and their lives than the country gentleman, Wordsworth, granting that the poet was never a laborer except in the art of poetry? Similar questions are raised for philosophy by David Wiggins.[4] Among the issues Wiggins shows to be central and not easy, perhaps the oldest is still the most important: "Are we not ourselves part of Nature?" For the arts this amounts to asking in what way the artist belongs to his subject. To give an example, I myself have never been sure that Wordsworth got *inside* the simple lives of the poor he so closely studied. But what difference does that observation make, if I do not also observe that he is very much inside his own remarkable poetic egotism and sublimity? If indeed a radical ideology motivated the younger Wordsworth, he would have had to counter this effect by an opposed attention to the diurnal, where the only revolution is that of the rising and setting sun, and we are left with Jonathan Bate's question about the politics of a relation to nature (if not to expedient policies regarding the use of natural resources). What counts with every diurnal art is that the forming mind begins with a deceptively simple grounding in the flux of change that we call life, and this grounding not only changes from moment to moment, but also changes with each successive historical era. While history is a strong and legitimate framework of understanding, it is clear that nature questions history, most extremely, for example, in the way significant time stretches out and moves infinitely slower in the geological domain than it does in the events of historical time. For the poet, dilating his diurnal perspective, significant long-term thinking is primarily never one of politics, despite appearances, since the poetry has to come from a source deeper and more personal than the group thinking defined in *political* terms. Justice is not a forbidden subject for this poetry; *however, the poetry must first discover the living moment in which questions of social justice are embedded for actual human beings.* In this sense poetry cannot proceed from the Platonic position, but instead must heed Hart Crane's call for a "poetic logic."[5]

Since living in the day is more or less immediate and given to us without the aid of large explanatory theories or scientific, philosophic, or ideological "laws" of thought, we must accept its sharp limitations. It does not imply progress, or even a progression of events, beyond the daily cycle. It seems often close to randomness, like the vague and mixed orders of happenings that occur during the natural cycle of the day. But one thing it does involve is the sense-experience of acquaintance. It comes to us, as Russell would say, "in sensation with the data of the outer senses, and in introspection with the data of what may be called the inner sense—thoughts, feelings, desires, and so on; we have acquaintance in memory with things which have been data either of the outer or of the inner sense. Further, it is probable, though not certain, that we have acquaintance with Self, as that which is aware of things or has desires toward things."[6] Russell holds that we can even be acquainted with universals, such as brotherhood or diversity, since these are concepts arising through the inward experience of conceiving. On the surface at least his concerns appear to be spatial, as if definitions belonged to an unchanging logical world. But for the descriptive poet the more pressing need is to confront the issue of temporal change, which requires looking at natural phenomena with precision, so precisely indeed (as was always said of John Clare) that even delicate temporal shifts are made visible.

Diurnal knowledge places us in a perpetual present moment. Hence change in this sphere is confined to cycles of returning events, and tends to defer any confident judgment of historical advance or decline as extensions beyond the diurnal. This confinement, as Russell observes (and great poets like Wordsworth instinctively recognized), can well be a limitation upon our thought. One can see the diurnal in this light: "We should only know what is now present to our senses: we could not know [for example] anything about the past—not even that there was a past—nor could we know any truths about our sense-data."[7] Caught up in the continuous onslaught of sensory stimuli, we would not be able to escape into ideas, even when these ideas (and their consequent "truths") derive from our inner acquaintance with what we call abstract ideas and universals. How these higher abstractions are grounded in a kind of acquaintance was a major intuition and question for Russell, and remains, I think, centrally problematic for the study of poetry, but even allowing for that, we can say that powers such as memory have a deeply acquainted character, despite their belonging to a "higher order" of thought than immediate percepts and sensations.

In *Other Traditions,* Ashbery raises a question of art fundamental to his own vision (as to Clare's and to Whitman's): the place in high art of fragmentary, momentary, and seemingly inchoate experiences. Since the circle precludes progress, the happenings have to be left just as they are, and we gain a grounded sense of things if we resist any temptation toward a too easy transcendental enframing. This is a universe whose catalogued parts define the miscellaneous character of life itself. This is buttoning up a shirt, putting on a jacket. To make a great poetry from quotidian events is no mean trick. This unassuming art requires a different kind of eloquence, the expression of a science developing out of natural history, even when the poet writes of human society.

Some years after Jane Austen's death, Sir Walter Scott praised her (and dispraised himself) in this regard. Observing her philosophical precision, Scott spoke of her "exquisite touch, which renders ordinary common-place things and characters interesting from the truth of the description and the sentiment."[8] Truth of description is a scientific goal, and we are reminded that scientific method is actually just a method of true describing. We often forget that the new precision of measuring instruments, initially optical like the telescope and microscope, permitted devices that make exact descriptions of mass and motion possible. This precision in turn has the effect of taking all fabulous late Renaissance "natural magic" out of the history of things in nature, allowing the scientist to develop equations of physical relativities. These equations have the power to reduce description as closely as possible to the form of mathematical laws. If we think of these scientific procedures as linked to the descriptive arts of language, we begin to see why so-called descriptive poetry had to be central to the eighteenth-century intellectual enterprise. New modes of description had to follow the impressive leadership of a post-Galilean mathematizing of science, so that, even though the *mathesis* of nature would appear to narrow and reduce all fields of study, in fact, as Foucault remarks, this rigorous classical ordering system (as it developed especially in France during and after *l'age classique*) "was equally true for all those approximative, imperfect, and largely spontaneous kinds of knowledge which are brought into play in the construction of the least fragment of discourse or in the daily processes of exchange."[9] Such approximating discourses would have to include poetry as its most powerful and concentrated example, as, let us say, in James Thomson's *Seasons*—a poem devising the discursive Georgic coherence of mid eighteenth-century thought. In all such accountings we have to remember that poetry never "obeys the rules," despite the dreams of Italian Renaissance academies. Yet one cannot doubt Pope's neoclassic admiration for the rule-bound character of Newton's celestial mechanics and optics. If indeed God said, "Let Newton be, and all was light," one was led by a natural course of thoughts to see how the couplet used its symmetry to mirror the balances of Newtonian mechanics. In a different direction, the pre-Romantic descriptive verse of *The Seasons,* with its extended version of diurnal knowledge, its sense of the onrush of seasonal change, shifts the emphasis from celestial mechanics to the field of natural organisms—the terrifying storm in Thomson's "Winter," like the storm in *Hiawatha,* resembles a wild creature. Even so, the light-centered universe of Newton's theory of gravity holds all together for Thomson.

> Our hearts would burn within us, would inhale
> That portion of divinity, that ray
> Of purest heaven, which lights the public soul
> Of patriots, and heroes.

These lines from "Winter" go on to show that there are lesser lights for humbler folk who dwell "along the smoothest stream / Of rural life," but in every case the universal system controls the operations of the mind, as much as it oversees and gives life to all natural beings. What follows in the poem is a typical exordium to the unbounded powers of mind rising from state to state, and world to world, "in endless growth and infinite ascent." This might as well be Milton cast in an optimistic mode, but the poetic treatment here differs radically, in line with the new episteme; the poem at once descends to a realism of describing peasant life in much detail, a level of precision that was to reach its acme in Cowper, Crabbe, and Clare. These poets directly raise the question of the difference between tropes and equations. Both know that metaphor, the cardinal inward burning source of poetry, is a kind of bad equation, an equation without numbers. Milton and Thomson, in their descriptive enhancement of the ancient anthropological purpose of epic, participate in the invention of a new field for testing poetic vision, where description creates a discursive paradox of vision and fact *inmixing* with each other. Such deep descriptions, as we may call them, in this paradoxical way maintain a close alliance with the felt reality of acquaintance, but on the other hand they tend also toward expressive romantic gestures, holding and yet attenuating the sense of balance that goes with the Newtonian order.

Rescuing Diurnal Knowledge from Journalism

Readers have long known that when Walt Whitman turned to a life of poetry, he turned his back on the hackneyed expressions that were needed for the journalism which he and his fellow newspapermen had known and practiced in and around New York. Yet David Reynolds has also shown that much free play with "news items" remained in the poet's toolbox.[10] It is usually said that he made this shift to poetry quite mysteriously, yet no doubt his outspoken political views brought him to odds with his newspaper employers on more than one disastrous occasion. My guess is that it was the poet in him that caused his troubles and his final break with the news business that he knew so well, from print shop and pressroom all the way up to the publisher's office. The poet in him had to slow up the pace of his perceptions, placing them at the service of diurnal knowledge, instead of yesterday's news.

Journalism in its most important form before the 1950s was usually called "the press," after the unbounded influence and omnipresence of printing. Speed is of the essence in this business. The press gave a new meaning to gossip, and a twist to the profession of hack writing that has perhaps been best caught in George Gissing's *New Grub Street.* "Haste makes waste" also takes on new meaning. Furthermore, the commerce of journalism is supported by advertising, and business forces have no inherent interest in the truth. Bill Kovach and Tom Rosenstiel emphasize the question of truth in reporting, with an important focus on the verification of fact and the journalist's responsibility for this veracity when approaching the reading public.[11] A Renaissance scholar like myself is only too aware of the early established battle between rumor and fact, as the most recent *wonders* were reported by the earliest of modern journalists, with their frequently inflammatory broadsides. Fact, certainly, is critical to the idea that newsgathering can be responsible, much as it is important in science not to *fudge* the evidence. Yet the news is seriously vulnerable, suffering from epidemic infant mortality. Only descriptions yielding diurnal knowledge can undo the instant senescence of news, its grotesque aging, by converting the passing event into news that cannot die. Nevertheless, the news promises to interrupt the eternal boredom of the daily round; it is exactly what the life of agriculture prevents, as if our need to eat forced upon our providers a cursed, never ending dullness. Hunting only appears to be different. But labor of all kinds is tiresome as well as tiring. Against this weariness the news should sparkle and inform, so that, as Tocqueville averred, "I approve of it from a consideration more of the evils it prevents than of the advantages it ensures."[12]

Unfortunately, certain secondary traits of the news conspire to weaken its tenure on life. Its reliance on sensation, however shrewdly manipulated, leads it to depend always on the cheaper tricks of rhetoric, most serious of which are appeals to what Richards long ago called "stock responses," or what critics of advertising, like Chuck Anderson, have called "the big lie."[13] Then too, the most effective news may be hot, but it cools down within days, hours, and minutes (even before the advent of television), as its conductivity is too high. By any definition, novelty cannot last. In his critical chapter on "Liberty of the Press in the United States," Tocqueville says that the American journalist makes "an open and coarse appeal to the passions of his readers; he abandons principles to assail the characters of individuals, to track them into private life and disclose all their weaknesses and vices. Nothing can be more deplorable than this abuse of the powers of thought."[14] Because passions shift interminably and without reason, it follows that this abusive journalism has no power to last. It contradicts itself. If it could not be sold, it would be completely worthless, with one exception: its momentary role in the incitement to free democratic thinking. Logically and ontologically, however, the news has no perdurable existence; it exists, by design and in theory, to cease to exist. Not even in memory can the news gain access to any fundamental knowledge of the day, although, as we shall see, a great memoirist can undo this grotesquely fast senescence of news.

Jorge Luis Borges, the student of semiotic blindness, once imagined a freak who could remember all the news for a week or a month or a year, and beyond. Funes the Memorious "remembered not only every leaf of every tree in every patch of forest, but every time he had perceived or imagined that leaf." Funes parodies Bishop Berkeley's god; he says to the narrator: "I, myself, alone, have more memories than all mankind since the world began," but then adds, "My memory, sir, is like a garbage heap."[15]

Memories of the Moment

In *Mimesis* Erich Auerbach devoted a brilliant chapter (which of his chapters is not brilliant?) to the Duc de Saint-Simon, the greatest of memoirists.[16] Commenting on the uncanny terror Saint-Simon experiences when he comes suddenly upon the Duc d'Orleans dying, purple-faced, tongue lolling, neck bent as he squats on his "pierced chair," on the toilet seat, Auerbach notes that it is not only the raw materiality itself that here shocks us and possesses such force. "The point is rather that these things are made to serve a completely serious character portrayal." The effect is modern or even ultramodern, while Saint-Simon reduces the world to the court, which allows him access to the most minute details of gesture, inflection, tone. His scene is an "everyday environment," given with absolute precision and so self-contained, says Auerbach, that "the whole work will have a unity of action"—the action of the observations being reported. Auerbach stresses that the details are unselected and random. There is no grand perspectival Claudian withdrawal to a high point of survey; there is thus no "general view of a situation in its entirety."

The apparent chaos of this arrangement, associated interestingly with Vico, acquires another unity, but only by means of an inner program, the urgency of the author's "inner impulse," which in turn "gives the language something unusual, at times something violent and immoderately expressive." The memoirist's method rejects any historicist theory of the schematizing of events by preferring always what individual memory prefers—the salient touch, the unselected gesture, the merest noticing. If for description this art of memory were plausibly to provide a central model, it would identify the unselected with the self-selected, and the form of the whole with the modern scientist's notion of a self-organizing adaptive system—Ashbery's "system." Auerbach observed that what seems in the Duke's memoirs "amorphously chaotic" unexpectedly produces a stable meaning through its use of the "absurdly personal" detail reaching down into "the depths of human existence."

Saint-Simon and indeed all the great journal-keepers give us a clue to the inner life of diurnal knowledge. The Duke expresses an intensity of emotional and experiential variability, a raw resistance to neoclassic rules. That events merely happen is the mystery. He establishes the idea of a journalism set free from its compulsion to seek always the newest thing, opting instead for the characteristic thing, the intimate revealing gesture. This is a private journalism, journalism for the family truth. But in this very success the memoir reveals the inherent dilemmas of the journalist, whose yen for public accessibility in fact prevents the news from ever really being new, in the sense that no gesture ever exactly repeats itself, and its deep personal idiosyncrasy has the only newness there ever really exists. The subtlest memoir is journalism saved by privacy.

Time and its gradual or sudden unfolding pulsations in experience will have to lose whatever shadowy substance they are felt to possess if journalism is to fulfill its role of dispossessing time of its felt pressure, while another consequence of thus de-realizing the record of human affairs will be a widespread illusion that we can possess ideas, whereas all we have is the iconography of ideas, labels for thoughts instead of the thoughts themselves. Since in all journalistic cases the news story is ideologically selected and shaped, the ideas of the ideology are subjected to the contradiction of a story reduced to the demands of some supposedly ideal "construction" or interpretation. This seems to democratic peoples like ourselves to lead to the self-evident virtue we call "freedom of the press," and we can argue that without such freedom there could have been no United States of America. Certainly it felt that way to Walt Whitman! But there are clear ambiguities in the ideal of a free press, because one adjacent freedom—almost frighteningly obvious in this present dubious period—is that free enterprise makes the liberation of truth subservient to the wishes of economically powerful interest groups, so that truth can be, as it were, bought and sold into slavery. The line between the news designed to entertain and outright advertising is the finest of lines. The truth always has its price, but woe betide if it is traded in a monopolistic market system, whether state-run or private. Given this difficulty, what happens is that news may come to be defined not so much as true or false, but as (a) fit to be printed, for ideological reasons and (b) printed to the extent that it merely fits a quantity the newspaper's advertising revenues will permit. "All the news that's fit to print" sounds good, but in fact is a covert admission that truth has little or nothing to do with journalism. Opinion and even verification of sources, yes; but truth, no—for the simple reason that by imprinting stories of the moment, stories destined by virtue of their being "newsworthy" to die with their instant loss of novelty, the journalistic media conspire to destroy true journal reality. One reason modern readers like excessively fat biographies is that such books promise manifolds of facts that look for a while as if they will last for maybe a week or two. Ralph Cohen's *Art of Discrimination,* his 1964 study of James Thomson's poetry, shows how eighteenth-century philosophers disputed over the difficulty of description ever achieving its goal of expressive sparkle. Their endless chorus that descriptive poetry, competing with a new magazine business, should be *vivid* focuses a debate all the more critical as prose romances had rapidly (in English) turned into novels, into the verisimilar fiction of "what's-new-without-being-new." The novel melds with romance, a critical dimension of its success. We can interpret a similar shift in the descriptive poem as a traveling, touring chorography, which had perhaps begun a century before with Bishop Richard Corbett's "Iter Boreale," which combined topographical vision within the frame of a journey.[17] As long as the mythological understanding of the powers of day and night persisted, there would always be a residual reverence for the Goddess Diana, but as clocks and timepieces took over, that aura of prophecy would slowly atrophy among novelists and poets. At times it seems that the destined task of poetry is to preserve this prophetic awareness, and certainly we find this enterprise among the great Romantics, who make no pretense of backing away from prophetic utterance. Alongside this great effort there is the second effort I have been discussing, where on a humbler basis the poets of empirical fact seek to embed such fact in the ever-flowing river of passage itself.

The Seasons of Diurnal Knowledge

Throughout I have been following notions found throughout the late *Essays* of Montaigne (Emerson's model), and most strikingly in "Du repentir."[18] There the essayist says: *Je ne peins pas l'êstre, je peins le passage.* ("I do not portray absolute being [as a translator has it], only becoming-and-passing-away.") The translator suggests something very like the form of journalistic continuity. Each essay, he claims, is merely a chapter in one long meandering book of melancholy investigation. This wavelike presentation of a living inquiry is one more case of the argument of form, to which I have referred; Plato's ideal forms are not part of the natural order of things, at least not here in Montaigne. If journalists want to convert logos into mythos, to shape saleable ideas into stories, they cannot evade the tyrannical myth of progress, which gets them from yesterday into today, and on to tomorrow. The very different poet of the diurnal has only the most primitive pre-industrialized body clock for his timepiece, the rhythmical signals of rising, eating, working, resting, eating, and sleeping, or perhaps just ritual bells ringing in the distance. This is not the mechanized secular time the late Roy Porter described so well in the story of a foreign traveler who noted in 1719: "There are now a great many large Clocks in London; almost every Body has a Watch."[19]

We have reached our goal, in that we can now say that diurnal knowledge is connected to the most basic human needs—living, breathing, sexuality, health, sickness, getting and spending even—but in all cases the knowledge of a life that has not yet been fully mechanized. It is above all seasonal knowledge, a function of natural order. Unlike the man of affairs in the city, the country-dwelling descriptive poet inhabits a less clearly measurable time and space of the day, a more Bachelardian day. With Thomson and *The Seasons,* a whole manner of living had been more concerned with time as an aspect of dwelling, as had been true in the poems of Andrew Marvell, whose "world enough and time" had given Auerbach the epigraph for *Mimesis.* If the descriptive poet seems to resist narrative, his resistance may result from a distrust of the *progressive* implication of storytelling in general. A strong contrast with progress needs to be drawn for Clare "making his rounds" or Montaigne's *branloir pérenne,* where pacing with nature is everything. Night and day still exist in this descriptive, circumscriptive world, unlit by perpetual electric light. Here it is possible to hold onto the insights of Montaigne when he spoke of the seasons of life—"as the peasants say, from seven years to seven years"—meaning the ages and days and nights of life, making no apology for an imagined lack of enlightened progress toward better things.

After the Enlightenment, of course, we are not likely to forget the acute connection between the press and revolutionary (French or English) liberty, nor should we ever seek to deny the central import of the press for our civil liberties. Tocqueville found he had to write at length about the virtues, if also the dangers, of an American freedom of the press. In Britain the noted nineteenth-century travel writer and historian of the Crimean War, Alexander William Kinglake, wrote classically in *Eothen* of the "wise and watchful press" which raises all citizens, high and low, into a wiser rejection of superstition.[20] At its best journalism is a useful mode of informational travel. Owing to a benign journalistic enlightenment, the citizen will not wish "to entertain a foolish belief about ghosts, or witchcraft, or any other supernatural topic." Kinglake might seem almost quaint, but if Enlightenment skepticism tells us anything, it is that superstition will result from the political misuse of any totalizing medium of propaganda, not just from a church, but equally from plutocratic monopolies on news dissemination. In short, all informed opinion depends upon genuinely open access to a relevant and broad source of fact.

Finally, there is formal clarity about Clare's way of ending-the-poem-without-ending, to which John Ashbery drew our attention. This poetic habit connects with the unclosed messiness of natural process. Often it seems almost that war is a form of psychic denial, intended to divert us from our hapless sense of this chaos and complexity. With Dylan Thomas we ask what order governs "the wood of weathers."[21] There needs to exist some formal working of the unenclosed, of the edgeless circle. David Herd, in a splendid book on Ashbery, suggests an answer.[22] He discerns a strong Pascalian strain guiding *Three Poems,* an Ashbery strain noticeable elsewhere as well. Here the note is explicit. "Running through this restless syntax is an argument about chance," says Herd. Parallels between Pascal and Ashbery abound, as evidenced in "the accumulation of verbs, the vertiginous shifts of perspective, the paradoxical logic." Pascal himself might be describing the modern poet: "Chance provides thoughts and chance sweeps them away; there is no art of keeping or getting them." The Pascalian vision of thought in the process of emergent appearance and disappearance accords with the Montaigne of the late *Essays.* The source of awareness of chance might be read as a recrudescence of the ancient problem of fortune, so powerful for Renaissance writers. Inherently, it would seem to involve a conflict between the random cyclical turning and returning of the daily diurnal round, on the one side, and the almost scientific controlling of random chance through the journalist's belief in progress, on the other. But the news is subject to an early death, as we have seen; hence its odd pathos. The journalist's progressive fictions may indeed be the sturdiest of Lyotard's *grands récits,* and hence no less mythical than a belief in spirits of the deep. But since the shape of this grand narrative is clearly designed to control chaos, so that history is seen "progressing" toward a goal of some sort, nothing could be more unlike the descriptive poem.

Deep description accepts chance as built into every day, as virtually its uncontrollably random truth. This we have distinguished from expressions of novel information, leaning on myths of progress. Journalists who have sold out to the power structure and the happiness industry must deny Emerson's (and Nietzsche's) circles, because they do not get anywhere. It follows from these considerations that if we are to understand poetry like Clare's or Ashbery's, and I think Whitman's, we need an open sense of what constitutes their freedom from a desire for closure, a desire surely nourished by a collateral sense that humans are a species designed to negotiate chance—as so many modern authors have thought. Such notions lead inevitably to the idea that poets like these are bent upon showing that design itself is beyond design, that shape and form are always about to be brought into the flux of emerging shape and form, but never allowed to acquire this from a predetermined pattern or convention. The space of this freedom from template is the space of the diurnal, and its being known and expressed is always what I am calling diurnal knowledge. The secret is that there is nothing but the day, which is always disappearing, reappearing, disappearing, reappearing again in a perpetual sequence.

6

The Whitman Phrase

"Notwithstanding the beauty and expressiveness of his eyes, I occasionally see something in them as he bends them upon me, that almost makes me draw back. I cannot explain it—whether it is more, or less, than human. It is as if the earth looked at me—dumb, yearning, relentless, immodest, inhuman. If the impersonal elements and forces were concentrated in an eye, that would be it. It is not piercing, but absorbing and devouring—the pupil expanded, the lid slightly drooping, and the eye set and fixed."[1]

When John Burroughs in 1863 wrote about the experience of being looked at, in this case by Walt Whitman, he was indirectly drawing our attention to "something" we notice in the poetry as well, its scarcely definable close-up distance, its power to radiate an absorption. We need to be reminded, many times, that Whitman was one of the great gazers. He studies the vista, not just when he writes about the promises and corruptions of democracy. His work contains a complete philosophy of seeing and looking, extending all aspects of the sense of sight while maintaining the power to absorb. Like a Stoic, Whitman sees *into* things, although often he may appear merely to notice them in passing. Some have wished to say that he stares like a man cruising the streets, looking for a sex partner. That might be, but I would rather explore Whitman's sight in terms of his wish for theory, a desire which historians would normally treat under the heading, "The Defence of Poetry." One cannot help feeling the influence or the affinity with Shelley's *Defence,* for example. Whitman, however, does not think poetry needs defending so much as expounding in the first place; he is very American. He knows what it is, and he is going to tell you. He believes poetry needs no defense as long as its visionary function is made clear. He reminds me of John Donne preaching a sermon on the text: "For now we see through a glass darkly, but then face to face; Now I know in part, but then I shall know, even as I am known." Clarity on earth comes from a way of thinking in vistas, including analogues to vista. Thinking in vistas is a general sight. As Donne says: "*All* the senses are called Seeing."[2] In his famed prose introduction to the 1855 *Leaves of Grass,* Whitman proclaimed the American bard would be a seer: "the expression of the American poet is to be transcendent and new," and when in the next sentence he rejects what he calls the "direct or descriptive or epic," he is imagining a new role for these traditional poetic impulses. Specifically, as we shall see, he loosens the idea of the descriptive, as Clare had done and Ashbery was later to do. *A Backward Glance O'er Travel'd Roads* (1888) celebrated the poet's sixty-ninth year by announcing the time had arrived "for democratic America's sake, if for no other, there must imperatively come a readjustment of the whole theory and nature of poetry."[3] In fact he had already achieved this readjustment, which depended upon his assumption of the role of prophet.

When the poem "Salut au Monde" (Sec. 4) begins line after line with the phrase "I see," the meaning clearly is "I imagine, I envision, I perceive in my memory, or finally, I behold," and this parallels a similar use of the formula, "I hear."[4] Such invocations of the senses are just that, invocations of the powers of prophecy. Invocation is then what the poet means to be doing, and after a while the "I see" formula ceases to strongly suggest the visual. In an unusual perception, like Galileo's father, Whitman grasped the importance of opera as another mode of seeing, seeing through sound.[5] Whitman is sharply concerned to show that he is actually looking at things in order to see them; he hears things because, in fact, he is listening to them. As a poet inventing his own tonalities, he is paying a special kind of close attention. A bird song, heard as aria in a lament, is something he might actually listen to, though it is hard to distinguish that warbling from his imaginary version of Rossini or Donizetti played by a brass band in South Dakota.[6] There is a problem, fundamentally, regarding imagination, which I note because of the status of the detached image in Whitman. In a purely hallucinatory way the imagery in *Leaves of Grass* recalls the definition of a thought in Shakespeare's Sonnet 27: "Like a jewel hung in ghastly night." How un-actual, one asks with Whitman generally, is any sense perception? He seems often to be *wondering at* what he sees and hears and touches, perhaps like a doctor diagnosing a patient's symptoms. The wonderment is critical, the experience of actually *having the percepts* always being felt to be the "main event." The idea of vista therefore remains curiously teasing; in John Burroughs' description of Whitman's eyes, his look, it is not easy to tell which of the two is Tantalus—Burroughs the new friend (it was 1863), or Whitman himself, gazing like earth as to a sky promising rain, desiring to absorb.

If such a sojourning sensibility is to issue in poetry, it will have to find a language of absorption to create poems of our climate. Climates, in fact, absorb us. The problem of climate and also of environment is that they resemble the galaxy: they are a soup of sameness and difference. In them, differences are absorbed by the recurring samenesses. To express these relations, Whitman shifts vista into *vision.* All the things he "sees" come to him then as what he calls "thoughts." Given this remarkable range of sculptural plasticity, and his meandering vision, we ask: what is their principle of order?—for poets as authors are so called because they seek to increase order in the universe. In this light, the following is the outline of theory for discussion.

Three initial points need to be made. First, when Whitman speaks of poetry and its theory, he means the theory of the making of poems, which are *made* symbolic objects, *poemata.* He does not mean interpretation, that is, he does not mean anything like what scholars have been calling "theory" ever since about 1965 or so. His concern is poetics, and *neither* rhetoric *nor* any sort of hermeneutics, immediately making it remarkable that he includes in his poetics the idea that "these United States are the greatest poem," hence raising the question: what is the *poetic* theory of this political union? We are left holding a most bizarre hybrid—unless we know Vico's work[7]—namely that the USA and "Song of Myself" are equally "poems."

The second point concerns politics, very broadly understood, namely, the assertion that Whitman's political vision was formed on the model, under the influence, within the culture, of Jacksonian democracy as it evolved during Andrew Jackson's two terms (1829–37). This claim should occasion no surprise. The Jacksonian model is obviously complex, the subject of numerous distinguished historical studies. I have only one thing to say about it. With Jackson, American politics changed from the end of the Federalist period in one major direction that surely no historian would ever think to identify as such: the politics and political order defining the country shifted from a hierarchical top-down structuring, with many natural chains of descending authority, to an utterly different model.

The third point is that this new model gives the picture or conceptual scheme of what I have been calling an environment. As soon as Jackson effectively established the full force and credit of universal suffrage—despite its restrictions as to race or gender—politics in America became, as a unifying fact, the ordering of a vast social environment. The implications of this fact, including its special pressure upon the Union of free and slave-holding states, will become clear as we proceed. The key question then becomes: what is the coherence principle for this or any other environment? What is post-Jacksonian coherence? John Quincy Adams was the last American president to wear knee-breeches, I have been told[8]—how could those breeches survive in the new environment fashioned by Old Hickory?

Whitman's call for theory takes a critical turn, of course, after Darwin. Our culture and politics must now, to quote the poet, "conform with and build on the concrete realities and theories of the universe furnish'd by science, and [science is] henceforth the only irrefragable basis for anything, verse included."[9] My argument may not seem to value Whitman's serious commitment to science as expressed in 1861. Darwin had understood his own theory of evolution already in the 1840s, but did not publish *The Origin of the Species* until 1859. The implication is clear, though I will not develop it here: an active interest in science and its methods would be ongoing for Whitman during all his years as a journalist, so that he *did not suddenly* become a poetical scientist in the early 1850s. To Thoreau or Muir or Burroughs, one would never ascribe a sudden scientific conversion, and so equally with Whitman. He was converted to the attitudes and to the observational methods of science, but not suddenly; always he remained true to his calling, to be the great Bard, the new poet of Democracy.

Democratic Vistas

Whitman's *poem-en-masse* cannot be a matter of conventional structures; this is not a matter of whim. According to *Vistas,* the old feudal order had used superior force as "the only security against chaos," whereas in Whitman's poetic view democracy embraced "many transmigrations, and endless ridicules, arguments, and ostensible failures" such that democratic man "may and must become a law and a series of laws, unto himself, surrounding and providing for, not only for his own personal control, but all his relations to other individuals, and to the State."[10] Whitman would like to see poetry take its part in promoting his idea that American democracy is "life's gymnasium."[11] He most often promotes the metaphor of the healthy body, but also uses the Enlightenment image of the machine. To express the balancing of the individual with the demands of the mass, he speaks of a "compensating balance-wheel of the successful working machinery of the aggregate American."[12] He knows that money and money-making will not preserve balance, for they are based on raw acquisition. If the larger aim is "preserving cohesion, ensemble of Individuality," then the only answer will be to "vitalize man's free play of special personalism." Like a Miltonic tract, the *Vistas* finally launch a violent attack upon "savage, wolfish parties."[13]

Yet the poet wonders at his own degree of balance. He asks himself if his thought is simply "the splendid figment of some dream," and he answers No: "we stand, live, move, in the huge flow of our age's materialism—in its spirituality."[14] The criterion for the poem must be a "scientific estimate." Whitman wants to make of politics a natural phenomenon, as opposed to a law-driven social conventionality. He wants citizens to be good steersmen, letting each soul voyage "with the accompanying idea of eternity, and of itself, the soul, buoyant, indestructible, sailing space forever, visiting every region, as a ship the sea." This voyager is to discover "the pulsations in all matter, all spirit, throbbing forever—the eternal beats, eternal systole and diastole of life in all things—wherefrom I feel and know that death is not the ending, as was thought, but rather the real beginning—and that nothing ever is or can be lost, nor ever die, nor soul, nor matter." Thus among us "must arise poets immenser far"[15] who make great poems of death, for "we sail a dangerous sea of seething currents, cross and undercurrents, vortices"—and what are these false tides, if not demagoguery and greed. He castigates the "blind fury of the parties" battening on "scrofulous wealth, the surfeit of prosperity, the demonism of greed"—excesses hardly to be redeemed by "new projections and invigorations of ideas and men."[16] His final focus is on the political sickness and disease caused by "the depraving influences of riches just as much as poverty." It is in this context of a mingled personal and political health that he invoked theory: "In fact, a new theory of literary composition for imaginative works of the very first class, and especially for highest poems, is the sole course open to these States."[17] This medical doctor is discovering a new doctrine, "the average, the bodily, the concrete, the democratic, the popular," notions providing the base for a good future. If we imagine the largest bound of such a medicinal art, it would have to be ecology, as studied and practiced by our environmental guardians of natural systems. What Whitman means by "adhesion" and "cohesion" comes finally to be what such scientists mean by ecological balance, what the Ancients meant by *philia,* the precondition of any working state, what Lucretius meant by saying that in the nature of things *amor* had to command the cosmos.

In the mid nineteenth century it was hard to imagine the laws of such outlooks, and we are not at all surprised that Charles Eliot Norton wrote thoughtfully of *Leaves* that it was a "curious and lawless collection of poems."[18] Thoreau wrote to a friend about "a great primitive poem," the verse "rude and sometimes ineffectual," while William Dean Howells equally discovered this lawlessness in *Drum Taps.* "The thought is as intangible as aroma; it is not more put up than the atmosphere."[19] Howells could not have been more percipient, for what he calls *aroma* and *atmosphere* are perhaps the defining cases of environment. He noticed subtle indeterminacies in the poetry: "memories and yearnings come to you folded, mute, and motionless in his verse, as they come in the breath of a familiar perfume. They give a strange, shadowy sort of pleasure." Unlike young Henry James,[20] Howells knew, of course, that Whitman had rougher democratic interests in mind, attenuated, he thought, by a delicate willingness to pull back from "spoken ideas."

In that age of Jacksonian influences there was more than ever a need to consider the Founders' distrust of natural acquisitive and aggressive drives, along with the constitutional balancing of powers designed to divert predatory political desires into channels of rational benefit. It is odd that as machines were rising in physical importance, the machine metaphor of the balance wheel of the clock was diminishing in political force. All through Edward Pessen's important study of the period runs the thread of a contradiction, as epitomized in his remark that "neither in word nor action did Jackson reveal a consistent interest in, let alone sympathy for, democracy and democratic social change, during the first 62 years of his life."[21] Yet Jackson presides over the massive change in our politics that occurred through the widening of the suffrage, although the right of the individual to vote was still radically curtailed—excluding women and blacks, for a start. A widened political place for the individual, even if only theoretical, was bound to destabilize. The historian Robert Remini tells us that "Madison regarded democracy as an 'unstable' effort to include every citizen in the operation of government." Chief among the consequences of polity would be the use of majority rule, which, Madison thought, could only "jeopardize the personal and property rights of the minority"—an established, often wealthy minority, the class and the culture represented by the Founders. In true Lockean fashion a validated identity, a proper governmental role for the individual, was to be defined in terms of property, a basis thought to be the guarantor of underlying political stability. The virtual opposite of this system would be the shift to an unpropertied individuality, and from the poet's vantage point this would require a new poetic expressive language whose grammar would reflect the different basis of speech and communication in the new political climate—a new grammar of status relations. Grammar implies the concept of the social mechanism. The American sentence will actually have to change.

It would not be until the 1890s that a knowledgeable English novelist, George Gissing, would find himself "insisting on the degree to which people have become machines, in harmony with the machinery amid which they spend their lives."[22] Gissing was going to call his book *Gods of Iron,* "meaning machinery, which is no longer a servant but a tyrannous oppressor of mankind. One way or another this frantic social struggle must be eased." In America, the changes marking the mechanistic assault upon the individual craftsman belong initially to the Jacksonian era, but for Americans they were masked by westward expansion, over which Jackson presided in no small measure. Industrial changes would accelerate vastly during the Civil War, but the link between "this frantic social struggle" and Jacksonian democracy can hardly be doubted.

Whitman in his formative years had occasion to learn all about many aspects of the complexities of a great age of personal independence. New York City, as Sean Wilentz has shown in great detail, long retained a variety of shops making endless arrays of different things; and although I myself remember remnants of this old New York in Manhattan, where we lived, today this individual entrepreneurial activity is almost unimaginable. Wilentz states that by mid-century New York's manufacturing cityscape demonstrated "immense diversity of scale and its complex range of journeymen, contractors, small masters, and independent producers bridging the gap between the largest manufacturer and the lowliest outwork hand. It was not, contrary to the most cataclysmic images of the early industrial revolution, a setting where all opportunity had been destroyed by invading merchant capitalists—where all artisans were plunged into the ranks of proletarianized wage labor."[23] On the other hand, the individual New York craftsman slowly came to participate in an incorporation of working men into large self-representing groups, encouraged by speakers and leaders like Fanny Wright or Robert Owen. Furthermore, as Wilentz and David Reynolds have also shown, the Jacksonian influence in New York had the effect of radically stimulating party politics, so that although a poet or a journalist like Whitman might see deep into the fate of the individual working man, the major shift gave power to organizations of political power groups, that is, to the parties dedicated to the game of colliding with each other, as groups. "Song of Occupations" reflects the legacy of craft and the small manufacturing businesses; meanwhile, when politics was imagined as craft, it remained an intensely local affair and hence occupied a middle ground between massive financial powers and the abject personal isolation of the poor. With the construction of the Whitman grammar, which was the chief artistic novelty of his 1855 *Leaves of Grass* and all his ensuing poems, we reach the area that chiefly concerns us, the imaginative vision that enabled him to become the poet of all these instabilities and changes.

The Whitman Phrase

The conditions and consequences, social and linguistic, of this new poetry may now be summarized under three headings:

I. Whitman, known for inventing free verse, even more radically invented a new kind of poem, which we must call the *environment-poem.* His poems are not *about* the environment, whether natural or social. They *are* environments. This generic invention, though not entirely without precedent, and not without affinities in certain nature writings, is a strange idea. Stranger than one might at first imagine.

II. The principle of order, form, expressive energy, and finally of coherence for such environment-poems is the *phrase,* which I mean in a grammatical and in an extended gestural sense. The paramount use of phrase accounts for the Whitman style, and more important for his poetics, for the way he arranges the boundaries and the innards of his poems.

III. The phrase, as it controls the shaping of the environment-poems that are required if he is to express any truths about a

Jacksonian world—whether pragmatic, political, mystical, aesthetic, or otherwise—takes its physical correlate and its metaphysical function from Whitman's obsessive analysis of wave motions. To put it iconically: when John Ashbery wishes to overgo his own Whitmanian prose-poem, "The System," or his vastly complex *Flowchart,* he simply writes "A Wave."

A few ideas for Whitman have thus emerged and are worth repeating: (a) that for theory we must deal with poetics and not much with rhetoric; (b) that the world in which these poetics evolve is a Jacksonian world; (c) that Whitman invents a new poetic form, the environment-poem; (d) that the chief method of such poems is the eccentric deployment of phrase-units, an extreme grammatical endeavor; (e) and finally, that the Whitman phrase is itself modeled on the virtually infinite translation of the wave—in nature, art, thought, and human experience. If one keeps these five avenues or vistas in mind, which are drawn from theory, politics, poetics, grammar, and physics, then one will begin to see what Whitman meant when he spoke of "a complete readjustment of the whole theory and nature of poetry."

Let us begin then with grammar in the poetic line. Virtually every single poem in his original manner is structured out of a single stylistic process: the *phrase,* but the phrase inflected in a particular way. Most readers of Whitman have seen his obvious discontinuities, but it seems no one has asked what larger structural principle is implied, in a formal sense, by the union of these discontinuities? It is as if readers delighted in saying Walt is just chockfull of colorful phrases, but they never ask what poetic principles of formation would allow the plethora to work. They do not ask how the coherence of the plethora is maintained. They do not seem to remember that Whitman writes poems which seem unbounded, but are in fact enclosures. The theory of poetry demands that we ask always what forming principles conspire to make the work into a poem, rather than a casual discourse or rhetorical exercise. The issue finally has to do with Union and Civil War. In a strict sense, every poem is a state. Leaving grammar aside for the moment, theorists should pay attention precisely to what Emerson may have meant by his colloquial expression, "part and particle,"[24] especially since for him, as for Whitman, states live only when they are always changing shape.

Theory demands that we isolate the phrase as the minimal life-unit of coherent expression. Hence, to construct modern literature's largest poetic environment, Proust built *Remembrance of Things Past* around the dynamics of the (musical) phrase, epitomized in *la petite phrase de Vinteuil.*[25] Broadly, by aggregating his own identity into an ensemble of parceled phrases, Whitman is able to insert his own personality into the drifting climate he invents, for ensemble is context in motion. Through the phrase and its clausal surrogates, the poetry gains particular control over the drift, the ensemble, the *en masse,* the average. Without subliming the grammar—a dangerous game, as Wittgenstein observed—let us consider more deeply what phrase does for Whitman.

Originally, the word comes from Greek *phrasis* and *phrazein,* to tell. A phrase is a short pithy expression, the shortest of telling expressions. In dance, it is a series of movements comprising a pattern. In Western music, Webster tells us a phrase is a short musical thought at least two, but typically four measures in length, closing with a cadence. A cadenced thought, coming through inflected cadenced melody. Most important of all, in grammar, it is any group of two or more words that form a sense-unit, either expressing a thought fragmentarily or as a sentence element not containing a predication but having the force of a single part of speech—hence we have prepositional phrases *(west through the night),* or participial, infinitive or gerundive phrases. The key idea here is that without predication the phrase expresses a thought, with the *effect* of the thought always being a fragment or part of a larger union.

My sail-ships threading the archipelagoes,
My stars and stripes fluttering in the wind,
Commerce opening, the sleep of ages having done its work,
 races reborn, refresh'd,
Lives, works resum'd—

When phrases like these pile up in "A Broadway Pageant," they are employed in chanting a plethora of gifts, where number is the chief metaphor—the metaphor of metonymy.[26] Classic philological skill and a deep study of *stimmung* enabled Leo Spitzer to reach into the inner form of the Whitman list, to show he is never simply itemizing things.[27] He is itemizing things which occur to him, which is different. Spitzer called the technique "chaotic enumeration," which he found also in the poetry of Paul Claudel, Blaise Cendrars, Aimé Césaire, and Rubén Darío, and we might add Pablo Neruda. He went on to show that instead of narrated events expressed in conventional syntax, we find on the contrary that the poet's "nominal style" employs a "coupling of nouns with adjectives or participles, without benefit of finite verbs or copulas." In a way this yields an impressionist effect because the style uses unconnected ingredients, touches of color, a general suppression of superordinate control. Explicating "Out of the cradle endlessly rocking," Spitzer wrote, "I see in these participles nervous notations of the moment which serve not to re-enact actions, but to perpetuate the momentary impressions which these have made on the boy when he was perceiving them." Spitzer identified the present participial ending, repeated over and over, with the rocking motion of the sea. Perhaps, ironically, this undulant numerous lapping is also a harbinger of death, the final message from the sea, a message borne upwards by the aria anchoring the elegy. The sense of rocking has many dimensions, like the rolling of images in Stevens's early homage to Whitman, "Sea Surface Full of Clouds."[28] The undulant in that poem initiated a perpetual prelude, holding and holding, while as the ocean imagined an end, "the water-glooms / In an enormous undulation fled."

With Whitman and *his* theory of poetry, however, Spitzer's chaotic enumeration is a thinking which expresses "the complexity of the modern world." Such thinking seems mainly a matter of individual consciousness, hence nonpolitical. But this is only an appearance; the politics run deep, right into the heart of grammar. Historical awareness underwrites an interrogation of the poet's "I," but simultaneously asks, purely pragmatically: what lies beyond the self? The limits of the present tense are obvious, in this historical perspective. A mindless favoring of the present tense (like the television commentator's use of the historical present) is bound to dissolve the sense of history, the sense of hierarchical concatenation or indeed any logically *enlinked* furthering of probable steps in a development—none of the hierarchical orders are supported any more, they dissolve, they liquefy, while complex enumerations in parallel quasi-biblical rhythms are allowed to verge on chaos. But, with Whitman, they do so in the interest of presenting a drama of the poet's own thinking, that is, the drama of his having what he called, systematically, his "thoughts."[29] It is apparent that among the few central theoretical questions to be raised regarding Whitman, none is more important than his paradoxical, elusive, and doubtless evasive relation to the problem of history.

Whitman seems early on to have found his phrasal method, not without influence from journalistic prose, and he clearly thought this linguistic method would neutralize interpretive problems of the relation between American and European history. Virtually unstructured sequences of phrase would allow for translation from the one conceptual scheme, to the other. A similar quest occurs with the fiction of Henry James, where a questioning recursive style betokens a pragmatic skepticism, whether about Europe or about American origins. Whitman seems to believe that these

United States are engaged in a great transition, separate and yet not entirely detached from European custom, and therefore his poetry specializes in all forms of intransitivity. To "see" is his main occupation (and then to sing), and this means in general that his expression of what he sees almost never rests on transitive verb action. There is almost never any strong sense of subject, verb, and object, although transitivity is always a further implication on some level of *interest,* as we shall see in our discussion of the middle voice. Whitman's hammer never hits the nail. Instead, he catches, as in a snapshot, the hand holding the hammer in midair in all its intrinsic hammerness. The Zenonian trajectory is what counts, or if you wish, an arrested liminal passage between and between and between. The lack of transitivity is staggering in its consistency. On reflection, of course, this persistently intransitive manner would necessarily have to be the Whitman method, given that vision and the full range of sense perceptions is archetypally his mode of response to the world. Perception and the naming of percepts, as with the Wordsworth poems on the "naming of places," are not material action.

To say that Whitman thinks intransitively, veering always toward the middle voice, is to claim that he sees rather than narrates, taking the word *see* in its prophetic sense. It is also to claim that he finds this seeing a sufficient index to a possible action implied in the gesture, a Neapolitan gesture, caught by the instant photo of what is seen. We do not forget that when he put his own engraved photograph opposite the 1855 title page of his book, he meant to suggest to the readers to read his book in a new way. Besides the wide format permitting the long lines to remain long on the page, he meant us to follow those lines as a picture-taker follows a subject. Everything is a brilliant sketch, almost a cartoon (and again his journalism is an influence). We are invited to catch glimpses of outlines, and that requires us not to be trammeled by ideas of logical or material concatenation. To read Whitman aright, we have to remain perpetually intransitive, like the vast majority of his middle-voicing verbs, his verbs of sensation, perception, and cognition.

Wishing to intensify the phrasal unit, he insists on the phrase of the pure verb, the verb before it is locked down into predication. Whitman's favorite and most effective phrase is crafted from the present participle. Take one example, out of thousands, a fragment found among his uncollected manuscripts. As so often, the piece has no title and is unfinished—or is it unfinished? The method prohibits a definite answer. Whitman's usual title for two lines like these would have been, simply, "A Thought."[30]

> Undulating, swiftly merging from womb to birth, from
> birth to fullness and transmission, quickly transpiring—
> Conveying the sentiment of the mad, whirling, *fullout*
> speed of the stars, in their circular orbits.

Here the effect of the floating present participles is to enhance an unusually cosmic sense of activity, as Ezra Greenspan has argued, and yet also this is personally felt by the poet.[31] He wants to be able to express his belief, "I know that Personality is divine," hence must intensify his verbs of mental activity. He also wants these devices of presence to express ideas about the land and country where he lives, and we are surprised to discover that the phrase is a device of political implication as well as personal expression.

Phrasing Jacksonian Democracy

The "buried past" with all its power over the evolution of custom and government has somehow to find its language in Whitman's verse. Our theory must now widen its perspective, for it is not enough that the phrase permit a wondrous play of the present participle. In a more general way the phrase also allows ideas, images, and thoughts to be distributed across and within the boundaries of each environment being described, and since each phrase is such an elemental part of the grammar, composing whole poems out of each description, it plays a central part in the idea that for Whitman each poem constitutes a state.

Note then what follows. The chief rivals the phrase contends with are *clauses.* ("When it rains, I carry an umbrella.") As every schoolboy knows, or used to know, this sentence is composed of two clauses, and in English these are the main building blocks of predication. In grammar we call these the main clause and the subordinate clause. Our language is completely controlled and expressively driven by the chief property of these clausal forms, namely, that they express superordinate and subordinate relationships between the main parts of the predication. A language of this type is constantly seeking to affirm a system of subordination, that is, what we may call a top-down hierarchical order, which was the order for America the Founders believed to be best for the country.

The only way for a Jacksonian democracy and its refusal of subordination to thrive, in symbolic terms, would be to get rid of the clauses of sentences as much as possible. This excision of the clause is only partly possible. Whitman carries it as far as he can by assimilating clausal forms in phrasal gesture, thereby weakening the hierarchical stranglehold of traditional English literary grammar. If you read William Cullen Bryant's nature poems along side Whitman's lyrics, you will see that Bryant is virtually locked up inside the traps of clausal grammatical units. Whitman uses the phrase as if he were a student of the Sapir-Whorf Hypothesis—in *Colors of the Mind,* I showed that Edward Sapir regarded Whitman as an extreme case of idiosyncratic expression, the master "of a larger, more intuitive linguistic medium than any particular language" (263). We know to what lengths the poet studied and noted down his language experiments. The phrase provides the fundamental technique Whitman uses to become the poet of democracy. No phrase is ever *grammatically* superordinate, superior to, any other phrase, although vocal intonation may confer greater importance on this phrase rather than that phrase. Examples of this ordering by intonation abound in paratactic poetic languages, such as Old English, where we see that anarchy does not follow from the abandonment of the grammar of subordination. Through powers of intonation poetry thus may need to learn how to inflect complex relations without resorting to the hierarchical top-down structure, and probably the best model for such intonation is the wave. By empowering the phrase Whitman averts a secret vice foreseen by Proust. In a passage of *The Guermantes Way* about the survival of etiquette in a decadent aristocratic milieu and in "an egalitarian society," he asks, "Would not society become secretly more hierarchical as it became outwardly more democratic?" "Very possibly," he answers.[32]

We have to imagine the rhythms produced by a phrasal style, undulant rhythms. The wave and the participle are not things; they are virtually agencies of thought, like waves of reminiscence. Whitman composes so as to *assimilate* all his units of expression, no matter how clausal and hypotactic they appear, to the participial idea, to the phrase. Throughout *Leaves of Grass* one notices a resistance to poetic argument, which, on a local level, would require controlled predications along with their extension into further sequences of predication, leading in logical fashion to clear conclusions. The example of Christian epics such as *The Divine Comedy* and *Paradise Lost* tells us that logical consequence is not alien to poetry on a large scale, but in fact may severely control the fable through the argument. Whitman's desire for a phrasally expressed chorographic vision of himself and of America leads him away from argument toward a visionary simultaneity without progress toward an end. His conclusions are deliberately expectant, suspended in liminal space before any arrival at a permanently defining closure. Such closure as he achieves is given by the anthropologist's model of ritual ending to initiations, that is, the stage known technically as aggregation. If we imagine a poetry dedicated to the idea that life is primarily a passage from birth to death, anthropologists will teach us the precise structure of this conception, namely, that the passage has three phases—separation, liminal passage, and aggregation—where the final stage marks the arrival of the initiate at a completely new status. The initiate is aggregated into a higher group within the society, and by analogy the poem following this plan would reach closure and climax when the protagonist reaches a higher level of insight, status, or home and belonging. When this last stage is reached, the protagonist is free to move around within a new language of equality, no longer disturbed with doubts about his or her own subordinate position. These anthropological facts of social ordering are one of the ways in which any "social environment" comes to possess its structure.

Aggregation and the forming of the ensemble allow the phrase to become the centrally natural linguistic expression of democracy, for good or ill. The phrase bespeaks thought in its most immediate, unreticulated, even fragmentary form, which in a later chapter I will identify with Whitman's use of waves deriving from particles. When he entitles poems simply "Thoughts," he names his general procedure, almost as if he were Amy Lowell calling her famous imagist poem "Patterns." The Whitman procedure is to vary the shapes of the poems—the complete poetic enclosures—so changingly, with such architectonic variety, that he can find places for a seemingly infinite number and variety of previously unreticulated thoughts. A prior reticulation would have occurred only if the present thoughts had been shown to follow from a series of previous continuous predications from which the present thought logically derived. Participial thinking in Whitman's manner holds the grammar of his ideas in a continuous present, which frustrates all sense of historical continuations. At the same time, it enhances the orbital vision the poet wants, displaying him, in Emerson's words, as the "man behind the poem."

Such thoughts can only be spoken in the present tense, as

thinkings, equivalent to collisions between Emerson's "atoms and their elective affinities," as Emerson alludes to Goethe's novel.[33] This allusion is packed with a revolutionary change in ideas about the forces binding or dispersing adjacent persons, whether in a love story or the founding of a nation. The ideal Goethean democracy would have to be a nationally constituted elective affinity. The landscape of wildness described initially in some of Thoreau's nature writing and most recently used as a model for preserving the environment could only suggest a parallel wilderness in politics. There was thus no conflict in Whitman's mind when he related his politically grounded poetry to the wildness of the Rocky Mountains, which he saw for the first time from the seat of a railroad train:

> "I have found the law of my own poems," was the unspoken but more-and-more decided feeling that came to me as I pass'd, hour after hour, amid all this grim yet joyous elemental abandon—this plenitude of material, entire absence of art, untrammel'd play of primitive Nature—the chasm, the gorge, the crystal mountain stream, repeated scores, hundreds of miles—the broad handling and absolute uncrampedness—the fantastic forms, bathed in transparent browns, faint reds and grays, towering sometimes a thousand, sometimes two or three thousand feet high—at their tops now and then huge masses pois'd, and mixing with the clouds, with only their outlines, hazed in misty *lilac,* visible.[34]

The above passage could almost be notes for a version of Shelley's *Mont Blanc.* Along with the artless wild plenitude goes a sense of the mathematical sublime. Whitman seems most himself when he notes not simply the numbers, but more important, the "uncrampedness." He assimilates the mountain scene to pulsations of free movements, breathings of rock and gorge. Such wild is the external terrain of a vast natural heartbeat pulsing in the world's body—a thought from Wordsworth perhaps, but more closely tied to the thought that in nature one finds the "law" of an art. To a degree, this is High Romantic doctrine, employing Bloom's American sublime.[35] Since the Renaissance, it had been customary to believe that art would tell nature what it was to be natural, but now in Colorado nature will tell art what it is to be artistic, so that a complete art/nature reversal has occurred. Whereas the English Romantics would still have to subordinate their interest in nature to a higher concern for hierarchical political order, Whitman's new world dream of America would permit him to fuse ideas of nature's sublime external power with the genuinely wild forms and actions of the new and often adolescent American polity. He admitted liking the society of roughs, but only on condition that they would not descend into "the herd of independent minds," as Harold Rosenberg ironically labeled the new fakery of yuppie freedom.[36] Abraham Davidson's book, *The Eccentrics and other American Visionary Painters,* shows what real artistic independence looked like during Whitman's lifetime; notably, the artists in question all looked for new "light" in the wilderness of nature.[37] Description here demands luminism.

It was left for Whitman to discover the wildness of the city. His early manhood was spent in a jungle of personality, his newspaper world, and democratically he made a theory of poetry centered on the idea that if the poet could only express his thoughts so as to insert them into a larger vision without claiming logical necessity for the insertion, the result would be a new social coherence, which I have identified with the coherence of a living environment. Man was to him a sublime animal, whose society could only be understood in the ecological terms of a grand scale, whose terror was essential.

In *Democratic Vistas,* Whitman spoke up against the mainly urban commerce in shams and simulacra. In "Our Real Culmination," a final story in *Notes Left Over,* the poet makes a plea for "comfortable city homesteads and moderate-sized farms, healthy and independent, single separate ownership, fee simple, life in them complete but cheap, within reach of all."[38] He attacks excessive wealth and its "anti-democratic disease and monstrosity." Late in life, Whitman has had his fill of "immense capital and capitalists, the five-dollar-a-day hotels well fill'd, artificial improvements, even books, colleges, and the suffrage." Behind his acute dismay and outrage at the side-effects of Jacksonian democracy, one perceives an older or more radical thought. His love of the machine had always been keen, but one hears another understanding here when he tells us "there is a subtle something in the common earth, crops, cattle, air, trees, &c., and in having to do at first hand with them." His feeling for the diurnal could not be more powerful. This may be a utopian version of agriculture, "the only purifying and perennial element for individuals and for society," but he is not wrong to glamorize this laboring utopia. Remembering he is a city dweller, one has to include in this cultural account an awareness that one of the most popular American poems ever written was Edwin Markham's dismal elegy, "The Man with the Hoe."[39] Yet Whitman at least asks the right question: "What fortune else—what dollar—does not stand for, and come from, more or less imposition, lying, unnaturalness?" He finally had to worry about the decline of craft in the Jacksonian legacy. He had always been a more serious thinker than his idling manner suggested, and when the Civil War left him shocked and saddened by a carnage that reached its tragic scene in the death of Lincoln, he could only accept the dark side of his initial optimism. Three years before the poet died, Oscar Wilde wrote a review, "The Gospel according to Walt Whitman," where he commented, "If Poetry has passed him by, Philosophy will take note of him."[40] This was often a primitive natural philosophy, of the kind I associate with the Presocratics. "He has begun a prelude to larger themes. He is the herald to a new era. As a man he is the precursor of a fresh type. He is a factor in the heroic and spiritual evolution of the human being." This makes the poet a virtual demiurge.

Although Whitman discovers how his poetry could fit democracy, he never writes as if the two institutions were all there is. That was much of his message, his continuously praising the things humans do, in all walks of life. When, as I claim, he invented the poem-as-environment, he never believed this was a literal fact. The environment-poem is, as any good poet would know, an imaginative discovery and an imaginative product. Given the form invented, that would be enough. But what a strange belief it involved, this belief in the mystery of the vastness of our ecological home, as if the earth momentarily looked at us!

7

The Environment-Poem

Imagine, as the model for an environment-poem, as I am calling the most intensely deep descriptive poetic form—the *chorographic* poem—the following lyric by Emily Dickinson.[1]

From Cocoon forth a Butterfly
As Lady from her Door
Emerged—a Summer Afternoon–
Repairing Everywhere—

Without Design—that I could trace
Except to stray abroad
On Miscellaneous Enterprise
The Clovers—understood—

Her pretty Parasol be seen
Contracting in a Field
Where Men made Hay—
Then struggling hard
With an opposing Cloud—

Where Parties—Phantom as Herself—
To Nowhere—seemed to go

In purposeless Circumference—
As 'twere a Tropic Show—
And notwithstanding Bee—that worked—

And Flower—that zealous blew—
This Audience of Idleness
Disdained them, from the Sky—

Till Sundown crept—a steady Tide—
And Men that made the Hay—
And Afternoon—and Butterfly—
Extinguished—in the Sea—

In this poem where so much is happening, the butterfly sets or surveys a scene in which a surrounding ambience of things and forces impinges upon a ghostly imagined perceiver, an observer, or even more abstractly, someone floating in space. The word *choro-graphic* as applied to a poem like this will emphasize its sense of space rather than place, as the ancient Greek word *chora* means space, while the word *topos* means place. We are most familiar with *chora* in the dance, where we speak of choreography. Here Dickinson does not define any particular placement of the physical action, so much as she glimpses a distance receding from an actual garden into a larger, but oddly undefined circle of reality. After the harvesting is done, we are left with light itself, the light of the butterfly's wings, whose extinction marks an edge, as Wallace Stevens said in one of his early poems. We discover what the horizon includes in its Parmenidean plenum, its *chora,* a lot of things merely surrounding the observer.[2] For these things, the reason for being is that they surround, they environ, and are felt to be significant by virtue of this circumscription.

These elements in the surrounding must somehow fit together, despite differences of type, so as to achieve a life-process. If all were dead, we would not speak of environments. We would speak of a blank all, a blank totality, but environments (in common speech) rightly connote life, such that we use the term to mean a living system. In Whitman's poetic tradition, Ammons's meditation on trash value, *Garbage,* is all alive.[3] Ashbery's *A Wave* and *Flow Chart* are equally living systems, as is his long prose-poem, "The System," in *Three Poems.* There may sometimes be a spotted owl to play the hero in such systems, but the system overrides the role of the particular hero, or rather, the hero is made that chiefly by being a singular participant. We could ask how to identify "the hero of the environment." Our answer must connect to the perpetual demonstration in *Leaves of Grass,* especially in "Song of Myself," that the self is a function of its world, its "context" in the sense of J. L. Austin when he observed that there may be many "breakdowns of grammatical criteria," but there are nevertheless "a great many devices . . . tone of voice, cadence, gesture . . . (to show what act it is) including, especially, context."[4] Tenney Nathanson has shown with great subtlety just how various unusual performatives are essential to the projection of Whitman's voice in its liberation from and use of *writing,* as the inner life of the mind meets the outward existence of the world, with each defining and speaking for and through the other.[5]

Voice in Whitman is intended to surround us. He is often uncanny, owing to the *unheimlich* character of this combination of the remote and the familiar, which, as Freud noted in his essay on "The Uncanny" (1919), is a central paradoxical attribute of "home."[6] Ending a poem is here like knowing the windows or walls of one's own house. In contrast, as Ashbery observed, Clare's final lines tend often to drift away, into the promise of a new reverie. As if in the midst of a movement begun, already forwarding and yet partly finished, Clare concludes a poem as if its description were for the moment tired and exhausted, having reached a perimeter which turns out not to be the horizon. Given this seductive deception, the poems refuse to go further, as if to say: this is enough, since what you imagine must be the ending of an environment-poem cannot end; it can only reach its circumference whose circular form provides an edge, but not an end. Approximating conclusions only, the environment-poem always drifts off toward the horizon, which in turn leads to another more distant horizon.

The trick for Whitman, and those like him, is to express enormous force driving toward a conclusion, but then to allow this force to dissipate as the poem reaches its ending. The mere use of the phrasal makes this a natural effect, but when the phrasal is intensified by participial presentness, the sense of tidal outflow increases subtly. That is what Whitman does, most famously at the end of "Song of Myself," where he comes to the end of his poem at exactly the place where the poem begins. The action of the poem, as is generally true for Whitman, is never really an action driven by a strong belief in material causality, but is rather a seduction of the reader into a search for the author, who emerges only through a crisscross motion within the mental space correlated to some physical space the poem describes. For the outer world in its letter gives the coordinates of the inner world, with its thoughts. This is the meaning, typically useful to ponder, of a later Whitman-like poem, Roethke's "Journey to the Interior," which (as Northrop Frye once noted), uses an environment perfectly balanced between inner and outer.[7] At the precise moment when the boundary is reached, the seeker, the one seduced, wants always to ask: but is he not here? I have lost him, where is he? The poet answers, typically enough,

> Failing to fetch me at first keep encouraged,
> Missing me one place search another,
> I stop some where waiting for you.

This "some where" is a two-word phrase for a surrounding. Among the twelve original songs of the 1855 *Leaves,* where each part is actually only a section of the larger manifold and no section may exist without a participation in the aggregate of all twelve, the poet is always asking: is this piece an aspect or avatar of the larger surround? If it was, then he included it, for he knew that in the nature of environments there was common space. The book had to expand, to fill this common ground. While individual literary tastes may vary, it has always seemed to me that Whitman knew what he was doing when he allowed the 1855 edition to keep on growing, changing, and evolving. He knew that everything in 1892 followed from and was born out of "Song of Myself." Unless this plan is understood, readers will never really understand "Song of Myself." Whitman moved his materials always forward, so that his book might, in a sense, be read backwards, as any work aspiring to simultaneity would need to do.

In a sense, *Leaves of Grass* is an ideal theater or a show. An early modern example of such would be John Donne's *Sermon No. 9.* The central Christian topic of the metaphysics of light underlies both Dante's and Milton's epics, and owing to the nature of the universe it must underlie all works of widest visionary scope, such as *The Divine Comedy* and *Paradise Lost.* Donne's sermon I have already quoted; he delivered it in St. Paul's Cathedral on Easter Day, 1628, drawing his text from I Corinthians 13.12: "For our sight of God here, our Theatre, the place where we sit and see him, is the whole world, the whole house and frame of nature, and our medium, our glasse, is the Booke of Creatures, and our light, by which we see him, is the light of Naturall Reason."[8] Donne imagines reason as an aspect of "the light of faith," and he goes on to say that "sight is so much the Noblest of all the senses, as that is all the senses." The preacher concludes: "and so of the rest of the senses, *all is sight.*" For Whitman vista is confluent seeing, such that inhabitants dwell where paths and rivers meet, as they do in New York City.

And I know I am solid and sound,
To me the converging objects of the universe perpetually
  flow,
All are written to me, and I must get what the writing
  means.[9]

This naturalist is deciphering a system of natural networks. In nature he finds "endless unfolding of words of ages . . . A word of reality . . . materialism first and last imbuing."[10] If there is room for contradiction here, the poet admits it; he permits contradicting swirls and "hefts of the moving world . . . scooting obliquely high and low." His democracy has to work from the bottom up, not hierarchically from the top down. His axioms are partial, not controlling; intermittent, but not absolute. One always has the sense with Whitman and others like him that they depend upon oral cultures and old customs directing the right way to live.

"I take part . . . I see and hear the whole"; but he refuses command, preferring the middle voice, as we shall see. "You can do nothing and be nothing but what I will infold you."[11] This *inleaving* vision is the main poetic method; it can go so far toward the surreal that one is not really startled to hear the poet say: "My head evolves on my neck," for one knows he has a vaguely scientific thought which is active at the very moment his locution is invented as an uncanny joke.

Environmental Belonging

Having several times asserted that an environment-poem *is* an environment, that such a poem does not merely suggest or indicate an environment as part of its thematic meaning, but actually gets the reader to enter into the poem as if it were the reader's environment of living, I need here to mention again the difficulty of knowing how to describe such a distinction between mind and living. Any literary artifact can induce an imaginative belief that one has "entered" a world, as Alice entered Wonderland by passing through the looking glass, but then we ask if these entrances are daydreams or hallucinations or the disconnected flights of fanciful association. With Donne we thought of theater as a scene of theory or fundamental philosophical action, as the *Poetics* characterized drama in contradistinction from history. In the theater, more sharply than at the movies, spectators and audiences admit to experiencing rather complete identifications when they attend brilliant performances, while readers of the great nineteenth-century novels commonly report a feeling of being "carried off into another world" by such realism, as if these readers descended from Don Quixote, who went mad because he believed so completely, if not so coherently, in the romances he read. A vast essay on mimesis, *Don Quixote* studies all forms of hysteria, to show how the mimetic principle works in the human psyche. At the same period it was written, our literature generated many new archetypes of identification—as Bloom would say, in Shakespeare this art marks out in modern senses the "invention of the human." A person in love will weep tears at Shakespeare's *Sonnets* or Spenser's *Amoretti,* and we may easily continue to list all the imaginative powers possessed by endless kinds of literature.

What differs here is the systemic character of the world or scene developed in the environment-poetic. For environments are a special kind of natural ensemble, where drama and story are not the issue, where emotion is subordinate to the presentation of the aggregate relations of all participants, rather than the striking enhancement of singular or single heroes and heroines. We can therefore ask if the environment-poem is a genre like the funeral elegy, or Pindaric ode, or Horatian satire, or classical epic. It almost looks as if this type were not a genre at all, because it evinces a careless want of traditional form, rejecting hierarchical shapes and grammars. We might say that its democracy is shapeless, but in that case we must ask what it seeks to achieve formally, that being the aim of art—to shape our sense of things.[12] To pursue the political analogy, the environment-poem seems destined to follow in the footsteps of philosophical anarchy, a fine idea that does not work! If in this sense it is to be a mirror for a society, we would need to ask how the representation of reality here becomes a model for representation itself, for modeling our critique of the body politic, such that some persons or elements or creatures or interactions with the fictive environment can subtend or generate our belief that "we are being represented," as in a House of Representatives. Nature's economy calls not for a House of Burgesses, of Lords, of Commons, but more radically for "representatives" with whom we interact in a system of mutual co-representation.

The relevant modes of environmental and ecological identification seem particularly important to sketch, even though we cannot yet define the form in traditional ways. How indeed does the reader *enter* such an environing symbolic or semiotic space? The strongest identifications seem to occur in fictions representing persons we never could "know the likes of" in our own familiar world, and I suspect this is true even when we discount changes in the class structure. Audiences knowing nothing of kings, nothing of Dark and Middle Ages, nothing of ancient dynasties, can still identify with King Lear and his daughters and even with his Fool. This is only possible because in such dramas the environment is reduced to a mere handful of factors—division of land, filial love and filial hatred, the storm, eyesight, eyes, white hair. These reduced elements allow focus on single protagonists—the classical aim of drama—and prevent atmosphere from taking center stage. As soon as action develops character, and character isolates the story from its atmosphere, the environmental effect diminishes—we see this process in reverse, in *Lear,* for the storm seems always a romantic wrenching or evasion from the play's central, classical action. The storm pits the King against Nature, and removes the play from its socio-political scenario; it then makes the play elemental as it approaches the later stages of its action, so that finally Shakespeare can speak of dogs, horses, and rats without losing direction. The test of any *Lear* production is somehow, therefore, to maintain the forces of identification while the storm is raging—very much the point of Albert Finney's playing Lear in the film *The Dresser.*

If we turn to the poems of our climate, as Wallace Stevens called them, we find extreme pressure put upon the classical aim of focusing image and action, and we ask how any reader could be expected to identify with the whole of an environment, as it were "all at once." Furthermore, remembering that we are mostly stirred by stories of actions we ourselves could never perform, Lear's for example, we wonder if environments we do *not* know are capable of stimulating us into any identification at all. The issue is put in terms of: *I am to become One with the Many,* a manifest if powerful misreading of Plato's philosophy. His One was a supreme abstraction out of the material Many, while the Many itself was an abstraction from the actuality of all changing things. How is the individual to become such a One? Cities and citizenship perhaps rescue our thinking here. It might be asked if city people can identify with the land, the country, or the wild. Suppose ways of life designed to follow the law and not to follow nature; suppose a freedom that devalues attachment to the land, enhancing social, urban attachments instead. And suppose then the city dweller's removal from all immediate contact with unimproved or cultivated nature (as on farms)—then how, for example, can a good environment be much more than a purchasable commodity (or a setting one may like, but cannot afford), and hence how could the environment-poem achieve any lasting humane importance? An individual person has, to say the least, a troubled relationship to any commodity; as such, a commodity is designed to subvert individuality. We must return to the question of our powers of identification, where the example of Whitman helps to clear things up. He found a way to array the many species of inhabitants in his New York, permitting the reader to enter the poetic catalogue of the city, which then is read as a democratic-leaning ensemble of innumerable interactions between those species. This in the novel is what Dickens achieved for London, or Balzac for Paris and other French cities. In our time Ashbery, as we will see later in more figural detail, has arrayed the ambient conditions of the largely exurban scene located outside commuter range. If the model for reading such works is to be found in authors like Clare, we should ask how a poem on this order provides a certain kind of knowledge, that being Clare's word for experiencing the environment.

Much can be learned from the struggle of Wordsworth to invent a language of common life. In the 1800 Preface to the *Lyrical Ballads,* he dwells on what I take to be one answer to the question of this "knowledge." It is clear that he foresaw the risk of banality to which I have alluded, a risk Clare could not suffer. At the same time Wordsworth seeks to invest his ballads and lyrics with mood, feeling, emotion, and a recollection in tranquility—the poet's exact terms. What Clare knew without study, Wordsworth had virtually to invent. Of his "Lucy Gray" he remarked, having said that the dead girl's body was found in the canal, "the way the incident was treated and the spiritualizing of the character might furnish hints for contrasting the imaginative influences which I have endeavoured to throw over common life with Crabbe's matter of fact style of treating subjects of the same kind." Since the poet believed he was showing how the child experienced her own solitude in a way no actual village child would ever have managed, he decided he would take deliberate counter-measures; he would "exhibit poetically" such an experience. One wonders if this poetry is not an atmospheric fabrication, all the way down to its deeply affecting "exhibit." Yet the generation of emotion is a possible artistic goal, and one is inclined to say that Wordsworth's emotive investments comprise one legitimate method of entering the village environment. What he calls "a complex feeling of delight" becomes the basis for our active response to the environment-poem. Only such a complex feeling draws the reader into the aggregate of village life, by triggering the desire to explore its environment, its ensemble. Again Clare and his fellow describers could be naturals, lacking a contrary higher education. They could follow the anarchic, nomadic, gypsy model of learning. If this village life were replaced by a great city like Paris, Walter Benjamin's "capital of the nineteenth century," we would exchange the gypsy for the *flâneur*.

For such wandering observers the actual or potential human participation is generally the critical factor. For expressing this participation, the simplest literary model might well be Aesop's fables, or in modern times the poems of Marianne Moore, who followed in the tradition of Aesop, Babrius, and Phaedrus. It might lead to novelists and poets like Hardy or even to historians like Marc Bloch, who wrote of the medieval forest that it was a "whole world of woodsmen, upon whom more sedentary folk looked with suspicion, traveled through the forest or lived in huts: hunters, charcoal burners, blacksmiths, honey and wax gatherers, ashmen employed in the fabrication of glass and soap, and bark pullers who supplied bark used in tanning leather or making rope."[13] To render and convince us vividly that any environment exists, the writer must always connect the elements of the scene with humans. Indeed for poetry, unlike science, human belonging and not belonging is the criterion for membership in any environment, and all environment-poems strive to present this structure on two levels: (1) the poetry will express the mere existence of those creatures who belong or do not belong, and (2) it will show how this belonging occurs, especially tracing the boundaries that define inclusion and exclusion. In widening circles of analysis, this poetry therefore studies boundaries, edges, hedges, and horizons. The least creature among the flora and fauna, "rolled round in earth's diurnal course / With rocks and stones and trees," belongs in the manifold and deserves its space, so that the poet's almost unimaginable chorographic persona must be that of a second creator, a demiurge of the scene. An earlier American world virtually imposed such a stance upon our nineteenth-century poets.

Personalities of the First Cause

Whitman, like the other poets who interest me here, is not unlike a Presocratic in that he is utterly amazed at the fact of the world's existence. Characterizing those philosophers, the physicist Roland Omnès speaks of "an eagerness to know never seen before."[14] Whitman went immediately beyond James Fenimore Cooper of *The Pioneers* and William Cullen Bryant of "The Prairies," in that while Cooper and Bryant already lamented the passing of the old untouched nature of early pioneering days,[15] Whitman could see that all times give their environment, and we have to deal with what we have, and value and reform it if need be. To him New York was as wild as the Rockies, and that is why when he saw the Rockies he understood what he had always been saying. He specialized in truncated recognition scenes, of course; he was always circulating to find them. As the *Oxford Dictionary of Ecology* reminds us, the environment is "the physical and biological surroundings of an organism." These surroundings include "the complete range of external conditions, physical and biological, in which an organism lives. Environment includes social, cultural, and (for humans) economic and political considerations, as well as the more usually understood features such as soil, climate and food supply." In the end Whitman built his greatest poems around those two scenes that are for all of us the final environment, death and the sea. On these, as George Saintsbury observed long ago, Whitman is especially eloquent.[16]

Some critics and poetic observers of Whitman, like John Cowper Powys, intuit the link between Whitman's descriptive techniques and his virtually shamanistic approach to poetry. "The composers of fiction aim at an aesthetic verisimilitude which seldom corresponds to the much more eccentric and chaotic dispositions of Nature. Only rarely are such writers so torn and rent by the Demon within them that they can add their own touch to the wave-crests of real actuality as these foam up, bringing wreckage and sea-tangle and living and dead ocean monsters and bloody spume and bottom silt into the rainbow spray!"[17]

This rhapsody on Whitman's rhapsody paradoxically makes the environment a transcendent fact, a One that is embedded in the shape or mere number of the Many. "All through, all conscious feelings belonging to living organisms, in a particular spot upon the earth's rondure, mount up and radiate outward from such a spot, overtaking in their ascent the sound-eidola and the sight-eidola which accompany them!" For Powys the Whitman *eidola* are here divided as to sense, but the main effect remains one of larger fusions and con-fusions, which I associate with the desire to develop environments *for all the senses.* This environing must make space to include what Powys called "the much more eccentric and chaotic dispositions of Nature." Poetry itself would have to probe the chaos, as Whitman understood when he saw his affinities with the wilderness of the Rockies, a wildness doubling the poet's inner prompting. The chaos had to become cosmos so that Powys wanted to argue that Whitman always followed a quest for "the magical unity of rhythm."[18] The occult must, of necessity, lie buried, encrypted in nature, while for Whitman, with Emerson and their dreaming contemporaries, this necessity always implied a song of the self. Nor was it even possible for a poet with Whitman's artistic independence to avoid developing his own law—he was exactly *not* lawless, which was obvious to friends at the time. New Englanders like James Russell Lowell were also becoming academic, following Longfellow's example, so wildness was out of the question, except as a lost stage of colonial history.[19]

The genius of Hawthorne in all of this was to develop what he called Romance, in order to bridge a significant gap between history and contemporary attitudes, fixing them in the frames of an iconography etched by his surreal photographic image-making.

We should never underestimate the magic of instant picture taking, where the *apparent* simultaneity is the main source of the magic. Whitman too is the owner of a "picture-gallery" which "has room for all the shows of the world, all memories!"

Reminiscing in the Direction of Essence

In his book on Proust, Gilles Deleuze so describes the relation between impression and essence that from our American point of view we can draw a parallel.[20] Reminiscence as chronicled by Whitman is a memory based on a Proustian sort of "impression," which evokes (in the classic terminology of Deleuze) a Platonic essence. We might say that for these two authors the role of reminiscence is to define whatever is or was essential to the poet's life and experience. This way of putting it is too loose, however. Proust's key word for search and research, *recherche,* catches the real issue. For both authors the Platonic idea is always only searched for, in the process of being searched out. As Deleuze says, "Plato's reminiscence has its point of departure in sensuous qualities or relations apprehended in process, in variation, in opposition, in 'mutual fusion.' But this qualitative transition represents a state of things, a state of the world which imitates the Idea as best it can, according to its powers." It follows that the Idea is always *before,* absolutely originary. But for Whitman and for Proust in the *Recherche* a quite different order of expression pertains. Here, Deleuze remarks, "Qualitative transition, mutual fusion, and 'unstable opposition' are inscribed within a *state of soul,* no longer within a state of things or a state of the world. A slanting ray of the evening sun, an odor, a flavor, a draft, an ephemeral qualitative complex owe their value only to the 'subjective aspect' to which they penetrate." In the example I cited while discussing Whitman's phrase, the *petite phrase de Vinteuil,* psychic intensity certainly does arise as a subjective aspect of the music. But Deleuze is willing to limit the absolute claims of the Platonic One. In his account of Proust the One is an end or ideal terminus of thought; for the novel the One marks a final boundary. Thus Deleuze argues, "of course, the subjective aspect is never the last word of the Search . . . The individual, subjective associations are here only to be transcended in the direction of Essence."[21]

When the Whitman poem ends with the line, "A reminiscence sing," an entire aesthetic is mobilized to follow in a certain direction, to inform us that reminiscence moves back toward the Platonic forms of being in the direction of an essence that might otherwise pass undetected, that is, unimagined. The journey never ends. Whitman the impression-gatherer would like to be a Platonist, but he never gets there. Here "more is meant than meets the ear"—these slanting rays of the setting sun, these perfumes, these winds and waves of water challenging the sailor and swimmer are all held in the transient grip of sensation and mere impression, held momentary in the mind, until they are experienced as reaching back through the *anagnorisis* to the unattainable Idea. At that moment of deep reminiscence the impression momentarily suggests what it had been "before," an ideal form. As Deleuze expresses it, "the direction of Essence" commands the order of narration. Whitman, of course, looks out toward a natural horizon, a Lewis and Clark horizon, we would say, across the visual array of his ocean of leaves. So like Proust, he is nevertheless an American primitive, and an eccentric.

In 1949 André Malraux wrote (from his monumentally French point of view) that "an American culture, as distinct from our own as Chinese culture, is purely and simply a European invention."[22] We are incorrectly assumed to be derivative in our *imaginaire*. Malraux went on to say, "There are no specifically American cultural assumptions in conflict with our own except precisely insofar as Europe has abdicated its beliefs and responsibilities." Cultural assumptions are, we might say, Malraux's cultural ideal, and here this ideal has to be markedly Eurocentric. So it does not occur to him that perhaps America has a special problem with the

Platonic forms. Not to be too material about the matter, it needs to be remembered that "America" got started in an utterly new way, as the experience of a new world, a new idea. The country had a weird sort of virgin birth, and this had to leave its mark on the thought that here even ideas had to detach from a higher order of philosophical thought. This was certainly true in politics after the Declaration of Independence. The United States could be "the greatest poem," but only if the Union could expand and leaf out, along with settling and exploiting the country. In both Whitman and Proust the literary work doubles a political or personal history, by thaumaturgy. All depends upon the powers of our approaching the new. The aesthetic of this approach drew Borges to rhyme the name *Whitman* with the Spanish *ritman.* The rhyme pays homage to an invention of the natural rhythm of the New World.

Thus the sonnet of the voice of the old poet dying, "Camden, 1892," ends:[23]

> Su voz declara:
> Casi no soy, pero mis versos ritman
> La vida y su esplendor. Yo fuí Walt Whitman.

We have only the rhythm of approaching a limit. As Wordsworth expressed this thought, we have only "intimations," or as Whitman himself expressed it in his gnomic utterance: "The sea whispered me." This expression through the middle voice intends to speak that consciousness inherent in self-reflexive awareness, for to reflect the self is to have a consciousness of the world surrounding the self, especially that world we call "the body." As we shall see, without a sense of the soul residing in the body, there is little place for the middle voice. Another aspect of the humanizing of the environmental array is to treat aspects of it as reveries of a coherent society.

One afternoon in the summer of 1948 the novelist Julian Green was idly "dreaming in the big public bathing establishment" of Merano, an eminently pleasant resort in the Dolomites.[24] His diary records that he was struck (as *he* would be) by "the chastity of nakedness," which led him to think of the body in its approach to the soul. "People talk about the body and the soul," he goes on to note, "as if the two could separate at will, be distinct, whereas more often they mingle, a little as earth and water mingle in mud." There is no perceptible borderline between the two, or at any rate no borderline that is not breached continually at every minute, as though it did not exist. Elsewhere in his *Diary* the novelist quotes Meister Eckhart, who had said, "A soul can save itself only in its own appointed body." Here in Merano Green was clear about a more modern, more American affinity. He began by paraphrasing Eckhart and then moved on to Whitman. "The soul is reached through the body and the body through the soul, and therein lies the whole tragedy of the human lot, which makes us such deeply mysterious beings. 'Oh, body, thou art the soul!' cried Whitman." Julian Green, obsessed by religious scruples, seeking to "write them out" in novels like *Moira,* nevertheless took reassuring pleasure in Whitman's joy: "He is an American after my own heart, a grand person, ignorant, crazy, generous, and inspired."

These words refer us to a social criterion of value, and indeed Whitman always raises questions about such matters, projecting as he does the theme of democratic friendship. One sees in him a logic of connection between the body and the body politic, and this too may irritate European intellectuals or others of like mind. The critical issue is to admit the societal point to be investigated. Again, Julian Green: "There is something barbarous about his intemperate speech, but a deep feeling for human fellowship and a contempt of all meanness rank him among the very first." It is probably still true, despite any American academic pieties, that "America is secretly ashamed of the *enfant terrible* she has given the world." Such a thought is somewhat puzzling, of course, because it is not clear whether any advanced civilization, ours included, could ever deal easily with a poet as distinct as Whitman. Green, who so admires Whitman's "bravely artistic sombrero," seems to have forgotten the way his French friends and predecessors could make art into a heroic act requiring flamboyant stance. We get a sense of yet another way Whitman eludes criticism, as if we always encountered this receding prey, when Green's *Diary* goes on to say, "in Whitman lies a sort of childlike nobility that Europeans cannot appreciate because a certain type of ingenuousness irritates them. I know very well that Whitman's extravagances can raise a smile, but who could resist his way of clapping you on the shoulder and calling you Camerado!"[25] This, from one of the more elegant writers of the twentieth century!

We are told that on one occasion one of the framers of the Constitution, a Southern gentleman, in a moment of unguarded admiration and friendship approached George Washington and put his hand on the General's shoulder, whereupon Washington coldly detached the gentleman's hand and walked off, offended at this touch of the "Camerado." A long road would stretch out before reaching Julian Green's very different, yet still Southern, response to the poet's generosity and warmth. Admittedly, Walt Whitman was not the hero of the Revolutionary War. Instead, his open gestures belong to the heroes of the Constitution, of union rather than independence. In this shift the body has to provide the foundations of metaphoric play. The body figures union as the space of friendship. For Americans the body may be an obsession, now because cholesterol rules our diet, but once because the soul was felt by us to be inseparable from the body, which is the depth, the sea in which the soul swims. The medium aspires to a classless fluency, as Bonnie Costello has suggested of Ashbery's landscapes.[26]

To read Whitman you need to think like certain Thomas Nelson editions of my childhood. Printed on exquisitely fine India paper, these books were bound in what was called "limp leather." Reading Whitman is like holding a book bound in limp leather. You savor the creamy texture of the binding; you can almost eat the letterpress print; though most books are common enough, this one is a rare thing. You gaze on its soft green color, tracing pliant thoughts. Today scholars may believe they have explained everything. But our explanations and glosses, even in paperback, are thick, stiff, and heavy; they do not bend.

Experiencing the Environment-Poem

If we pull the American environment-poem away from its journey in the direction of essence, we find it examining a singular present, as if such a poetics could subtract the oneness from the One. Such poetry asks in what way our environment is our possession, our property—hence, it tests belonging in all directions. If we experience a poem as a singular event in life, is that the model of genuine possession? Yet if it is singular, it surely cannot last, except in thought, except perhaps in the poem.

A few connected issues at once arise: we need to ask to what degree an environment-poem is designed to increase our knowledge, as distinct from our experience, and if the latter, must our increased knowledge be of a factual nature? The chief obscurity of what happens to the factual in eighteenth-century descriptive poetry is that poets interlard facts and material names with personifications. While this device has been much discussed, it seems we should more strongly emphasize the ancient purpose of the figure: it bridges between material and spiritual worlds, sharing in both, announcing the ideal, but always embodying some kind of personhood—the face, the masking *prosopon,* the visage of a believed ideal form. Personification seems to express our need to believe that ideas are only existentially significant if they appear to us as living beings, as thoughts capable of *personal* agency. For the poets I am considering there is another matter as well: is it possible that Clare's perceptions of the creatures of his village, Whitman's phrases of note as he confides his vision of democracy and democratic variety, Ashbery's wandering asides, while he perambulates through the landscape of his own thoughts—is it possible that these are all a new variant of ancient personifications, new *persons* always on the lookout for their own discovery? If so, the knowledge imparted by such a poetry is already half way into an experiential training ground. "Experience" is what William Empson would have called a Complex Word, like so many of the other major critical terms the present book introduces; but customarily it means *living through an event,* with an accent on the word "living." Experience has an emotive side, also, as when we say "Well, *that* was an experience"—what the Hungarians call *élmény,* where the living through is in the verb *élni,* or as in the German *Erlebnis,* while the coursing aspect of experience is caught in the word *Erfahrung.* An environment would seem destined to impose a kind of learning and wandering about inside it, at least with sentient human beings, if not with the "dull and speechless tribes" of whom Shakespeare spoke. That being the case, a descriptive poetry that renders environments is bound to stimulate an awareness of varying conditions of life and living through, and these will by themselves engage a willingness or a refusal to experience these or those particular represented conditions. Modern technology allows us to air-condition the tropics and heat the arctic, but we have not changed those environs, unless (as today) we kill them, having decided that their death is not really worth serious concern and foresight. This is to deny the value and being of human experience. If we deny our species its nativity, this implies limiting or curtailing the power to explore our thoughts, in effect to study ourselves. If in turn this is not to be a narrowing self-exploration, its process must include a willingness to discover *where* the self is and *where* it lives through its experiences.

In principle there is an obvious question as to the scope of this "where." The term "nature" is well known to denote the widest possible extent of life, among many senses of the term. Then it must be asked how, for the environment-poem, it is possible to distinguish this extended notion of nature from any locally confined notion of any singular environment, any singular ecosystem. Here it helps to notice that in environmental studies *scale* is everything, that is, the research looks at parts of the universal natural manifold as these parts relate to other parts—say, the setting of a village in relation to a county, or a single species interacting with many other species sharing a single ecosystem. The research always examines the relativities within its defined and limited purview. In this way the research manages to avoid drifting into the *hypersurround* or *hyperscene,* as we may call it. Today we increasingly deal with such a massively large scale of perception, and we call it "the global." If on average the jet stream drives the main wind currents around the world every five days, all localized winds and weathers provide almost infinite variety within this larger pattern.

On the plan of such a more localized life-world, each environment is understood to be a region within the ultimately much larger natural surround. What could be more obvious? And yet the great achievements of High Romanticism have sometimes obscured the point; they have certainly made it hard to perceive the different scope and purpose of the environment-poem, while they have occluded the role of description as an underlying base of Romanticism. We need no deep analysis of examples here, but we must observe the tendency in the great Romantics to write a poetry of the hyperscene, as distinct from the quite different chorographic tendency, which tries to limit the scene to a known environmental array, that Timaean space John Clare called "my knowledge." These two scales of vision imply different motives and experiences. Perhaps Shelley is the most revealing instance of a poet moving in both directions, but always tending toward the hyperscene. When in *A Defence of Poetry* he calls poetry "something divine," we are not to forget that for Shelley its primary function is that it "creates new materials of knowledge, and power and pleasure," and hence is never more to be desired than during periods of history when "the materials of external life exceed the quantity of the power of assimilating them to the internal laws of human nature."[27] Shelley speaks at one moment for both science and art: poetry "is at once the center and circumference of knowledge; it is that which comprehends all science, and that to which all science must be referred." It is clear from the ensuing passage that Shelley believes inspiration to be both necessary and natural, as distinct from the mastery of a mere *techne.* The model for this freedom to create is "the inconstant wind." While poems like "Ode to the West Wind," or "Mont Blanc," or indeed many other similar poems seem to extend our vision to the outer edges of comic speculation, to the most sublime conceptions of time, life, universe, and destiny, there is in Shelley almost always a scientist's interest in the exact natural object. In short, he constantly shifts back and forth between the poet's own environment, let us say "the Euganean Hills" or some very different English countryside from which details are drawn, and that sublime hyperscene toward which his imagination seems always to have drawn him.

Our task as readers is then to move back and forth between different scales and sizes of natural phenomena and natural events. Though it may not be fashionable to use such words, I would say that this scale-shifting has a spiritual aspect, which in our poetry is signaled by the descriptive use of personification, along with other signs of animation in the scene. Something has to shift us beyond the materiality of observed fact, and yet hold its specificity in a representation of the passing of real time.

The environment-poem, by attending to nature's cyclical system, assures a place for the *animate* aspect of the life process. In antiquity a personification such as Iris—the rainbow—bridges thoughts of material and spiritual worlds, by voicing or imaging the messages her power enables her to carry between regions. Personifying figures generally prevent fact from having the last word, as if poets using them knew that no fact were sufficient without a spiritual and in that sense symbolic spin of some kind. As a Neoplatonist would claim, the poem and the scene mimetically encode the same phenomena as two modes of emanation, as of course all living creatures emanate from their own identities, as we now know, by virtue of a genetic code.

Certain sentences in the last of Montaigne's *Essays,* "Of Experience," illuminate our human relation to this equivalence.[28] "It is an absolute perfection and, as it were, divine for a man to know how to enjoy rightfully his being. We seek other conditions because we do not understand the use of our own, and go out of ourselves because we do not know what it is like within." Because literature of the surround gives attributes of the participant's selfhood, the heroic stance becomes less interesting, and one prefers to meditate upon the field of interactions between many inhabitants. Field is a technical term in physics that enables us to understand electromagnetism. But field is an even older term for nature's appearance and actuality. Francis Ponge wanted his modern reader to learn this link of ancient and modern from his environment-poem, *La Fabrique du Pré* ("The Making of the Meadow"). Ponge writes his poem as if it were part and parcel of all the explorations underlying a final version, and hence his poem displays a seemingly systematic relation between this type of poetry and the essay. All is finally provisional, because the details of the chorographic scene are constantly changing, day to day, month to month. Like a chapter in Emerson or Thoreau, each larger work draws upon an ever-changing diurnal source of passing observations. Allegorical controls disappear. As Ponge seems to have wanted, his *Fabrique* works best when accompanied by all its preliminary drafts, as if the notebook of such sketches were the "living through" his poem wishes to express.[29] Our reading of the work lets us see that environments express the character of nature in a certain terrestrial space, where every ecosystem is an expressive unit within a larger field.

Every such unit then concentrates the forces of a field, and the poems rendering this confluence, like Clare's innumerable "studies," are always focusing down onto small details. Among many poems on different nesting scenes, he writes of a ground lark's nest:[30]

> Close where the milking maidens pass
> In roots and twitches drest
> Within a little bunch of grass
> A groundlark made her nest . . . ,

However precise, this nest is also a universal. When the local people "came to mow the hay / They found an empty nest." The nest is beyond understanding, because it asks, emptied of its builder, what is the meaning of our lives in the first place? In another poem men hunting a marten for its fur are tricked into losing their prey, when he is defended by an old owl who ". . . leaves the martin twisting round his den / Left free from boys and dogs and noise and men."[31] These lines provide an ordinary case of the poem mimetically articulating a surround. We are the boys and dogs and men, and we are also more importantly the surrounding we make, the noise; we are the noise of war. The story, seeming circuitously to get nowhere, presents an array of complex social relationships.

If Clare is the simplest yet most intense of our three poets, there is no convenient way to epitomize the wide range of their works, except to notice certain gestures they make. Whitman helps us to understand the gesture language, when he says, "You sea! I resign myself to you also—I guess what you mean." "Resign" and "guess" express the basic principle, which we may call Invitation. Thriving on invitations, we can choose to be nature's guests, with a slender leave to stay. This ghostly inviting and visiting is surely what Gerard Manley Hopkins instantly found in Whitman, and he heard it linked to a belief that society adds up to an aggregate nature, requiring a new language of invitation in which to express belonging.

As for Ashbery, his whole body of work is an invitation to "hang around," savoring the indeterminate borders of shapes in so much modern painting. But he is also the poet of the age of Joseph Cornell, often meditating on the house and the outdoors. If he were not such a coolly ominous poet of apocalypse, he might appear the ideal Fireside Poet. But to quote John Clare, "the mirrors change and fly."[32] Ashbery's poetry expresses Tocqueville's observation of American instability, as if the poet were always moving in, and hence must be the master of that miscellaneousness of which Emerson said we were all dying. In Ashbery this miscellany is clearly a kind of wilderness ecosystem, a house of things just unloaded from the cosmic moving van. Ashbery's collected works might well be titled "After the Move," and happily the sum of the whole will be less than the inchoate mass of all its parts. The main principle is epitomized in a phrase from "I Found Their Advice"—"A change takes place." In Ashbery the tones reverberate off the far end of the cathedral. The reason for the reflex delay is that he is in fact representing the real character of a so-called "simultaneous" perception of events that in material truth appear one after another. If you represent such a sequence, you can only do it by introducing a slight sequential delay, which may be disconcerting, but is in fact accurate. It is as if each event in an Ashbery poem, like the cathedral organ tone, exists *simultaneously* at two different moments on the temporal continuum. Most of the poetry is perspicuous to a careful reading; it is just that Ashbery plays subtle polyrhythmic games with sequential order. Strange connections between disparate things enable us to see how much bizarre variety goes into the making of any complex habitat.

Our own multifaceted thoughts surround us with dream-like perceptions. When our personhood splits several ways, we paradoxically are enabled to follow a new perseveration of Being, resulting from various voices all living together—at least, that seems to be the model. By saying to ourselves as readers, "Let's move in," we get to be where we need to be, where Being is tested in experience, as it always is for children. They, unlike the poor grownups, do not experience buyer's remorse. For them the place is a poem supporting a way of life and, as Ashbery has so often said of his work, a questioning affirmation of friendship, even love, in an ominous world.

8

Waves and the Troping of Poetic Form

Whitman developed a theory of poetry and of its imaginative partner, democracy, precisely by recurring to the paradigm of wave-motion. Waves of change will permit the poem and the nation to become a unity arising from a diversity, exactly as the aggregates of environment compose a composite unity, according to a pragmatic rather than Platonic resolution between the One and the Many. In "I sing the body electric," he writes of "undulating into the willing and yielding day," in "Out of the Cradle" he sings "the word up from the waves," and in "Song of Myself" he cries out, "I know the sea of torment, doubt, despair and unbelief," and he identifies this torment with the fish haled savagely from the depths "with spasms and spouts of blood." At the other end of the spectrum there is a gentle "lapping of waves" in the great rhapsody, "From Pent-up Aching Rivers." The scale of the working of this "irresistible sea" is unimaginably wide, as the poem says: "Out of the rolling ocean the crowd came a drop gently to me," a weird triple catachresis (the ocean the crowd a drop), yet that is the effect of ocean, a seemingly infinite accumulation of drops, a drop of infinity. Readers have long noticed Whitman's fascination with the undulant forms of nature, nor is he alone in this American preoccupation. In a recent book, Eric Wilson has shown how such imagery is a source of wonder for Thoreau, while generally the American ecological defense of the wild belongs with this interest.[1]

Analogies of the Wave

Sizeable waves, readily apparent to the eye, say aboard a boat, are capable of upsetting our sense of balance or maybe so sharply disturbing the semi-circular canals of the inner ear that we get seasick. When wind and tide go against each other, the waves cease rolling; they hit the boat hard, slapping it around, and yet meanwhile they are still perceivable as obvious waves.

But when wave motions are reduced sufficiently in size, as with light, they become seemingly two different things; they display the paradoxical character of the kind of poetic language Whitman discovered—they are now unfaithful to their undulant form to the point of divorce; they become separate particles. In science the actual laboratory setup makes all the difference. Recalling early work in this field, Richard Feynman says, "You had to know which experiment you were analyzing in order to tell if light was waves or particles," and it was Feynman's view that the aim of quantum electrodynamics, where he pioneered basic new methods, was to show how this "wave-particle duality" could be understood and how the physics of light was entwined with the physics of so-called particles. "It was jokingly said by someone that light was waves on Mondays, Wednesdays, and Fridays; it was particles on Tuesdays, Thursdays, and Saturdays, and on Sundays we think about it!"[2] In literature we need not vainly seek to become scientists, but we can profitably observe that with poets like Whitman a similar duality occurs. For there is no doubt that the Whitman phrase is a kind of linguistic particle, while his main larger effect is to create waves of expression and meaning. Feynman himself asked the Whitman question: "It is natural to wonder how far we can push this process of splitting events into simpler and simpler subevents. What are the smallest possible bits and pieces of events? Is there a limited number of bits and pieces that can be compounded to form *all* the phenomena that involve light and electrons? Is there a limited number of 'letters' in this language of quantum electrodynamics that can be combined to form 'words' and 'phrases' that describe nearly every phenomenon of Nature."[3] For the scientist this set of questions works on the level of analogy, though in reverse. Among the many interests of the mutual comparison there is a further aspect revealed by modern science, namely, that wave-functions in quantum mechanics are only describable in terms of probabilities. This is well enough known in general—an event in this physics has only a probability of occurring *here* or *here.* The event cannot be exactly located as one puts a pencil on the north-northeast corner of a writing desk, as in "An Evening with Ramon Bonavena," Borges's satire on early versions of the Robbe-Grillet style. ("At any rate, descriptionism is on the march.") The pencil will only probably be somewhere, within greater or lesser degrees of certainty. This science is content to be statistical, in the proper scientific sense of that term. Our analogy suggests that within the domain of the descriptive field, Whitman's poetic seeks only to convey what he knowingly called the *average.* He was not just talking vague large numbers of people more or less doing this or that; rather, he perceived that his language experiment showed that meaning was a matter of approximate location, mass, motion, and momentum.

Whitman early began to derive such understanding from the motions of water. He grew up on an island. Whenever he crossed the fast-moving East River by ferry, he could watch what waves actually do and what they look like. Ever since the seventeenth century, if only by rowboat, one could get to Manhattan by some sort of ferrying. Gradually traffic came to use grander transport, so that by 1814 the Fulton Ferry Line was using steamboats (the street and the boats being named after the inventor), and since 1835 there was the South Ferry, then since 1849 the Broadway Ferry. Among other things this meant that Manhattan also was known very much as an island (as much later that sense was still felt by those who took the Hoboken Ferry over to the Lehigh Valley Railroad terminal, to return to Philadelphia; nor should we exclude the Staten Island Ferry). Manhattan, an island reached from another larger island—Long Island is to this day colloquially referred to as "the island"—remained "unique" in the way all islands are, a quality not to be changed until the 1883 opening of the Brooklyn Bridge. Thus the poet's city was doubly surrounded by water. With its inland bays to the East and with its fishlike Paumanok shape, Long Island exerted a lasting influence on the poet, who knew from early years that one could know proximally two different kinds of seas (and hence waves of the sea)—the Atlantic Ocean, in those days still guarded on the south shore by a long unbroken barrier reef of sand, and to the north the Bays and Long Island Sound itself. When the wind dies in Gardiner's Bay or on the Sound, the surface of the water goes dead flat, while on most occasions it ripples, though a storm can turn this flat surface into a turmoil of wild, short, choppy waves.

Late in life Whitman told his friend Horace Traubel that his work was a part of Ocean. Whitman was never a literalist of natural forces, yet he knew from nature the shaping of the turns of verse. Characterizing the "rhythmic patternings of long and short lines, aligned, variously interjected, refrained, extended, receding," John Hollander reminds us that the analogy is just that: speaking of his *Leaves* as Ocean, Whitman said to Traubel "its verses are the liquid, billowy waves, ever rising and falling, perhaps wild with storm, always moving, always alike in their nature as rolling waves, but hardly any two exactly alike in size or measure, never having the sense of something finished and fixed, always suggesting something beyond."[4] Hollander goes on to observe, "He might just as well have likened his long anaphoric catalogues to urban crowds through which the reader himself will pass, jostling, pushing, sometimes striding, sometimes pausing." One can imagine that these phenomena could provide a ready source of metaphors and images and *eidola* for the poet. What counts is that these are conceptual metaphors, since, as Erik Gunderson says in his handbook of physics, "A wave is a traveling disturbance that moves energy from one location to another without transferring matter."[5] If the reader of any Whitman poem grasps this concept, there will be no further fundamental questions to ask about how he writes poetry. All other secondary questions, including those of historical fact and background, will flow from the theory of undulant form.

Still, as poet, Whitman shows no signs of encoding a scientific theory in the Enlightenment style of Darwin's grandfather, Erasmus Darwin.[6] Waves for Whitman are *eidolons* of passage and transport, signs of his own fervor; they correspond in this communicating function to his democratic leanings. On the other hand, Whitman's scientific side emerges in the way his sense of the wave pushes his thinking toward such paradoxes as later appeared in modern physics. If the motions of liquids, sounds, and light provide one model for his image-making, there is an apparently opposite component, the discovery that wave-forms may shift into the massive accumulation of bits, particles, pieces, quanta. There is a vaguely mathematical side to Whitman, and Ashbery, for that matter; they incline to an appreciation of isolated fact, and that inclines them to merge the canonical principles of prose and verse together.

In his most pragmatic moments Whitman imagines groups of people forming into ocean-swells of force, which then spread or propagate; his individual participates in the propagation. The issue for politics after Jackson, given all the material change Whitman chronicles and critiques, is to see how such gatherings of force into ensembles can occur. When such gatherings occur, they accumulate like a build-up of waves. The exploitation of natural resources on an industrial scale, organized in the United States under the influence of railroad expansion across the continent, made a Tennysonian, feudal allegiance and its chivalric expression an instant archaism. Archaism is of course a trope, and it goes with Spenserian forms like *The Encantadas* of Melville.

Troping Poetic Form

John Hollander has said that poets do not so much imitate the world, as *they trope poetic forms.*[7] Poems are made by troping their own shape, that is, by making a metaphoric or other figural change in some previously invented available *form.* Suppose that a predecessor had used a sonnet-form to express something. Later poets, powerfully inspired, do not stretch their *subject;* they stretch the *form* in which the subject is to be expressed or presented or represented. Metaphor and other tropes thus live beyond their common local function; now they transform larger shapes of expression. Form and genre, in short, become the chief occasions for metamorphic treatment.

With the larger literary forms it is always easier to see Hollander's principle at work. Cervantes tropes the forms of romance, and then later on Lawrence Sterne tropes the forms of Cervantes, weaving them into the counter-narrative of *Tristram Shandy.* With poems also, when they follow ampler narrative dimensions, we can see form-troping at work: Spenser's *Faerie Queene,* Milton's epics, Byron's *Don Juan,* Coleridge's *Rime* or *Christabel,* Berryman's *Homage to Mistress Bradstreet,* are all examples. Another way to put this is to say that far and away the most important poetic invention resides in this troping of forms, after which the rhetorical and poetic manipulation of lesser effects naturally will fall into place. A failure to grasp Hollander's principle will lead to such beliefs as that Spenser is "all about the Protestant Reformation," or Hopkins is "all sprung rhythm," or that Whitman is "all language experiment," with his lexicons and lists of words.[8] What these poets required was troped *forms* in which to deploy their materials, so that their words could easily, not to say naturally, come alive in sequence.

The notion that the highest poetic act is to trope or reshape the larger poetic forms themselves, rather than redecorate them like old rooms in a palace, is akin to the Romantic vision of political revolution and behind that, an order of political philosophy imagining radically new political dispensations. Ernst Cassirer, in a chapter on Romanticism and the state, notes that Hegel's *Phenomenology* regards philosophical truth as a partially processual, even processional, effect: "the real subject-matter is not exhausted in its purpose; . . . nor is the mere result [of thought] attained as equivalent to the concrete whole itself, but the result *along with the process of arriving at it*."[9] Without process we have only "the corpse of the system." It follows that the vision of politics shares in the evolving curve of thought. If the goal of the nation is to raise each self to a higher level, "in point of fact the notion of the realization of self-conscious reason . . . finds its actual fulfillment in the life of the nation. Reason appears here as the fluent universal substance . . . which at the same time breaks up into many entirely independent beings . . . They are conscious within themselves of being these individual independent beings through the fact that they surrender and sacrifice their particular individuality, and that this universal substance is their soul and essence." The troping of form translates into a larger reshaping of our ideas of representation, since politics is itself a figural game whose paradigms are simply very large-scale metaphors.

Cassirer's Romantics, such as Friedrich Schlegel, wished to poeticize the state. All significant social and intellectual actions were to be imbued with the "poetic spirit," again an idea Whitman inherits, and in which (with Herder particularly) there is a turn towards finding the poetry of the individual. In this Romantic context, we learn, the Romantics "had a deep respect for all the innumerable and subtle differences that characterize the life of individuals and nations."[10] "To Herder every nation was only an individual voice in a universal, all embracing harmony." Hence began a literary search for the individual who is the integer within larger collectivities. The individual as political entity is required if we are to counterbalance Romantic beliefs such as those of Schleiermacher with his religious philology, where "religion is love but it is not love for 'this' and 'that' or for a finite and special object, but love for the Universe, the Infinite." A visionary in both these ways, Whitman is able to imagine poems based on a cosmic sympathy with universal orders of nature. He seems to share a belief in continuity between individual humans and nature with Herder and Schelling, for whom there is, to quote Isaiah Berlin, an "assumption of continuity between, on the one hand, natural forces of this kind and human activity, including intellectual or imaginative, on the other."[11] That Berlin should thus (though not unexpectedly) distinguish these and other *Naturphilosophen* and Romantics in general from Giambattista Vico is perhaps critical, since in so many ways Whitman seems to share Vico's idea of a general poetics by which civilization comes into being. As John Hollander put it:

> A map of the "greatest poem," the United States themselves, shows us shapes formed by natural contours—seacoasts and lake shores, demarcating rivers and so forth—and by surveyed boundary lines, geometric, unyielding, and ignorant of what the eye of the airborne might perceive. Whitman's poem of America purported to have dispensed with all surveyors, with arbitrary strokes of a mental knife that score out legal fictions like state boundaries or city limits. It declared that all its component lines, stanzas, and structures would be shaped only by the natural forms they exuded. Which meant, as in every great poet's high ulterior mode, that the art that shaped them would teach older formal paradigms and patterns to dance, rather than negate them utterly.[12]

Poems are not uniforms made to be spangled with medals, the "figures." For the true Romantic and perhaps for all poets in all schools, the formal modes of the poets, "as well as their complex articulations of those modes are all in themselves subtle and powerful formal metaphoric versions of more traditional ones." The poet here tropes form, but not substance; the latter act comes into play to serve the former, more fundamental poetic purpose. The naturally contoured geography here ascribed to Whitman's poem remains one of the most massive known cases of troping the form, and if we do not grasp this principle we cannot appreciate individual poems as they exist both within the volume and independently of it. The poet had to be expansively confident that his book could extend to the horizon, way beyond the slim volume of 1855. One can hardly doubt that Whitman had envisioned the whole of the expanded *Leaves of Grass* when he began with the 1855 edition of only twelve poems. The whole evolved work was to build out, in the classic architectural lean-to method Whitman would have known from his Long Island childhood, and it would lean upon "Song of Myself."

In my enlarged sense of *descriptive poetry,* tropes are also no longer local decorations or particular swerves of particular meanings; tropes go beyond any turbulence in the text. Whitman and Ashbery, who is so like him, take the object of description and turn it into an *objectified form of the object of description.* They get the object to speak. *Leaves of Grass* aspires to the condition of a vast contour map of America, its lands, its peoples. As contour maps show undulations, so here in this spirit "the fixer and finisher, the poet himself, is far more crafty a puller of waves than the coldly regular moon"—and Whitman seems to have known all about this art and artfulness, even to its tricks. He knows the rhythmic measures of his poems are never "exactly alike in size or measure, never having the sense of something finished and fixed, always suggesting something beyond."

One might compare the Whitman sound with an early poem of Hollander's, "A Theory of Waves," which resembles French seventeenth-century lyrics by Saint Amant or Sponde or, to mention a specific poem, "Description de l'étang" by Racine. (Both Whitman and Racine give voice to the turbulence of formal transformations.) Here is Hollander's sonnet.

Having no surface of its own, the pond,
Under the shifting grey contingency
Of morning mists, extends even beyond
The swamp beside it, until presently
The thinning air declares itself to be
No longer water, and the pond itself
Is still for a moment, and no longer air.
Then waking bass glide from their sandy shelf,
And sets of concentric circles everywhere
Expand through some imaginary thing
Whose existence must be assumed, until they meet,
When incorporeal ripples, ring on ring,
Disturb a real surface, as if, with dripping feet,
Some dark hypothesis had made retreat.[13]

Whitman imagines even the art of carpenters and joiners as subject to the dark hypothesis. He is fearless. He always responds, in Hollander's phrase, with a movement "toward hyperbolic envelopment."[14] That excess is what I prefer to call movement toward the horizon within the environment, an exfoliation. On the varied senses of the word *leaves* and on "Whitman's difficult availability," Hollander comments that these include an organic sense of *leafage, leaves* or *pages* of books, *leavings* (one thinks of Hopkins's lyric "Spring and Fall," with its opening lines, "Margaret, are you grieving / Over Goldengrove unleaving?") and of course all the particular appearances and realities of *the grass itself,* from the Bible to the present-day environmentalist's groundcover. I wonder myself if Whitman did not also think of the word "lief," which we still have in the phrase "I would as lief," meaning to desire, to do something gladly, from the old word *lief,* meaning dear, or beloved. The note of connecting affection with leafage is always strong in the writings of Whitman's friend, John Burroughs, where waving and fluttering leaves are of a parcel with the waves of the sea, the waves of grain, of wild flowers.[15]

Finally, in a biographic sense, we know that Whitman never really abandoned the wave song of his Long Island childhood, coming to him from the edge of the sea. Numerous naturalists have expressed fascination with the edge of the sea, most notably Rachel Carson, but one of the moving accounts is Thoreau's *Cape Cod,* where he remarks at one point that "the sea-shore is a sort of neutral ground, a most advantageous point from which to contemplate this world. It is even a trivial place. The waves forever rolling to the land are too far-travelled and untamable to be familiar. Creeping along the endless beach amid the sun-squall and the foam, it occurs to us that we, too, are the product of sea-slime."[16] The ocean is the source of life, yet he writes in the ensuing paragraph that the edge of the sea is "a vast *morgue,* where famished dogs may range in packs, and crows come daily to glean the pittance which the tide leaves them." We need to recall, and I can remember this from my own childhood at the beach, mostly in winter, that the seashore is a perpetual epiphany of "whatever the sea casts up." Thoreau's first and coolly sublime chapter was entitled "The Shipwreck," followed by his penultimate chapter, "The Sea and the Desert," both of which recur to the same strict and arresting thought: "The carcasses of men and beasts together lie stately up upon its shelf, rotting and bleaching in the sun and waves, and each tide turns them in their beds, and tucks the fresh sand under them. There is naked Nature, inhumanly sincere, wasting no thought on man, nibbling at the cliffy shore where gulls wheel amid the spray." It would be hard to exaggerate the importance of shipwreck to the novel, as in *Robinson Crusoe,* or the cry "man overboard," as in William Cowper's "The Castaway," for reasons that Hans Blumenberg developed in a philosophical essay.[17] Blumenberg was asking about the paradox of land-living humans so often wishing "to represent their overall condition in the world in terms of a sea-voyage." From antiquity "two assumptions above all determine the burden of meaning carried by the metaphorics of seafaring and shipwreck: first, the sea as a naturally given boundary of the realm of human activities and, second, its demonization as the sphere of the unreckonable and lawless, in which it is difficult to find one's bearings." A line in an old Restoration song, "Love still has something of the sea," catches this idea of passionate turbulence commanded by the god of ocean.

Anaphoras and Waves

Thematic approaches to poetic effect are always bound to mislead, or else lead us away from the poetics of the poem in question. The trouble here with thinking simply in terms of the iconography of waves is that it does nothing to explain how the poem comes into being as a powerful poetic form; it merely shows the allegory of the poem, its use in this case of the symbols of the undulant. But Whitman in his way, and my other descriptive poets in their ways, write less *about* waves of life than they actually write *in waves.* Arguing that Whitman manages this undulant effect by means of his lists would be true, as long as we understand that the lists themselves are not catalogues, as they always violate categorical order. Their systematic-looking orders are subversively dismembered, as much as possible, until finally these lists are not lists at all, rather, they are phrasal processions of thoughts.

Their expressive, ceremonial mode is dependent upon a well-known classical figure of speech, anaphora. Anaphora is a device of organizational decorum that produces the sense of ritual, procession, or when let loose produces an opposed sense of onrushing elemental force. Anaphora reinforces belief in a ritualized spell binding poetic rhythm, whose force attains sometimes to religious ecstasy, as in the mystical poems of the seventeenth-century

Catholic poet, Richard Crashaw. The technique requires waves of segmented phrases whose repetition builds into pulsations rather than points and predications. Ritual rhythm—to what purpose, one must ask—is thus the almost inevitable anaphoric consequence. A classic example would be these lines from "The Ocean to Cynthia," Sir Walter Ralegh's unfinished rhapsody expressing his unrequited love for Queen Elizabeth, a poetic aria that abounds in seemingly desperate ensembles:[18]

> But in my minde so is her love inclosde
> And is therof not only the best parte
> But into it the essence is disposde . . .
> Oh love (the more my wo) to it thow art
>
> Yeven as the moysture in each plant that growes,
> Yeven as the soon unto the frosen ground,
> Yeven as the sweetness, to th'incarnate rose,
> Yeven as the Center in each perfait rounde,
> As water to the fyshe, to men as ayre,
> As heat to fier, as light unto the soonn. . . .

These phrasal repeats may be read as ritual and hence a vaguely magic device, like casting a spell. The broad effect is elemental—an invocation of the elements. In highly evolved texts like the *Bhagavad Gita* spell translates gradually into ritual, then into recognitions of the world around us, until anaphoric gathering devices are required if the text is to suggest a cosmic range of reference and value. Critics who see lists in Whitman are seeing him as a Western thinker whose anaphoras and similar repeating iterations serve a conceptual purpose: the listing is believed to organize a description into its classified, connected, catalogued parts. Some have thought Whitman was in charge of the Parts Department, but looking back we find a more exalted usage, as in earlier philosophic poetry, where ritual naming has an honored place.

Take Spenser's "Hymn in Honour of Love" (the first of his mystical *Four Hymns*):[19]

> The gnawing envie, the hart-fretting feare,
> The vaine surmizes, the distrustfull showes,
> The false reports that flying tales doe beare,
> The doubts, the daungers, the delayes, the woes,
> The fayned friends, the unassured foes,
> With thousands more then any tongue can tell,
> Doe make a lovers life a wretches hell. [259–65]

Here, because the parallel phrases add up to a full catalogue of the "wretch's hell," their formal arrangement leads a series of lines to a climactic ending. A vaguely anaphoric order organizes the material of different poetic lines and thence influences the order of items *within* lines, so that every element or every "thought-rhythm" (G. Wilson Allen's epithet for such items in Whitman)[20] is placed in apposition to its neighbors, the apposition yielding the total sum of a certain state of mind. This is portraiture by numbers, unless we say that by loosening poetic rhythm, Whitman creates what we should call *a neighborhood of images and ideas.* Whitman's aim is less to express or depict persons exerting power over each other (which would yield allegory), than it is to express the adjacency of people, places, and things. This adjacency, when articulated as a complex living neighborhood, is exactly what I am calling an environment.

If, to achieve this symbolic neighborhood, the chief figuration of thought and image will be Roman Jakobson's metonymy as used in the fashion of Pasternak and Ashbery, then the chief type of image and concept will always aspire to the shape of the wave, for metonymies come in the shape of waves, even trivial small waves. In Whitman's case a poem will often bend actual waves into wave-like forms, rhythms, and structures, such as the scallop shell or the "living, fierce, gyrating wheel" of "The Dalliance of the Eagles," where the undulant motion of the wave is translated, as in math, by the transverse movement of a rotating wheel. The eagles' gyring dance is the pantomime of sexual freedom, in the sense that Noverre, the great classical choreographer, understood pantomime: "a bolt which the great passions discharge; it is a multitude of lightning strokes which succeed each other with rapidity; the scenes which result are their play, they last but a moment and immediately give place to others."[21] The issue is indeed balletic, since all those slight "lightning strokes" call eventually for a larger order in which their wavelike purpose is reinforced, not lost. In this search for a choreographic order of composition, Whitman achieves the shaping poetic principle of his chorographic poetry of our living-space, and always these undulant motions come at us in parcels of meaning, those unexpected, if not wholly paradoxical particles involved in the wave-particle duality.

This paradox always returns, for Whitman "disturbs our classifications," as Edward Dowden said in his lengthy and important 1871 review. The Homeric Whitman so valued by friends like William D. O'Connor eccentrically develops his own way of expressing personal sentiment and feeling.[22] One such "disturbance" arose through Ossianic influences. Whitman's poems use the old heroic simplicities to convey a modern complexity, and Dowden was right in seeing that Whitman's idea of democracy, while touched everywhere by science, is oddly connected to archaic and seemingly tribal visions of life and society.[23] Some of the unconscious humor that so troubled his early readers derived from the fact that in moments of extreme sensitivity Whitman remained the naive hero of Schiller's treatise *On Naïve and Sentimental Poetry.* This *naïf,* and perhaps only this *naïf,* can discover the dream of democratic "adhesion."

The Phrase and Its Intensifier

Randall Jarrell called Whitman "the poet of parallel present participles,"[24] and Ezra Greenspan has developed this observation. For Greenspan the *presentness* of this verb-form lifts the poetry into openness, into a promise of indefinite future, which imports an almost perpetual motion.[25] Present participles raise the traditional philosophic question of presence as guarantor of existence. Any present participle of the verb makes an implicit claim for existence, not least because this claim involves at least momentary stability in the midst of change. Perhaps only a poet of the "greatest and oddest delicacy and originality and sensitivity" could extract such force from a mere verb form, so that we truly believe the poet when, in "The Song of the Open Road," he writes:

> I and mine do not convince by arguments, similes, rhymes,
> We convince by our presence.

Participial elements belong to a general effect, which is that all predications are assimilated to a phrasal function, that is, to act as formally incomplete but psychologically complete utterances.

We need to think beyond the immediate confines of Whitman's page to the broader connections with the question of horizon. Consider the comments of John Cowper Powys, whose novels fall under Whitman's influence: "The 'free' poetry of Walt Whitman obeys inflexible, occult laws, the laws commanded unto it by his own creative instinct. We need, as Nietzsche says, to learn the art of 'commands' of this kind! Transvaluers of old values do not spend all their time sipping absinthe."[26] Powys calls this a "spheric law." He praises Whitman for his rare ability "to convey to us that sense of the unclassified pell-mell, of weeds and stones and rubble and wreckage, of vast, desolate spaces, and spaces full of debris and litter, which is most of all characteristic of your melancholy American landscape, but which those who love and know where to find, even among our trim gardens! No one like Walt Whitman can convey to us the magical ugliness of certain aspects of Nature—the bleak stunted, God-forsaken things." Powys then writes his own version of a Whitman paragraph, and concludes: "these are the things, the ugly, terrible things, that this great optimist turns into poetry." What Powys calls "the magical unity of rhythm" gives Whitman's verse its power to extend out toward the horizon.

Many times, however, Whitman uses the chopping, discontinuous rhythm of *asyndeton,* of which Longinus, writing in late antiquity, speaks in chapters 19 to 22 of the famed treatise, *On the Sublime.* Here are some examples: *He came . . . he saw . . . he conquered; I am the man . . . I suffered . . . I was there.* These jagged bits of *asyndeton* force the listener to imagine hidden meanings and connections lying between, which in turn lead the reader to imagine a cohesion and coherence which is all the more powerful as it is merely suggested by ellipsis, by the whole having been perpetually cut into phrases. These phrases are units of perception, as when the poet writes of the flag of peace being "quickly folded" ("By Blue Ontario's Shore," line 164), or more deeply when he writes: "does not all matter, *aching,* attract all matter?" and "I am he that aches with love," [line 2] or "Nose, nostrils of the nose, *and the partition*" [line 135, "I sing the body electric"].[27] There is a seemingly infinite variety of perceptual events here, to produce the delicacy Jarrell famously noted: "Even a few of his phrases are enough to show us . . . greatest and oddest delicacy and originality and sensitivity . . . so far as words are concerned."

If then Whitman is the "poet of parallel present participles," those present participles are for him *intensifiers* of the phrasal order. Such intensification is cultural as well as psychological, in the sense developed by the great American linguist, Benjamin Lee Whorf.[28] In his studies of the Hopi tribes, Whorf discovered that "the strange grammar of Hopi might betoken a different mode of perceiving and conceiving things on the part of the native speaker of Hopi." The Hopi were able through their grammar to express a universe full of vibrations ("vibratile phenomena") which were becoming the primary concern of modern physics. But the grammar allowed primitive intuitions to go beyond any language possessed by "normal standard English." Whitman is a born Hopi. Less metaphorically, he would have known the Indians of Long Island. Owing to his phrasal grammar, a Hopi "progressively adjusts himself into the action, and throughout the action is maintaining this adjustment, either to develop or to stabilize and continue the effect. Hopi includes here sleeping, dying, laughing, eating, as well as most organic functions and most alterative operations, e.g., cutting, bending, covering, placing, and thousands of others." By insisting on the environmental model, I insist on this strange kind of energy, action and exhaustion marking the completion of a poem. This is not the cadence of a dramatic solution to a storied question, rather it is the texture of filling the *chora*. Whitman is always waiting, peering ahead, testing his own expectancy. In this he shares the life of the women he abstracted and idolized, beginning with his own cherished mother, who plays such a part in the myth of his manhood. The Gaian poet of gatherings, he is in that sense Presocratic, a maker not unlike his successor in another field, Charles Ives, who knew how to mix three separate brass bands all at once in a single piece of music, while Ives's own successor, Henry Cowell, went all the way to the tone cluster.

Standing in for such a tone cluster is the famed engraving of the author's full-length portrait appearing across from the title, *Leaves of Grass* (1855). Most readers of Whitman have read this picture rhetorically, for the *effect* it has. This is not quite what Whitman wanted. He wanted it to be understood as *integral* to the poem it faces. The picture is a poetic, not a mainly rhetorical element, as Ed Folsom has observed, noting also the care with which the poet advised his engraver on technical matters.[29] True, Whitman, like many of his contemporaries, was a showman. There is an obvious bravado here, like the angle of his hat in the picture, suggesting he is one of the rough and tough New York fellows. The streetwise angle of the body also gave Bayard Taylor just what he wanted for a splendid parody of Walt's personal and poetic style. But more subtly and powerfully, Whitman seems to have meant that his picture should be, in effect, the first phrase of "Song of Myself."

Ossian and Phrasal Sensibility

Walt's engraved self-portrait is pure sensibility, and behind it stands the great underestimated influence upon Whitman's poetic vision and rhythm, Macpherson's *Ossian.*[30] This work, famous in its day, though in some quarters suspected of being a forgery—Dr. Johnson was an early doubter of its authenticity—had been confected into prose poetry by James Macpherson out of putative *original* Celtic poems, which the author claimed to be translating. In passing, we should say that there is something inherently romantic about forgery, and *Ossian* had sufficient sensational power to have converted young Werther from Homer to romantic effusion and sentiment, as soon as the young man read the poems of Macpherson; its strong and dramatic effect played a critical part in the hero's suicide, which in turn led to a rash of actual suicides all over Europe.

The vogue of Ossianic enthusiasm was immense, and it traveled across the Atlantic. When in 1782 the Marquis de Chastellux journeyed into Virginia and the Appalachian Mountains to see the Natural Bridge, he stopped en route to pay a visit to Thomas Jefferson. The Marquis was struck deeply by attitudes he shared with his host. His narrative of the event speaks of openly communicating feelings and opinions. He goes on:

> Not only our tastes were similar, but our predilections also—those predilections or partialities which cold and methodical minds hold up to ridicule as mere "enthusiasm," but which men of spirit and feeling take pride in calling by this very

> name of "enthusiasm." I recall with pleasure that as we were conversing one evening over a "bowl of punch," after Mrs. Jefferson had retired, we happened to speak of the poetry of Ossian. It was a spark of electricity which passed rapidly from one to the other; we recalled the passages of those sublime poems which had particularly struck us, and we recited them for the benefit of my traveling companions, who fortunately knew English well and could appreciate them, even though they had never read the poems. Soon the book was called for, to share in our "toasts:" it was brought forth and placed beside the bowl of punch. And before we realized it, book and bowl had carried us far into the night.[31]

Chastellux does not say that his other conversational experience of Jefferson (at home) followed immediately that night upon the bibulous reading of *Ossian,* but there is an odd sense of connection when he at once continues: "At other times, natural philosophy was the subject of our conversations, and at still others, politics or the arts, for no object has escaped Mr. Jefferson; and it seems indeed as though, ever since his youth, he had placed his mind, like his house, on a lofty height, whence he might contemplate the whole universe." This anecdote confers authority, as if any were needed, on the claim of Ossianic poems to inflame strong feelings in the late eighteenth century. When James Macpherson (1736–1796) fabricated and composed his versions of ancient Gaelic epic verse, he called his hero Fingal and around such figures he wove rhapsodic and enthusiastic simulacra of originals which he did not in fact possess, or even have the ability to translate from their original tongues. Perhaps his most daring creative act was to establish the verisimilitude of his forgeries, which became instantly popular throughout Europe. The story of his fabrications and their vogue remains one of the most fascinating in literary history, and even serious critics like Johnson felt obliged to puncture the Ossianic mystique. The poems known then collectively as *Ossian* were so powerful that they for a long time established, even if they did not single-handedly inaugurate, the associative rhythms of the Age of Sensibility. *Ossian,* as much as any other prior poetry, stands behind those breathless, often fragmentary surges of word and phrase of Whitman's phrasal structures. The rhythms are pure Whitman, and they suggest how important to his own voice was the work of Macpherson. "He [Fingal] opened the hall of the maid, the dark-haired Everallin. Joy kindled in our manly breasts. We blest the maid of Branno. Above us on the hill appeared the people of stately Cormac. Eight were the heroes of the chief. The heath flamed wide with their arms. There Colla; there Durra of wounds, there mighty Toscar; and Tago, there Frestal the victorious stood; Dairo of the happy deeds: Dala the battle's bulwark in the narrow way! The sword flamed in the hand of Cormac. Graceful was the look of the hero! Eight were the heroes of Ossian. Ullin stormy son of war. Mullo of the generous deeds."

Macpherson was the master of cut and paste (the "narrow way" goes back to *Cymbeline* and beyond to Old English poetry), but for a poet like Whitman what counts in the poetic example is the rhythmic variation within a paratactic, iterative order. Whitman's own reading of *Ossian* is on one occasion dramatically suggested in *Specimen Days* when, reflecting upon the ghostly absence and presence of friends, he recalled a wild Ossianic night, crossing the Delaware ("a real Ossianic night" he called it).[32] He remembered the "Gael-strains chant themselves from the mists" inciting him to commune as much with the vanished spirit of Ossian as with the spirits of his absent friends, O'Connor, Bucke, Burroughs, Anna Gilchrist: "friends of my soul—staunchest friends of my other soul, my poems." Whitman, obeying a call from the imagined bard, could offer up the same prayer, a poet's prayer: "Bend forward from your clouds, I said, ghosts of my fathers! bend." The whole passage is a Whitman chant, and a model for his chant, expressing an expansive mind desiring that discontinuity be controlled by wild associative rhythms. In a helpful passage Gérard Genette explores the borders of such enthused relations between fact and fantasy.[33] Of poetic language he says: "Poetic language reveals here, it seems to me, its true 'structure,' which is not to be a particular *form,* defined by its specific accidents, but rather a *state,* a degree of presence and intensity to which any statement may be led, so to speak, on condition that there is established around it a *margin of silence* which isolates it from its surroundings (but not from the gap) of everyday speech." The phrasal method finally insists upon projecting such "states" as partial awarenesses or, to use a word from Wallace Stevens, as the *credences* we enter into when seasons and their different weathers unfold before us.

9

Middle Voice

Sometimes, when we perceive things, we notice we are crossing back and forth between an inner self and a world out there, as if in a peculiar way perceptions resembled gifts exchanged back and forth between persons. Such mental activity is both inside and outside at the same moment, while we the perceivers stand between. Surely, if perceptions are neither active nor passive, they must acquire a grammatical form for their expression, a middle voice of some kind.

In English grammar, however, we do not have the middle voice, although we have both active and passive. We strike nails on the head, and nails get struck. In other languages, most notably ancient Greek, this middle form of the verb does exist, and in English we can create its effect by stressing the use of certain verbs of interaction and indwelling, transactions which lie half way between acting and being acted upon. Such, for example, would be many verbs of personal involvement, such as ponder, sense, move, dwell, loose and lose, hold, attach and detach. All these concern Shakespeare's question: what shall defend the interim? Their locus of commotion is the *limen*—Whitman's door slab—and insofar as a poetic art is devised specifically to speak for them, it has often been understood as a poetics of passage, much as that notion was developed by Arnold van Gennep in his classic *Rites of Passage.* In his work on linguistics, Emile Benveniste begins with a basic Indo-European example, the difference in verb form between sacrificing for someone else's benefit and sacrificing for one's own benefit or on one's own behalf; these two ideas shift grammatically from the active to the middle voice.[1] The latter always suggests that the agent has an "interest" in the action performed. The grammatical form virtually defines the meaning of interest, the middle-voice expression says that one is interior to the process in question, whether sacrificing or dwelling or whatever. This is Whitman's idea that he is concerned or involved in whatever he finds it worthwhile to tell us about, no matter how grand or trivial the *whatever* may be. Akin to the reflexive, as in the French verbs *s'emparer* or *s'habiller,* whatever is middle-voiced becomes part of one's sense of belonging to a certain thing, person, experience, or action, and hence there is a vague undercurrent of temporality, suppressed but inevitable in the usage. One's interest in the event is so much interior to oneself that it requires a duration over time, even though the purport of that duration will not reveal itself all at once.

For ancient Greek, as Herbert W. Smythe's *Greek Grammar* makes clear, the role of interest is widely extended in sense.[2] That is, middle-voice verbs denote that the subject acts often on herself or for herself, on himself or for himself, as the case may be. Thus I would "defend myself," and this middle state is enhanced if I take action by using something that belongs to myself, as when I wash my hands or I sell my house or even command my platoon. The direct and the indirect reflexive middle voices denote that the self is the direct or indirect object of a reflexive verb. The former would include as examples placing oneself, showing oneself, preparing oneself, even destroying oneself, while in the second category one might provide for oneself, keep guard for oneself, choose (for oneself), furnish a place for oneself, and even present an offer for oneself. Among the most important ancient Greek uses there is the denotation covering cases where "the subject acts with something belonging to himself," which might include the use of physical powers, means, or property. By extension the middle voice is used to indicate promises, excuses, setting forth an opinion, making professions of faith, hence even believing; and even further, making speeches, bringing about wars, signing treaties, and arranging hunts and explorations. No matter how varied the situation, there is an expression of a sometimes obscure but nevertheless intimate involvement of the self in the action taken. This type of expression transpires whenever the subject finds himself or herself in the midst of an environing situation and seeks to express this fact of interest in, connection with, whatever surrounds the self.

Consider an example of voice from Whitman, the nineteen lines beginning "What can the future bring me more than I have?"[3] Included in the 1856 edition as part of a 34-line poem, these lines were altered and then finally dropped from 1892. There are twenty-five verbs in the nineteen lines, starting with the sacrificial "brings." What sorts of action or passivity do they refer to? Almost none, in the ordinary sense. They are verbs of connection, copulars. *Suppose* occurs four times. *Believe* occurs four times. *Know* occurs three times. We get words like *wish,* phrases like *am not; am to be believed;* verbs of extreme involvement such as *like, love, enjoy.* We get phrases like "here I grew up," "have good housing all to myself," "the studs and rafters are grown parts of me," and then combinations of middle-voice expressions in one sentence: "And I *know well* that whatever *is really* Me shall *live* just as much as before." The most ample middle-voice term here is simply the verb *comprehend,* which occurs twice.

None of these verbs expresses direct action upon, or being acted upon, while they all suggest in some way that whatever is going on, the important aspect of the verb is the way it expresses a relation to experienced change. The verb, as "aspect," expresses continuation. When Whitman uses the verb "to find" twice, it points to the deepest effect of the middle voice: recognition of interiority. Whitman uses this effect of voice and aspect continuously, and he identifies it with what he typically calls "thought" or "a thought." Hence these nineteen lines end: "And I believe I have this night thought a thought of the clef of eternity." He puns on clef as "key," suggesting a mystery to which his thought gives him the key, and also a musical key-signature which on this occasion amounts to our learning on what scale the melody of thought is being played. In a musical way the poet searches for the particular right note, as when, in "Native Moments," he says: "The echoes ring with our indecent calls, I pick out some low person for my dearest friend."[4] To *pick something out* is about as far as Whitman ever goes toward the active verb. Choosing is always for him a passage through an intermediate state of cohesion, a sense of apprehending a presence, so that only in that rather indirect way is he active, although he gains in intimacy and interest *for* the apprehended object. The grammar for such a poetry has to be mainly written in a middle voice.

A similar, better known poem, "We two, how long were we fool'd," expresses the desire and the state of mutual love, affection, desire, in similar middle-voiced neutrality and interaction. The poem is full of verbs like "bedded," "swimming," "balance," "rolling," "interwetting," and the like, so we do indeed come to believe the lovers are like two clouds driving overhead, seas mingling, waves rolling, that they have become particles of an atmosphere transparent, receptive, pervious, impervious, that they are indeed "each product and influence of the globe." Benveniste and also Eric Charles White show the difficulty of relating the middle voice to the opposition between transitive and intransitive.[5] White quotes Jean-Pierre Vernant to the effect that in antiquity the middle voice finally disappeared when the subject became author of his actions, rather than remain intransitive participant. A modern version of this shift would be to observe the way a poet—Whitman—improvises, following in the kaironomic tradition of the ancient rhetorician Gorgias, who could jump in and instantly talk on any subject whatever. Without much play on words, one could say that in *Leaves of Grass* the persona of the Answerer underlines the middle voice—a lexical rather than grammatical effect, since in English we can only approximate this voice through a range of intransitives and reflexives. Experience in the *Song of the Answerer* is always in the midst.[6]

> A young man comes to me bearing a message from his
> brother,
> How shall the young man know the whether and when of
> his brother?
> Tell him to send me the signs.
>
> And I stand before the young man face to face, and take his
> right hand in my left hand and his left hand in my right
> hand,
> And I answer for his brother and for me, and I answer for
> him that answers for all, and send these signs.

Whitehead's 1938 remark, sharply anticipating Lacan, perhaps influenced by Wittgenstein, that "language dictates our unconscious presuppositions of thought," indicates that on the level of the unconscious answering is the speech act of all this watching and waiting.[7] The epigraph to *Drum Taps,* with its verbs *aroused, thought, urge, failed, drooped, resigned, sit, soothe, watch,* shows how often Whitman is interested in the unconscious presuppositions of thought. His verbs "involve an infinitude of alternative potentialities," to quote Whitehead again. The poetry depends upon an intransitive alternative to what the philosopher calls the "factual occasion." Using jump cuts and dissolves, this poetry treats all ideas, images, theories, other poetry, even dictionaries, biographies, and essays as "relative and interfused." The ensemble produces a grand resemblance to nature,

Fitted to the sky, to float with floating clouds—to rustle
among the trees with rustling leaves,
To stretch with stretched and level waters, where ships
silently sail in the distance.[8]

Following Whitehead, if the ancient Greeks sought to "discard the factor of transition" and chose instead "the realm of the completely real," we would have to say that such Platonic beliefs have been immeasurably powerful. Platonism and its legacy in Neoplatonism, and also Platonic beliefs such as those of the mathematical theorist Gottlob Frege, all suggest their power over Western philosophy and science. However, with the gradual onset of the observation of temporal changes in the earth's history, the timelessness of Platonic ideas came under question, and the poetry I have been discussing directly exemplifies such questioning. During the nineteenth century the Platonic dream lost its grip, as philosophy began to make "a survey of the vague variety, discernible in the transitions of human experience."[9] Montaigne meets modern science, and logic pays attention to the paradox of the heap.[10] In Whitehead's view this new approach is almost a requirement of modernity: "A power of incorporating vague and disorderly elements of experience is essential for the advance into novelty."

The Eloquence of Continuing Conversations

Anecdotes from Helen Price suggest Whitman's approach to modernity. Reminiscing how he visited her family (her mother was Abby Price, a well-known advocate of women's rights and a good friend of Whitman's), Helen Price described his way of listening as if to acquire his listener's ideas.[11] Often when asked to give his opinion on any subject, his first words would be, "'Tell me what you have to say about it.' His method of considering, pondering, what Emerson calls 'entertaining,' your thought was singularly agreeable and flattering, and evidently an outgrowth of his natural manner, and as if unconscious of paying you any special compliment." A considering and pondering style appeared also in his way of speaking, as Price reports.

> Mr. Whitman was not a smooth, glib, or even a very fluent talker. His ideas seemed always to be called forth or suggested by what was said before, and he would frequently hesitate for just the right term to express his meaning. He never gave the impression that his words were cut and dried in his mind, or at his tongue's end, to be used on occasion; but you listened to what seemed to be freshly thought, which gave to all he said an indescribable charm. His language was forcible, rich and vivid to the last degree, and even when most serious and earnest, his talk was always enlivened with frequent gleams of humor. (I believe it has been assumed by the critics that he has no humor. There could be no greater mistake.)

Helen Price is an important authority on the poet's command and use of language. She continues: "I have said that in conversation he was not fluent, yet when a little excited in talking on any subject very near his heart, his words would come forth rapidly, and in strains of amazing eloquence." One gets the impression from this memoir that Whitman thrived in the midst of common conversation, a prototype of democratic discussion. As Whitehead later observed, "the basis of democracy is the common fact of value-experience constituting the essential nature of each pulsation of activity . . . Nature is a theatre for the interrelations of all activities," where the essential feature of life is perpetual transition, as each living body seeks to be "unified" with its environment, sharing in what Whitehead calls "the togetherness of things."[12] Whitman says, "I name everything as it comes,"[13] because he wants to see how he fits and is unified with each pulsation of activity, always maintaining his difference.

There appears something impossible about this descriptive notion of a shared conversational poem that simply *is* an environment. For the claim to be literally true, the reader would have to be actually living inside a verbal construct. That can happen in science fiction, but can *such living* occur in ordinary life? The answer would be yes, if the imagined union of the poetic form and the reader's experience is in fact the most imposing aspect or part of that experience. Whitman writes as if being in a poem were his normal condition, and in our time, when Ashbery in "The System" writes that "chaos began to seem like the normal way of being," he joins in the aesthetic of the American river, where the poet is buoyed up and always open to new turnings, calm or threatening.[14] The aesthetic here assumes that the passenger on the ship is just as important as the captain. In a splendid modern critique written in the early 1950s, Charles Feidelson comments on the poet's theory of Personality that "his interest is not so much in the Personality or the environment *per se* as in the 'changed attitude of the ego.' The ego appears in the poems as a traveler and explorer, not as a static observer. . . . The shift of image from the contemplative eye of 'establish'd poems' to the voyaging ego of Whitman's poetry records a large-scale theoretical shift from the categories of 'substance' to those of 'process.'"[15] This shift has more recently been explored by Tenney Nathanson, in *Whitman's Presence.* My own desire as critic is to attend less to the issue of the poet's projected "self," asking instead: what are the poetics that would make it possible for the poet, and us, to believe that one can live inside a poem, inside *Leaves of Grass?* This question involves a rather public theory of poetry, instead of its ancillary problem of a theory of the self. One response to the question might be that Whitman and poets like him resemble the Vico whose *New Science* proclaimed a theory of culture based on a new notion of truth, namely, that we know only what we have made. This *verum factum* principle governs the making and exfoliating of *Leaves of Grass* as an evolving body of accumulating text. Feidelson states that "the poem, therefore, instead of referring to a completed act of perception, constitutes the act itself, both in the author and in the reader; instead of describing reality, a poem is a realization." This claim perhaps does not go far enough. Feidelson wants to name a peculiar mode of realization, a genre even, which would somehow collapse substance and process together, fusing state and change of state—exactly what would happen, if one could write an environment-poem. For in any environment substance is only known and functions only as (and in) process—precisely the subject matter of the new science of Complexity Theory, with its concern for emergent adaptations. The reader is asked to join in the formal experience of evolving with the environment created by the ever-expanding book. "The chant is neither pure self-expression nor pure description; what is talked about is oddly confused with the talking; and the audience is potentially both the subject and the writer." Here Feidelson catches the drifting participial character of "a process which renders a world in process."

It is known that when Whitman was writing "When lilacs last," he made a list of about ninety words connoting sorrow, and while we might instance section five of that poem to show how Whitman's phrasal atmosphere envelopes the fallen hero's death, speaking in words of passing and carrying, the original thesaurus of ninety sorrowing words signifies more powerfully the invention of an environing language. *To grieve* belongs exactly to this mode of belonging through speech. Whitman means his encyclopedia of sorrow to *surround* the elegiac moment, dressed in a sounding shroud of language.

In all such discussion the reader should remember that only under special and abnormal circumstances does sight envelop the viewer, whereas sound always surrounds us, as it resonates, although we may to a degree focus the sensation of a focused sound-source. Wordsworth composed an oracular formal ode, "On the Power of Sound." He considered this a major poem, while Coleridge had said "there are sounds more sublime than any sight can be, more absolutely suspending the power of comparison, and more utterly absorbing the mind's self consciousness, in its total attention to the object working upon it."[16] Sound possessing this degree of sublimity, this Aeolian harp, absorbs our powers of discriminating part from part, edge from edge, as sight alone permits us to do with complete accuracy. Whitman, we might say, subjects all vistas to the authority of a surrounding sound, and in synaesthetic fashion he invents his mode of environment-poem. These sight and sound fusions belong also to the poetry of High Symbolism, as Betsy Erkkila showed.[17] While they abound in Poe or in Tennyson's poetry, which Whitman esteemed, they are absolutely necessary for major French poets and they doubtless connect to Whitman's inventions of free verse, which later influence the French through the work of Vielé-Griffin. All this Paul Valéry affirms in his memorial lecture on Francis Vielé-Griffin. One can only surmise that the present participial sound conjoins with the concept behind that grammatical form, allowing sight and sound to intermix. The intensifying present participle makes the *sight* of process *resound* in our ears, with a sense that something is ongoing, continuing, flowing, moving through a moment that knows no start or finish. For sound and aural experience take precedence in the environment, as we have said, and this kind of resonance defines the meaning of interest in the middle voice. Caliban knew this, with his isle full of "noises, / Sounds and sweet airs, that give delight and hurt not." Other sounds might terrify, but they would no less surround the answerer, like the shores of an island, Whitman's home as much as the setting of *The Tempest.* The envelope of sound tells us where we really are, because, unlike most sight, sound in poetry has greater power to enter into us bodily.

10

Ashbery and the Becoming of the Poem

Asking how and at what stage of its existence a poem or any other imaginative work could be said to "come into being" might seem a philosophic inquiry beyond the simpler present account, but I include the question as a result of what I have already said about environments. To the best of my knowledge a study of environments and of ontology begins in Western philosophy at about the same time, with the Presocratics. For them existence and environment, taking this second idea in its broadest sense, occur simultaneously, since their questions about what "is" initiate a parallel set of questions about the actual world surrounding and environing us—are we surrounded by and hence formed by one of the elements, or by mind, or by an ideal Pythagorean harmony, by some other existent state or condition? Working with extravagantly fragmentary remains, modern historians of philosophy explain that the Presocratics needed this question about the universal surround, in order to begin their thinking about what is real. Some time in the early sixth century B.C., on the eastern shore of the Ionian Sea, Thales had asked: "What is the one single constituent of all that we see about us?" However much individual cosmologies differed, the question would sooner or later arise as to how the world comes to exist. Later in the game, in fact not long before Plato reordered philosophic priorities, a very different kind of philosopher, Democritus, would say that the originating fact was the existence of atoms and the void, out of which the world around us—analogous to Thales' sea around us, or Anaximenes' air around us—came to be organized into being. Democritean atoms comprise the elements in "the constitution of those things that flow upon (the body) and impinge upon it."[1] In the back of these thinkers' minds was probably some form of Parmenidean question: why is there something rather than nothing? So that if there is a world around us and we are living "in" that world, we need to know or find the fundamental principle by which that world "comes into being."[2]

Nothing could be harder to grasp than these fragmentary sayings of the Presocratics, mostly because they exist in minuscule portions of lost treatises, nor is the ontological issue inherently perspicuous. Only a highly trained professional philosopher can begin to disentangle all the possible lines of argument we can suppose them to have made, and for that reason I intend here only to suggest some ways in which what appear to be leading ideas could have a critical hold on certain problems of poetics.

Form and the Existence of the Poem

One central problem for the existence of the poem is the question of form. The orthodox view is that the poem, for reasons of aesthetic pleasure, comprises a deliberately formed linguistic artifact, a grouping and organization of words such that the very form of the poem is an inherent and strongest part of the aesthetic power. Poetry, as distinct from prose in all its uses and as a recognizable verbal art, is commonly and wisely thought to depend less on factual reference to things in the world, and more upon our imaginative relationship with those things and references. We are here reserving a place for a poetry which does entertain such referential and empirical language, but we need always to remember Coleridge's remark that the best poetry is never to be fully understood, for he knew that the determining role of metaphor changes the way poetry relates to reference. The extreme shamanistic use of metaphor and metamorphosis results in Rimbaud's systematic *dérèglement des sens.*[3] Any addiction to common sense makes problems for art, not because it is common, but because it may radically reduce the role of sense in human life, an ambiguity Jane Austen explored all through her novels, but which she directly addressed when she asked how sensibility could or should interact with plain good sense. That poetry is an art of formal achievements, achievements of form, is a long established tradition. Indeed it is hard to imagine that poetry ever could have played a part in human history had it not been a mysterious use of language, whereby a play of perpetual metamorphosis distinguishes the poem from all other uses of language. When Aristotle developed his notions of immanent form in the *Poetics,* he lifted Platonic Ideas down from the shelf of transcendental truth and left us wondering whether poems (unlike the Eternal Ideas) could achieve any permanence at all. On the other hand, it might be possible for the poetic search for the best forms of expression, for poetic shape, to amount to a reaching for the eternal; in the context of idealized love Shakespeare seems always to say this in his *Sonnets.* One does at least feel an odd inevitability in well-formed art, as if that were all we could ever know of the eternal.

If we begin with our everyday experience, we can say that on a lower level of argument there are at least two ways we can speak of the poem's existence:

(a) It has material endurance as an object, which we usually think must be a written object, or an aurally remembered object. For literature the so-called *text* puts the poem out there, fixing or establishing its objectivity. Whenever a text is lost—say the Nile River floods and a papyrus dissolves because the Nile Valley is irrigated—we can say with certainty that a certain poem on papyrus no longer exists.

(b) Textual existence implies the traditional response—interpretation—which then creates a body of *reading,* stimulating further responses that eventually enable the poem to endure as a social object. As text, the poem acquires social privilege, so that it comes into existence by right, as some may think, or simply is just there before the inquiring mind and from merely *being around* may come to be recognized as existing.

At times, as when commentary builds up around the extant fragments of ancient Greek poetry and philosophy, whole works seem to exist which are composed mostly of missing pieces; Ezra Pound depended upon this process when he composed his four-word, three-line fragment, "Papyrus":

> Spring. . . .
> Too long. . . .
> Gongula. . . .[4]

Here, whatever Pound may have thought, the reader *acts for* an imagined author, filling in the blanks, interpreting the sonorous remnant into full existence. If, as Parmenides wrote and Heidegger recalled, "thinking and being are the same," we will here have thought the poem "into being."[5] One might question the matter of the medium here, the mode of inscribing the poem—did Parmenides himself write or did he dictate his poem, or was it carried down by oral transmission until indeed it was finally written down? The literary object raises questions both about its materiality and its social construction, as academics often say today. The poem, for example, could cease to exist because its culture had radically changed, as the dinosaurs died because 11,000 years ago an asteroid hit the Earth. Such matters would seem to stay on the plane of material existence. Writing texts down certainly does bear upon the existence of what is presented and represented in that text.

Something odd does begin to happen if we, at least in our time, should ask, whose poem is it that has this existence? The French might say: "To whom is this poem 'proper'?" Whose property is it?[6] At such moments we seem to have inverted our original intuition; now existence seems to be deriving from a social practice that lies almost entirely outside the identity of the maker—society constructs ownership through copyright. Historians have studied the actual rise of literary ownership, and while its materiality has the comfortable promise of a world of things, we can hardly understand the full existent aspect of the poem through this limiting aspect of social practice. In earlier times, when poets were inspired, at least part of the poem belonged to the gods, and the author owned the poem without any material extension beyond creative selfhood. What conferred ownership on the author was that the poem existed through its *being,* not through any secondary textual extension of its material *existence.* The right of moderns to extend the existence of the poem is only a right to copy it, so as to establish a copyright. But then, by virtue of that legal mechanism, the modern owns the poem only as simulacrum.

Before this, and even now (if we allow the notion), the poem connected itself to existence through its phase of making, its *poesis.*[7] During that phase the poem was all process; A. R. Ammons, who died recently, said once that poems were "existences" full of contradictions—and "existences" catches what I have in mind, if the word is loosely understood to mean a process of coming into being.

A poet's notebook with its scribbles, lists, erasures, and second tries would catch the transition from nonexistence into existence. There is a note, then there are notes; there is a draft, then there are drafts; finally there is a poem. What I want now to say is that when this evolving creative process occurs, the poem's existence—its emerging into the light, as it were—actually displays a reversion to a more primitive state. The poem goes from *seeking* material endurance or duration, to wanting what the earliest Greek philosophers called Being. Charles Kahn, writing on the philosophy of existence, reminds us that the ancient Greeks for a long time could not name, and probably did not understand, any philosophical domain of existence.[8] They only spoke of Being and Becoming. Consider the terms, *hyparchein,* with its noun *hyparxis;* and the verb, *hypostenai,* with its noun, hypostasis, corresponding to the Latin verb, *sistere,* hence close cognate to *existere,* to exist—none of these arose until late in the game, until Islamic philosophy began to make "a radical distinction between necessary and contingent existence: between the existence of God, on the one hand, and that of the created world on the other." Kahn makes a broad claim, which bears on the question as to what is happening when a poem is made, although he is talking about the ontological question as such: "my general view of the historical development is that existence in the modern sense becomes a central concept in philosophy only in the period when Greek ontology is radically revised in the light of a metaphysics of creation: that is to say, under the influence of Biblical religion."

Plato's *Timaeus* [27a,b] presents the older ontology, of which Charles Kahn says

> the old Platonic contrast between Being and Becoming, between the eternal and the perishable (or, in Aristotelian terms, between the necessary and the contingent), now gets reformulated in such a way that for the contingent Being of the created world (which was originally present only as "possibility" in the divine mind) the property of "real existence" emerges as a new attribute or "accident," a kind of added benefit bestowed by God upon possible Beings in the act of creation. What is new here is the notion of radical contingency, not simply the old Aristotelian idea that many things might be other than what in fact they are, that many events might turn out otherwise, but surprisingly that the whole world of nature might not have been created at all: that it might never have existed.

Much depends on the reigning cosmogony. If one believes in a divine creator-god who makes the world, one will doubtless feel uncomfortable with the idea of existing things just drifting along somehow, somewhere, forever becoming. The belief in creation, of any kind, earthly or cosmic or divine, when it occurs at some point in time, will always favor the belief in existence as final, rather than Being as final. Kahn would say that the ancient Greek conception of being and becoming at some point collided with the biblical conception of creation occurring at a moment once-upon-a-time, or at an extended moment when history began. Here ancient Greek and Jewish beliefs are in radical opposition to each other, and much of the difficulty of traditional metaphysical discussion arises from their conflict extending through the Christian era. Imagine that if either being or a creator god are conceived as the grounds or sources of creation, then on a dependent level the poet will be attached either to the School of Being or the School of God, or perhaps oscillating between the two schools. What one might then call the School of Becoming is the school to which poets belong. The poets awake and look around, like Odysseus arriving on the shores of his homeland. They live through the actuality of perpetual change and they accept it as a given, with which they work as they make their attic shapes. In literature the stasis of the work of art is made especially ambiguous, however, by the way we write things down, one way or another. In a general sense, the Presocratic philosophy of being and becoming would logically have to favor the recited oral poem over the fixed written text. If poets work in the School of Being, they must lean towards silence and hermetic mystery. If on the other hand they work in the later School of Existence, again things are different, and we may say they are working for book sales and the copyright office. Oddly, this final option is underwritten by the archetypal model of the creator god, whose word is, in effect, "I own the world I have made." In our tradition of poems, which I fervently believe seeks separation from all religious dogma, as if there were an ideal paganism to which poets owe allegiance, the creative forces of imagination are closely tied to the poet's dreaming, as Freud opined in his famous essay on "The Poet and Daydreaming."[9] The poem has to dream its way toward being, before achieving textual existence. Orality and inspired improvisation—perhaps even a certain creative blindness—index the search for becoming, which is always a coming into being, and passing away from being. These alliances of literature with change and the unstable are more than anything else the mark of its independence from various irrelevant ideological orthodoxies.

"As Clouds Like Leaves Fashion the Internal Structure of a Season"

The recently published *Your Name Here* is the twenty-first book of poetry published by John Ashbery. Every poem in this and prior volumes, going all the way back to *Some Trees,* can be said to exist by virtue of a textual imprint. In this sense, many poems can be said to *exist* twice, because they were published initially in periodicals. They can all exist in hand-written drafts. Of all of them, we can ask, what does it mean to say that they came into existence? Printing is admittedly a weak criterion, since being and becoming pertain to forms of presence independent of being known to a public. In John Shoptaw's book on Ashbery's poetry you will discover that Ashbery's poetic always sees itself in flux, which seems to mean that letting new developments happen (for example, prose-poetry in *Three Poems,* or the double columns of "Litany" in *As We Know*) is the surest way to achieve a grip on being.[10] Ashbery devises forms (like *A Wave, Flow Chart,* or *Girls on the Run*) that always seek to "go on longer." With him, wholeness is not strongly bounded, or rather, is deliberately unbounded, as in Shelley Prometheus was "unbound." Mostly with him an elegant disarray mixes with casual détente, each poem almost calling, as if a person called out, for shifting sands and disappearing shores. In this poetry rivers are always questioning the land. Bodies of water exist by virtually contradictory means, as if liquid were more solid than stone.

Ashbery is noticeably what we would call a most *individual* author. Of such independent agents Nietzsche said: "Individuals are the bridges upon which becoming depends . . . the entire being of an individual takes part in every activity."[11] Down to the smallest cell, the individual is a complex unity, including all our experience and our individual past. Hence, says Nietzsche, we have the possibility of procreation. When Milton wrote in *Areopagitica,* his limited defense of what we would call the freedom of the press, that "a good book is not an absolutely dead thing," he implied that symbolic expression is as much a living thing as any bird or living creature. Guarding our thought against spiritualist platitudes, we can wonder if poetry does not try to establish a special domain for its becoming, a domain best named imagination. Fantasy and imagination are not just in a Coleridgean romantic interest; they occupy a sphere of thought as old as time. Poetry tends to evade problems of material existence, until very recent centuries, and even now there is an odd sense that when you go to the poetry section of a bookstore, you are stepping outside history. Poems are clearly not documents, speaking to us as if from a space outside both fiction and nonfiction. Surely Joyce was right to say that "poetry, even when apparently most fantastic, is always a revolt against artifice, a revolt, in a sense, against actuality . . . it makes no account of history, which is fabled by the daughters of memory, but sets store by every time less than the pulsation of an artery, the time in which its intuitions start forth, holding it equal in its period and value to six thousand years."[12] Joyce's allusion to Blake's *Milton* speaks for another way we might understand the poem's revolt against mere textual existence, namely as an endeavor of Blake's romanticism *before* Romanticism. No one could have been more hard-headed than Blake about the modern actual world in which he lived, yet no poet could have more clearly defended poetry and the other arts from the materialist narrowness history almost always recounts. Further, despite his persistent connection to biblical vision, Blake exemplifies the poet's desire to undo all uncritical, prefabricated world views. He would have us believe that poets never, *except in naive allegory*, decide ahead of time what their poetic logic and language will be. Rather, they look at the world. They invent a story, a lyric, a play, even a history—which they make into poetic artifacts as a consequence of looking around in the world. There are, then, two kinds of outlook, for this deeper thinking: (a) *There's a world and here's my idea of it.* And (b) *Here's my idea. Let's see if there is any world around that fits it.* The former type gives the basic model for the poet, the latter for the theoretical physicist. This world around us, this environing world, has usually seemed to proclaim being, whenever a presence of any sort appears. Being is the showing forth of things, as Heidegger might say. Then, in what way does a poem manifest itself? At a certain moment the poet is HERE. The poet sings a song; makes one up; imagines it; declaims it. In later times, the poet then writes it down and its existence begins. The poem is pulled out of the air, onto a ground. The text weaves it into a writing of infinite pathos. Textually the poem is preserved and then becomes an uncanny document. Its ground is not the philosopher's ground but is a mortal tablet, and on it the letters might as well be written on eroding stone, the lettering of Shelley's "Ozymandias."

But what middle condition, or flux, or state of change, occurs between the poem and its text? Maybe that is the question, the middle state, liminal passage, the transactional flux. Maybe the poem, as a being, inhabits a middle air. Poems do seem capable of living beyond their moment, and that is not because the text itself keeps them alive. On the surface, it might appear that the poem, as a text written down ("inscribed") and then possibly published or somehow preserved in an archive, keeps alive and living through commentary, through interpretation. But this, we have seen, is a life that ensures a disappearance into lost presence. Poetry thumbs its nose at interpretation, but we tend, perhaps in error, to know the poem as literature, as the letters of a text, which leads us around in a desperate circle, unless we have a theory of the *environment* of poetic being and becoming. In this last sentence, the key word is no longer being, but *environment.* The measure, the rhythmical and rounding order of personal lyric experience implies a strongly metaphoric control of poetic form. But with Ashbery the lyric "I" is forever being diffused into You, He, She, and We and They, and various kinds of It.[13] He has on many occasions spoken of his fluidity, even loss of personal identity, as a clear and strong ego. He has said his poetry is "disorganized" or "more disorganized than usual." Yet he is a master of classic forms, such as the sestina, which means that his forms are troped into an ontological game of their becoming, that is, always changing.

Metonymies of Becoming in Pasternak and Ashbery

Clearly Ashbery is always looking for a different genre of the medieval poet's *formosa,* which I am identifying with the phrase, *environment of Being.* To suggest exactly and poetically how this works, let us look at an article on Pasternak by Roman Jakobson (1935), not as well known but not unconnected to his famed essay on the two aspects of language.[14] Its background is an idea that the environment, the *Stimmung,* whose theory is a semantic version of ecology, involves looking around to see where we live. Environment may have simple effects, such as getting blown over in a high wind, but in its nature is complex. Environmental surrounds are never single, they are multiple, as befits scenes of becoming. If, like the weather, a poem should embody such a surround, it must furthermore share in the life-process, its language coming to life through a complex combination of interactions between all the elements and effects of its words. The verb here will always hold onto the becomingness of aspect and onto the *interest* projected by the middle voice. Jakobson wanted to show how poems actually shape the *Stimmung* effect. In his 1935 article, contrasting Boris Pasternak with Vladimir Mayakovski, he recalled that lyric poetry mostly speaks for the first person, in the present tense—a present toward which lyric always impels any past or future events.

Unlike Mayakovski, Pasternak heavily favors metonymy, so that "images of a surrounding world function as contiguous reflections, or metonymical expressions, of the poet's self. . . . Surrounding objects are thrown into turmoil; immovable outlines of roofs grow inquisitive; a door swings shut with a silent reproach; the joy of a family reconciliation is expressed by a growing warmth, zeal and devotion on the part of the lamps" and so on.[15] The same effects characterize Ashbery's work from start to finish. Adjacent objects work the greatest magic in him, as in Pasternak, and then metonymy leads the American poet into plays of synecdoche, causal figures, space becoming time, and all sorts of other games of showing that this goes with that and that goes with the next thing. We are always looking in these poets for the next thing, the next connected particle. Roman Jakobson identified personal character with the environment surrounding the person, and hence he thought that action could be replaced by topography, and figuratively in realistic literature by metonymy.

Suppose one did not know the source, one might identify the following sentences from Pasternak's influential prose work, *Safe Conduct,* with sentences by John Ashbery:

> "Suddenly I imagined, outside beneath the window, his life, which now belonged entirely to the past. It moved sideways away from the window in the form of some quiet street, bordered with trees . . ."
>
> "Somewhere nearby . . . a herd . . . was making music . . . The music was sucked in by blue-bottles."
>
> "Two rare diamonds were playing separately and independently in the deep nests of this half-dark bliss."

"Midday quiet reigned. It communed with the quiet that was spread out below in the plain."

"Lacquered sounds of giggling from a disintegrating order of life winked at each other in the quiet."

As Jakobson put it, "Pasternak's poetry is a realm of metonymies awakened to independence."[16] This freedom often "blurs the outline of things"—and, I suspect, leads to frequent animisms and personifications. "Spatial relations are mingled with temporal ones, and the time sequence loses its strict regularity." The poet, as Pasternak himself said, consciously prefers "the vicissitudes of guesswork to the eloquence of fact." He proclaims that " 'time is permeated with the unity of life's events,' and builds bridges between them on just those prelogical, 'ridiculous grounds' which he openly opposes to the syllogisms of 'adults.' " Note that the role of fact remains constant in this art, but it is gradually being subjected to a kind of uncertainty principle. Fact now becomes ambiguous event, much as scientists find in quantum mechanics, where without any loss of precision the factual falls under the discipline of statistical probability. In consequence, "material connectedness is subdued, sometimes to a mere glimmer." Such metonymies "show a persistent tendency to dispense with the object." Jakobson constantly presses the case for relational linkages taking priority over imagined single things, and yet this case in no way annihilates the existence of single particles of meaning, which we call things. "A connection once created becomes an object in its own right. Pasternak does not tire of underlining the inessential, random nature of the thing to be connected," nor does John Ashbery, we must add. Pasternak himself described his own style in this most extreme form: "Each detail can be replaced by another . . . Any one of them, chosen at random, will serve to bear witness to the transposed condition by which the whole of reality has been seized . . . The parts of reality are mentally indifferent."

Hence, as Jakobson says, "The poet defines art as the mutual interchangeability of images." Both poets in this way resist ordinary meaning, of which Jakobson says that here, in this basically nonmetaphoric style "meaning is inevitably etiolating, and plasticity deanimating."

Then we can only ask, what link between desire and figuration animates the poem of John Ashbery? Our answer could be put in one Pasternak sentence: "Show me your environment and I will tell you who you are." The Ashbery aesthetic is built of a web torn into endless synecdoches and metonymic approximations; Borges would call them "approaches." We learn in poem after poem to what the poet is "related, by what he is conditioned, and to what he is condemned . . . Action is replaced by topography." Or, as Jakobson puts it: "Following the path of contiguous relationships, the Realist author metonymically digresses from the plot to the atmosphere and from the characters to the setting in space and time. He is fond of synecdochic details."[17] Jakobson extended his general theory of the two fundamentals in language by showing that metaphor and metonymy appear throughout language, "be it intrapersonal or social." In dreams, for example, Freud's identification and symbolism rely on similarities and contrasts within classes, while his displacements and condensations rely on metonymy. Perhaps even more important for poetry, when we examine magic thinking, we find the two aspects playing out as homeopathic or contagious magic, which undergirds the two fundamental forms of allegory.

In terms of the present argument, this last connection implies an odd consequence, which I mention as an aside. It would appear that Ashbery, so often mocking high symbolism, instead necessarily favors metonymy. The predominance of this figure of adjacency leads to a new and original kind of allegorical writing, an instance of what we might call postmodern allegory. Traditional allegory projects the *received ideas* of a culture, and when inspired, brings to these orthodox ideas a new and pleasing analysis. In all such cases the aim is to provide a fiction of ideas in action. Quite different in tone and manner, Ashbery plays a parodic game with the stereotyped tokens of what "most people think." These stereotypes belong to an environment hostile to the subtle visions of their touching banality which his poems present. It is as if with Donald Davidson he questioned the very idea of a conceptual scheme,[18] and in a benign way asked, "who needs conceptual schemes anyway?" He writes an allegory avoiding or undercutting the grand personifications of received wisdom, of Lyotard's grand narratives. On the high level of the art he practices, he invents what one might call *allegory without ideas.* This is major art, and it translates the folklore of our time, including advertising and our sad universal hustle, into genuine poems. It abolishes the rigid terroristic schemes of the Book of Revelation and expresses a much more natural, if no less worrisome apocalypse.

With authors like Ashbery, agency usually manages to displace the agent through a perpetual middle-voicing, until the hero is translated into a condition of heroism. Pasternak masterfully expressed such indeterminate conditions. For instance, in a typical passage of *Safe Conduct:* "Everything that came from the parents to the children came at the wrong moment, from one side, provoked not by them but by certain causes that had nothing to do with them."[19] This could be an Ashbery sentiment. One understands why Ashbery borrowed an epigraph from *Safe Conduct* in an early and significant place, his first volume of poetry, *Some Trees.* His affinity with the Pasternak metonymy becomes the major stylistic attribute of his many and varied poetic works. It is his chief device of a poetics of becoming and of producing the environment-poem.

II

Meditating Chaos and Complexity

The common assumption is that we have first-hand knowledge of chaos, whereas only in total war, especially civil war, will advanced civilizations know chaos up close or at large. Terrorism plays on the ominously undefined fear of chaotic destruction, and although the physical fear of horrible pain may seem at first the most grievous social or political reaction, pain is not something individuals can *remember* for others, so that slowly over time a different and deeper fear of chaos begins to have a wider hold over the social ecology, as recent extreme terrorist attacks in the United States have demonstrated. Terrorism on a massive scale is only one of many indices to the new situation of the world we all live in, a world where masses and sheer numbers determine the fundamentals for intelligent decisions. Ecology may appear to depersonalize social thought, but ecology is nevertheless the sadly correct concept for initiating adequate *global* analysis. We have to accept that every developed society must think in broader and more systemic ways about these masses and numbers of people, these demographics, when chaos is contemplated. The masters of fantastic literature (I would nominate J. G. Ballard as chief among them) have analyzed mass numbers in fiction, where the excess numbers induce cognitive overload, a kind of psychic chaos.

If for *chaos of values* we substitute *complexity of images,* we discover Complexity Theory, a uniquely germane notion for studying chaotic phenomena in literature. Edward Lorenz, the meteorologist who discovered the "butterfly effect," chose the words "full chaos" to mean completely random disorder, complete lack of order.[1] To back away from Lorenz's full chaos into a less aggravated lack of order, we might ask: what *looks* like chaos, but is not? The reader will be ready for my answer to this rhetorical question: an Ashbery poem. If that is right, the poem will have to be an attenuated case of controlling chaotic disorder. This will have to be a chaos with rules. Literature and the other arts have traditionally played on the margins of disorder, and in stories have always shown us what happens when "life gets too complicated." We want a denouement, and we treasure ancient Greek literature for showing how such clarifications emerge, often tragically, when the Sophoclean plot of complexity is at last concluded. For confronting this question, Complexity Theory deals with theories of nature, theories that remain uncontaminated by teleological beliefs. In this field things are not imagined to be inevitable just because they have been called "natural." Poets are in many ways concerned with the primitive, but they should not uncritically be associated with blind fundamentalist beliefs in divinely ordered teleology, since poets employ the main scientific idea in Complexity, the notion of a self-organizing system.

For reasons that will emerge, the poetry of John Ashbery demonstrates the complex in a theoretical sense, and we need not shanghai him to make the point. A typical Ashbery poem lacks an obvious plot with stereotyped events whose sequence is standardized. Descriptions begin, are at once interrupted, turning left and right into other partial delineations. Voices come and go, fading in and out of earshot. Harold Bloom, ironically calling himself an exegete, admitted that "it was difficult to see how Ashbery got from point to point, or even to determine if there were points."[2] This sense of broken line inhered, for Bloom, in what he called the poem's "procedure." In this case a splendid reader and apologist for these poems, he seems insufficiently to measure the relation between procedure and process, which might come from our recognizing that Ashbery's meditative sequences lead to organized happenings. We no longer need the causal outlines of a logical or coherently compelling sequence of actions; rather, we need a coherence of perceptions, crowding each other for simultaneous recognition like children at a birthday party. If there is discontinuity, it recalls certain French authors, perhaps Raymond Roussel, or perhaps more poignantly Joseph Joubert (1754–1824), whose private Notebooks read in some ways as if they could be some sketches for of the longer Ashbery poems.[3] The accidental surreal and the aphoristic *aperçu* are equally at one with the style of *Flow Chart,* where, to quote Joubert, "in each true meditation a moment of rest follows each movement." Oddly, in spite of his increasing rage and dismay at the banal crassness of our world, Ashbery comes down finally always to a certain tenderness and, to quote Joubert again, "tenderness is the repose of passion." A French tonality touches this new surrealist style of sensibility, which to my ear recalls the rhythms of a poet like Robert Desnos. The "Ashbery tone" seems to need no violent assertion of its authority. At times he appears a park visitor idly taking snapshots of a dust storm in Death Valley, and in a sense the control of this desultory attitude is the poet's main accomplishment. As if its maker did not care where the poem is going, since quite happily it may be *going nowhere,* the typical Ashbery lyric walks at random through a landscape of insouciant irony.

Meditations on the Middle State

Traditionally and critically, the Ashbery poem might be called meditation. The profitable alignment will be with exercises like Donne's *Devotions upon Emergent Occasions* or Descartes' *Meditations on First Philosophy* or perhaps even Marcus Aurelius. The informality of the essay developed by Montaigne and Emerson also plays a part, modeling the flow and flux of consciousness. From the poet's angle of vision, of course, the fountain from which most Ashbery draws is Walt Whitman's *Song of Myself,* a poem simultaneously direct and oblique. Meditative disciplines play a central part in Oriental mysticism, even more than in the West. Like poetry, they too involve the most intimate transactions between a direct sense of self and an oblique sense of the world, while, as Tantric Buddhists might demand, the meditation uses detached images to block the intrusions of thinking.

Consider the term "meditation" itself: it ties directly to the most ancient words for the middle, for measuring, and for medicine. In his etymological dictionary, Eric Partridge explains: "Whereas the Latin *medicus* is a measurer of man's ills and injuries, *meditation* is the thought-measuring of an idea, a fact, a thing. The Indo-European root *me-,* to measure, is displayed openly in Old English *metan,* whence 'to mete.'"[4] We can still say that an authority metes out a reward or punishment. Meditation links to the Old Irish word *median,* which means to judge, and more importantly links all the way back to the ancient Greek *medesthai,* to attend to, to estimate. The etymologist gives us only the roughest road map, to be sure, but Partridge does point to one essential component of the meditative process—it is loosely "medical" in the sense of attending carefully, with the weight of meaning implied by the phrase "attending physician." Attention here is far more pointed than in Frank Kermode's phrase, "forms of attention," by which he merely means paying close interpretive heed to any textual imperative or call, the sort of call canonical works appear always to demand.

On this account Ashbery writes with a special way of paying close attention. You will say, all serious activities, including the activity in and around a poem, are surely attentive. But in fact most poetry is deliberately inattentive. It dwells in memorized formulas (ballads); it dwells in romantic exaggerations and hyperboles

("My love is like a red red rose"); it dwells in the great generalized traditions of myth, those stories appearing everywhere as the loosely ordered *structures* of poetry and literature; it dwells in a studied indirectness and obliquity which are the very opposite of attentively observed reality. Poems seem to be elsewhere, as booksellers know. Inspired, the poets' minds drift or fly to the horizon, as we found with Clare. Even neoclassic poets like Ben Jonson or John Betjeman are less haunted than might be expected by their societal facts; they are playing with societal principles. So it seems that a strictly attentive poetry is unusual, and will need a proper definition. But again, attentive in what sense? If there is something measuring and medical as well as meditative about Ashbery's verse, then there would have to be an underlying order to it, something like a search for health, or the self-examination of a body that is working well or not, perhaps the first stages of a diagnosis. Some rule of order operates here, albeit mainly hidden from sight.

Meditation gives us a method of diagnostic surveyal, at once precisely responsive and open to the drift of thought as it becomes one with an outer world. Meditative attentiveness points toward the symptom, toward the merest passing sign of an order or disorder, hoping to catch this sign as it emerges from the flow of consciousness. *Description,* as I use this word, always means diagnosis. The capacity to observe and record the symptom is only used when there is a hazard of disorder. The experience of accident, chance, and the unpredicted is what we know when we become conscious of the complexity of life and being alive. Whenever we are disturbed, we sense that somehow we did not expect some interruption to have happened. Keeping in mind that poetry as much as fiction can dive into a turbulence, we can observe another quality of Ashbery's work, its peculiar way of tripping up when it meets minute obstructions in the random walk. Already this notion of tripping up on a stone in the way gives us some answer to Bloom's puzzlement: the poet gets from one point to another by *trusting that he is going along a path,* which is among the oldest of all theories of meditation. Sir Philip Sidney's muse commanded to move along with two simple words: "and write."[5]

With Ashbery the typical lyric uses its being written down, its textuality, to carry the reader away from the focused materials into a flux whereby those materials are processed. Frequently with Ashbery the poem makes mocking comment on the idea that poems are printed objects that are readily interpretable. Ashbery's poem gives *voice* to the interplay between thoughts, pictures, and things. His eye shifts sharply from material, concrete actuality (often extremely sharp-edged bits and pieces of ordinary fact, like the smudge of newsprint on today's paper), to an ideal landscape. But this landscape is itself never fixed. In the tradition of Emerson's use of Montaigne, to discover the scene is to discover the self. Of this relationship between actual writing and actual seeing, Marie-Rose Logan has said, "In the *Essais* Montaigne explored through writing the process of self-discovery."[6] By writing in a certain way (and then publishing) the author creates a housing so that the poem may contain the meditation. Of the essaying technique and its precursor—the epistle—Marc Fumaroli has said, "The humanistic letter, in its Italian origins, was already an 'essay' with the meaning given to the word by Montaigne, in which all kinds of topics were broached by a meditating and central self, the only unifying principle within such a meandering diversity."[7] A typical early Ashbery poem would be "Young Man with Letter."[8] We are rapidly losing the genre of the "familiar letter," but we can still see that it mainly consisted of familiar particularities.

Diagnosing the Moment

Like Whitman, Ashbery writes in the middle voice of both a medical and a meditative approach to symbolism, preserving an open and unjudging formal principle, until the poem, like the day or night, comes to a close. The diversity of an Ashbery poem comes from its increasing and interactive circling around a center, that "central self" Marc Fumaroli found in the Montaigne essay. The poem becomes a special kind of fragment, produced by removing what is conventionally called the beginning, and the ending. The activity of the poem is not linear or causally clear, where one thing clearly would lead to another, to another, and so on, to an end point. The artistic aim is to enable the reader, for a moment, to live inside a poem. Ashbery's celebrated *Self-Portrait in a Convex Mirror* is only one of his more obviously mannerist and ekphrastic poems; most recently Ashbery (the former art critic) has published a "primitive" rendering of an *art brut* painting by Henry Darger, "Storm Brewing," which metamorphoses into the long poem *Girls on the Run;* by enclosing the poem in a fantastic reading of the picture, Ashbery avoids having to produce a linear story of whatever the girls in the picture are imagined to be doing, beyond running from the approaching storm. As with *Self-Portrait in a Convex Mirror,* the poet is in no sense literally tied to his pictorial source. Instead, the poem says the children may be doing this, or that, or perhaps even that other thing, and in any case the option is open for the poet to give the girls any names and lives his imagination may confer upon Darger's two-dimensional image. But picturing is an essential part of meditation, as the trained mystics have always told us. Picturing may go nowhere, but it encourages focus, the perceptual prerequisite for *paying attention.*

The Causeless Middle

If Dante begins his epic in the middle ground, *nel mezzo del cammin di nostra vita,* so also Ashbery in *Flow Chart:*[9]

> Still in the published city but not yet
> overtaken by a new form of despair, I ask

the diagram: is it the foretaste of pain
it might easily be? Or an emptiness
so sudden it leaves the girders
whanging in the absence of wind,
the sky milk-blue and astringent? We know life is so busy,
but a larger activity shrouds it, and this is something
we can never feel, except occasionally, in small signs
put up to warn us and as soon expunged, in part
or wholly.

Flow Chart, beginning with these clear allusions to Dante and Eliot, is about 200 pages in length. Other works, like "A Wave" or "Tuesday Evening," are shorter but still have meditative length. *Flow Chart* is a strict example of the poetry of diurnal knowledge. John Shoptaw has told the story of its composition and has provided a brilliant exegesis of its extended form. When, in the fall of 1987, a friend suggested that Ashbery write a one-hundred-page poem about his mother who had died the previous January, the poet converted this plan into an almost daily journal leading from the day of her death to his own birthday on July 28, 1988. "Starting on December 8, 1987, he wrote *Flow Chart* with his birthday . . . as his destination and deadline, making almost daily entries and nearing the end ahead of schedule (he finished 93 pages by the end of June 1988)." Some sense of the complexity of this diary may be gained from the fact that Shoptaw's severely concise commentary on *Flow Chart* occupies a full forty pages. The commentary, paralleled by David Herd's briefer account, performs two functions for the reader: on the one hand, we begin to see that diurnal knowledge adds up to an ever shifting flow in our currents of experience, as we live day to day; and, on the other hand, we see that these broad currents are punctuated by a seemingly infinite number of detailed discriminations of experience. To recall another more famous diary, even though Samuel Pepys ends every day's entry with the well-known words "and so to bed," the details of his daily life are within a certain range endlessly varied and precisely observed. The mark of this diurnal literature is always a striking combination of recurrent rhythms and singular turbulence. With all such poems the sentences are formed and deployed to achieve an effect of perpetual transition from one set of "small signs" to another to another. This system of portent yields Ashbery's recurrent image of the vaguely apocalyptic approaching storm. Large systems of causality seem to have lost their purchase. Night is coming on, like the murderer's rain in *Macbeth:* "Let it come down." A later poem, "Crossroads in the Past," evokes some kind of withheld omen.[10]

> We've got to change all the furniture, fumigate the house,
> talk our relationship back to its beginnings. Say, you
> know that's probably what's wrong—the beginnings
> concept, I mean.
> I aver there are no beginnings, though there were perhaps
> some
> sometime. . . .

If Ashbery's poetry expresses passage and passing from one moment to another, this *procedure* will not always follow a clear forward direction. This process-like vision, often but not always twilit, may even seem without structure, unless we understand the structure of this poem to be the movements of an interior flow like *Flow Chart* (". . . its itinerant birth some years back down the creek. First, / there was a lot of hammering. Then a blonde woman got out of the car to take pictures. / H'mm, this must be *the* night, a lot of people assumed. Then the thunder / Again."[11] Ashbery invents an art of elliptical juxtaposition, with just enough causal glue to hold the reader in touch with the stream of metonymies.

The units of attention will be figures of speech and thought, whose prime technique will be a typical sentence-shape. "Proust's Questionnaire" contains these lines:[12]

And I see once more how everything
Must be up to me: here a calamity to be smoothed away
Like ringlets, there the luck of uncoding
This singular cipher of primary
And secondary colors, and the animals
With us in the ark, happy to be there as it settles
Into an always more violent sea.

The cadences of the verse are gently modulated. A lightly paratactic style (here . . . there . . . and . . . and . . . and) allows the poet to slide forward without the stricture of a marching or dancing poetic step. The thought here is of ciphered relationships, questions (how shall I meet catastrophe?), perceptions ("an always more violent sea"), without the verse-form constraining the flux of consciousness. When Alexander Pope meditates in the *Essay on Man,* he is forced to tailor his meditation to the symmetry structures of the Augustan couplet; he cannot follow the trail of thought wherever it leads. Another poem ("Cups with Broken Handles") tells us something of the way the Ashbery free-verse syntax allows thought to *flow.*[13]

Meanwhile, you're
Looking stretched again, concentrated, as you do not pass
From point A to point B but merely speculate
On how it would be, and in that instant
Do appear to be travelling, though we all
Stay home, don't we. Our strength lies
In the potential for motion, not in accomplishment, and
it gets
Used up too, which is, in a way, more effective.

Another sentence, drawn from the great meditation "The System," approaches a passage about chaos beginning to seem "like the normal way of being" by letting the prose and its natural flow fall as if down a slope from a sublime height to a quotidian digression: "There is no cutting corners where the life of the soul is concerned, even if a too modest approximation of the wish that caused it to begin to want to flower be the result—a result that could look like overpruning to the untrained eye." "The System" specifically speaks to the idea of complexity, and links it with noticing all the details in an intelligent, percipient way.[14]

> Forget about the details of name and place, forget also the concepts and archetypes that haunt you and which are as much a part of the typical earthbound situation you find yourself in as those others: neither the concept nor the state of affairs logically derived from it is going to be of much help to you now. What is required is the ability to enter into the complexities of the situation as though it really weren't new at all, which it isn't, as one takes the first few steps into a labyrinth. Here one abruptly finds one's intuition tailored to the needs of the new demanding syndrome; each test is passed flawlessly, as though in a dream, and the complex climate that is formed by the vacillating wills and energies of the many who surround you becomes as easy as pie for you.[15]

"The System" continues with an elaboration on successful passage through the labyrinth of merely living, without prior concepts, archetypes, names, slogans, dates, places, and locations, as the addressee is told "to live in that labyrinth that seems to be directing your steps but in reality it is you who are creating its pattern, embarked on a new, fantastically difficult tactic whose success is nevertheless guaranteed." Our task is to believe the success, so it may happen. We have to accept a satire against silliness (. . . "easy as pie"). We have to accept the condition of our familiar drifting, which seems so at odds with the oppressively "successful" advances of technology.

The ideal quotation from Ashbery would discover that single step or phrase or sentence that *places* the poem precisely on its random walk. We will later find that metonymy is the chief device by which this placing occurs in the poetry, because metonymy is the figure of the symptom. Metaphor is not a conspicuous device here, except as producing the archetypal *framing symbol*—the river, the approaching storm, the labyrinth—such frames being necessary for the detailed diagnosis and meditation to begin.

The Fall of Parity

Ashbery writes in the age of *the fall of parity,* as it is called in physics.[16] Historically, ours is an age where symmetry is always eroded, where sequences of events often appear to slide forward into unbounded openness. The limitless *apeiron* of the Presocratic philosopher has reasserted its authority. Logocentrism and its reliance on the dialectic now generate their opposite, the hermeneutics of suspicion, which, once begun, knows no terminus. To counter these climates of perpetual doubt Ashbery has mobilized a moving army of metonymies, largely because his method of meditation requires devices leading one always around in a circle, as each name leads to another to another; there must always be a magic circle of naming and renaming to produce a sense of seemingly endless, asymmetrical, nonlinear sequence.

Partly because the meditations here always suggest the larger activity shrouding the business of life, they share in the ironies of T. S. Eliot and other moderns. Such irony in turn requires a language of sliding transformation, where mythic structures (the great Western stories) collapse, as *The Waste Land* collapses epic amplitude, a deliquescence which in turn calls for that mysterious figure, *metalepsis,* or in its Latin name, transumption. *Metalepsis* creates a magic effect in literature, because when a poet uses a word drawn from a previous poet, the second use is designed so that by evoking the first use, the repetition implies a magical anticipation. Single words and images are used transumptively so as to suggest that there is a mysterious continuity, not materially sequential in an obvious way, between earlier and later events. Such magic of naming calls upon a primitive human understanding of synchronicity, by which causality is, so to speak, trumped by occult resemblances. When, with this figure of traveling allusion, Ashbery's *Flow Chart* speaks of "metal fatigue," we have been already led through a series of associations and anticipations to recognize a pun on mental fatigue, and thence backwards in the poem to the final line of its first section, "the ground blue as steel."[17] If this procedure recalls the Wagnerian use of the leitmotiv, this is to be expected, because Wagner saw how repeated motifs could organize the very large structures of his *Gesamtkunstwerke.*

Metaleptic figures, like the play on "metal," are figures of promise; they give the future a place in the present, one thing always leading to another. Success of some kind lies ahead, a hope that *Flow Chart* expresses with casual sublimity, somewhat towards the end of the poem:[18]

> A hound-shaped fragment of cloud
> rises
> abruptly to the impressive center of the heavens only to
> fold itself
> behind itself and fade into the distance even as it advances
> bearing news of the channel coast. That is the archetypal
> kind of development we're interested in here at the win-
> dow girls move past continually. Something must be
> happening beyond the point where they turn
> and become mere fragments. But to find out what that is,
> we should be forced to relinquish this vantage point, so
> deeply fought for, hardly won.

In the common parlance of *ordinary language* such a vision is full of portent, but it is also inherently complex. The nonsymmetrical *infolding* of different planes of reality available only to an apprehending power of mind shows us a layering of experience—not so much of *meanings,* as would be the case with allegory, as an interleaving on the plane of experience itself. To articulate the interleaving process, a leading complexity theorist, John Holland, found that a seven-fold model gives a reasonably accurate picture of any complex process, whether it is the weather, or the market, or an ecosystem where quail and minnows have to survive.[19] In essence complexity theorists are writing about the same things as the naturalists Peter Matthiessen and John Elder. Their "natural history" ancestors are Gilbert White, Richard Jefferies, John Clare, even Sir Thomas Browne, who so influenced Thoreau and Melville. Ecosystems (as distinct from heroic stories) provide the archetypes for this literature.

Hidden Orders of Complexity

Following its seven-fold paradigm, Complexity Theory has focused on the idea of adaptation. John Holland's account, presented in two books, *Hidden Order: How Adaptation Builds Complexity* (1995) and *Emergence: From Chaos to Order* (1998), unfolds a picture of emergent phenomena which is to some extent familiar from much earlier speculations (Ludwig von Bertalanffy would recognize his idea that for living organisms the whole is greater than the sum of its parts, a biological concept that by itself almost defines "emergence"), and to some extent newly formulated (computers have opened the way to research into very large numbers). The guiding notion is that "emergent phenomena in generated systems are, typically, persistent patterns with changing components." Such a general principle resembles the oldest rules for making good works of art.

It is worthwhile to rehearse a sequence described in John Holland's *Hidden Order,* in which he proposes a seven-fold array of the elements of any such adaptive system: (1) The system (for us it would be a poem) begins by gathering its materials, this being a process of *aggregation.* We might call it the first stage of the logos. (2) By *tagging* its batched materials, the system puts a special sign on the ones that count most for the process to operate, as cells in the body are tagged by iconic banners that give them special functions and make them "recognizable" within the system. For literature this tagging occurs through the varying signals sent out by the *rhetoric* of the utterance. (3) The *nonlinearity* of the adaptive system is perhaps the most familiar of all its analogies to literature, where the effect of a poem or a novel or play is not produced by simply adding up the components, but instead by getting the components to interact, to *multiply* each other's effects. Nonlinearities are products, not sums. It was to show this feature of the artwork that the Romantics invented the notion of organic form. (4) The power of a system to adapt is enhanced by its formal character, which Holland calls its *flow,* by which he means that here we are talking about "patterns that reflect changing adaptations as time elapses and experience accumulates." This parallels the poem's generation of its own time, as it accumulates its own internally evolved "experience"—the development of the plot and characterizations of a novel, for example. (5) Another essential property of the adaptive system is internal *diversity,* to which literature affords many analogies. Broadly speaking, we need the diversity of agents, all interacting nonlinearly, in order for a complex system to come alive, as a city comes alive only if its citizens are various. (6) In order to survive changes by anticipating, the system needs an internal *model.* The model or schema gives a mechanism for eliminating irrelevant items from the initial aggregation. Artists planning their compositions are familiar with this charting function. Looking ahead, in chess, would show this charting, but all poems are written with much the same "look ahead." By internalizing the function of model or idea, its system, the poem can effectively change its environment. In that sense if the poem models the horizon by participating in it, that horizon ceases to enclose us, and instead guides us to look outward, yet without losing ourselves. (7) Finally, the system needs what Holland simply calls *building blocks.* In physics these might be the quarks and atoms and molecules and cells, and other repeatable and variable modules of combination. In literature they are the units or elements of composition, the mere words and dialects Stéphane Mallarmé had to recover for modern poetry.

Perhaps the most intriguing aspect of Holland's account is that if there is a difference, as he believes, between tacit and overt models, then the former allow the building blocks to be combined on an evolutionary time scale, whereas overt modeling speeds up the process so that "the time scale may be orders of magnitude shorter."[20] The distinction between overt and tacit orderings is not unfamiliar in literature, although we may not always notice this. All standard allegory, and this includes the chief place where allegory is used, namely advertising, makes use of an overt model of iconic organization; this overt model is what we usually call "the allegory" of a story. It makes the message of the work immediately available. By contrast, Realism, Symbolism, Impressionism, and all other similar modes convey messages according to a longer time scale. Even though the immediacy of a realistic story might seem to make it quickly available to the reader, the order of this realistic story is only more slowly revealed to understanding. A tacit model is always more fruitful over the long term. Complexity Theory aligns the open or hidden patternings with the materials of the process in question; Holland's building blocks are either more or less open or hidden. In either case, slow or fast, covertly or overtly modeled, the adaptive system and the poem use these recognizable building blocks in order to impose a measure of regularity on the final product. In literature we understand the role of tradition in this light, for while tradition is a holder of change, it is even more deeply a holder of stability. The poem, like the system, adapts *by itself* to meet communicative needs at many levels of contact with the environment. The intentionality of literature and art is clearly *in the work,* not in the maker alone; the maker's middle voice injects an interest and authorial intention in the action of making the author's own work, and in this way—half way between mind and object—the work finally organizes itself. The reader of complex meditations like *Flow Chart—the specific reader of that particular poem*—will at once recognize that for intentional *innering* to occur, there must already exist a chart of transaction. This chart in turn permits all the elements Holland described: flow and diversity, attentive tagging, aggregated and diversified building blocks, and above all the internally adaptive, nonlinear sequence Ashbery's poem achieves. This combinatorial power will not surprise the reader of *Three Poems* and other meditative works by this author, since the ultimate arena of complexity, as formally and scientifically defined, is the mind itself.

Mind and nature thus converge on the plane of complex nonlinear aggregates. In science the use of computers has given to Complexity Theory the requisite computational power, and this power is in effect the machine equivalent of human thinking. Again, literature today shares in what James Crutchfield calls an interest in "global coordination" of natural phenomena "in which highly-structured collective behavior emerges over time from the interaction of simple subsystems. Flocks of birds flying in lockstep formation and schools of fish swimming in coherent array abruptly turn together with no leader guiding the group. Ants form complex societies whose survival derives from specialized laborers, unguided by a central director. Optimal pricing of goods in an economy appears to arise from agents obeying the local rules of commerce." The scientist looks at the ways in which such coordination requires hidden skills that give the system (birds, fish, ants, buyers) new information needed for modeling new and ever changing conditions. What emerges is the capacity of a system to develop its own ensemble character, much in the manner of small chamber groups of musicians who play without a conductor, as in the eighteenth century.

Response within the adaptive system, complexity theorist James Crutchfield tells us, "pushes the observer inside the system," like the reader of an Ashbery poem.[21] Any poetry that pushes the observer inside the system seeks what Donne called emergent occasions. Poetry on this order seeks to obey the principle set forth by Crutchfield: "a process undergoes emergence if at some time the architecture of information processing has changed in such a way that a distinct and more powerful level of intrinsic computation has appeared that was not present in earlier conditions." As the poem proceeds, new states of awareness are progressively added to its intention to create its own environment, which ambiguously doubles the external natural environment. *Flow Chart* speaks of "the litany of all that has ever happened to me"; inevitably, then, the meandering plot of the poem is constantly undercut by the apparent triviality of its remembered events, "childish pranks included," but then the poem attends to its life's symptoms, the poet playing the role of the attending physician, or in regard to the poem's composition or birth, the attending midwife. Meditation is a matter always of learning how to pay attention at a higher level of thought, so that if "the readiness is all," this poetry will always be ready for accident, distraction, occasion, and the new insight. In the final analysis *Flow Chart* narrates and meditates the weaving of a life as lived diurnally over several months, a life experienced as an adaptation to stresses and hopes and fears. Complexity Theory shares this interest in adaptive outcomes, not only with poems like *Flow Chart,* but in its own terms with the governing ecological science of evolution, which virtually defines what we mean by adaptation. In this light, poems of this kind are dedicated to showing how we adapt to the environments into which we are thrown by life—a Heideggerian dimension of both the poetry and the science.

Ashbery's environment-poem, written out on a daily basis, risks one aesthetic disadvantage—the days resemble each other too closely. The poem needs what in music would be called a *stretto,* a concentration of themes in one massively converging contrapuntal treatment. This amounts to placing a monument in the scene, to interrupt the flow of reverie, so that in itself the flow will be sensed as the idea of the poem, by virtue of the aesthetic contrast. Such interruptions take many different forms, of course, but another illustrative musical example would be the use of a slow variation stabilizing a set of faster variations, a slowing which is always classically placed towards the end of the set—we find this, for example, in the *Goldberg Variations* and in numerous Mozart pieces. The slow treatment of the musical theme allows a gathering to occur, a settling, a domestication of the theme, before the final windup. In serious literature this may occur in much the same fashion, as when in his *Meditations upon Emergent Occasions* John Donne places his dramatic command, "Ask not for whom the bell tolls," at a late turning point in his drama of recovery. The late placement of the interruptive moment is exactly what we find in *Flow Chart.* The monument must control the larger flow by looking back over a broad stream of pages preceding it. Yet it must be followed by a final denouement, which again we find in *Flow Chart.*

12

"The Long Amazing and Unprecedented Way"

In a letter to Thomas Moore, his friend and fellow poet (November 30, 1813), Lord Byron exclaimed: "All convulsions end with me in rhyme,"[1] and the same is true of *Flow Chart* by John Ashbery. For Byron this meant a poem like *Don Juan*—rhymed, stanzaic, and Arabian, with one episode leading, casually or almost at random, to another—the whole tale unified less by a quest-romance (the apparent thread through the labyrinth) than by the wit of the local observation and the exact telling. The Arabian tale of a Romantic hero's life (Byron's own) projected onto the Don Juan story becomes a feverish revelation, in due course. It periodically convulses, and it needs a machine for closure and order, a device destined to control the fever. For the fever must run its course, whose turns and twists flow indeed and yet call for a charting—a stilling. Otherwise the poet loses the balance between state and process, loses control over "living on the plane of insistent self-knowledge," as Ashbery put it.[2]

Most of Ashbery's poems are relatively short lyrics, but the tendency of his art has always been toward longer, more riverine extensions. He is perhaps best known, indeed, for his *Self-Portrait in a Convex Mirror,* and more recently for the lengthy prose lyrics in *Three Poems;* the two-column poem "Litany" (so resembling

Derrida's *Glas*) in *As We Know;* "The Skaters," "A Wave," and "The Stars Were Shining"; the rhymed quatrains of "Tuesday Evening"; and most recently *Girls on the Run* (about 50 pages in length). The acidly sharp lines of "Grand Galop" in the *Self-Portrait* volume amount to what we might call a fairly long poem. The question of length is not absolute; it refers to a manner of sequacious continuity that most meditations require. If all these longer poems are in their different ways meditations, they grow naturally into their ample, loosened forms. One might ask, since Wordsworth wrote *The Prelude* (a book-length work), did his lyrics imply such amplification? Necessarily? One would have to say yes, to the extent that major lyrics, such as "Tintern Abbey" or the Lucy poems, call for an ever-developing mental landscape, in which the *mind* finds the ever-changing *chora* delineated in *The Prelude.* This could be aligned with the Stevensian long poem, where a lyric impulse is always yearning to discover its own cosmology. Wallace Stevens had a way of extending the lyric into meditation, as in briefer scope Andrew Marvell had amplified the lyric moment in "The Garden" or "Upon Appleton House."

Ashbery expresses similar poetic desires in *Flow Chart.*[3] This more than 200-page poem is not one I would care to summarize—suffice it to say that it drifts forward, in six sections, through the meandering course of the speaker's suffering, living, remembering, observing, commenting, and interpreting, touching, losing, hoping, even joking, through a segment of that dream we call life. From its opening lines, *Flow Chart* interrogates "the diagram"—the grand or merely pragmatic plan—which, as John Shoptaw says, turns out to be the poem itself. Like the Guggenheim Museum, the armature of the poem is an exoskeleton. It lives in its own *latering;* each moment of composition becomes an instant retrospect.

Adjusting Scale in the Longer Poem

We need a larger critical principle to appreciate what John Ashbery has achieved. This principle is central to all sciences, as it involves measurement, relativities, cosmology, the biological sciences of the differences between us, the ants, and dinosaurs; in fact, it is a fundamental of all applied mathematics in the fields of science and engineering—the *concept of scale.* Only by knowing scale can you map or chart any movement. Only by drawing to scale, or in relation to a given arbitrary scale, can you blueprint a structure. The trickier aspect of scale occurs when we speak of the scale of motions, of moving masses, as when a waterfall falls, a cloudbank rises, drifting sideways, or when some slower tectonic shift gradually *flows,* invisibly but no less actually. *Flow Chart* plays with all such motions, but, as *Self-Portrait* says, "not coarse, merely on another scale."

No doubt the most mysterious scalar questions involve time, which flows and does not flow—which, we could say, is always subject to Borges's "New Refutation of Time."[4] To make this latter paradoxical point—imagine the question: how would you establish the *scale* of a map of your own memories, as Augustine attempted in his *Confessions?*

Aesthetics also depends upon scale. It can be shown that six-inch pyramids, modeled by a child on a sandy beach, when photographed in a certain way, will appear to be the Great Pyramids in Egypt. The normal cue to scale has been removed from these tiny replicas. The monumental is thus only known as compared to its surround. The sublime, basic to modern and romantic allegory, is relatively the scalar inversion of the picturesque, that is, all the effects of sublime excess in the direction of monumentality are inverted by the picturesque, and what is large for the sublime becomes miniature for the picturesque. Crudely, the picturesque is simply the inversion of the sublime, when the scale of their elements is considered as a primary issue. Humans and human proportions are central to all aesthetics from the late Medieval period, because, as Erwin Panofsky showed, the human body is our most useful scalar point of comparison.[5] The fundamental flaw of skyscrapers is that they violate the modular unit provided by our bodies. Some architects, though not Corbusier author of *Modulor,* would say we must disregard the human frame. But art as humans may want it, make it, and treasure it will always seek a monumentality relevant to the human body. To argue otherwise is to argue for allegory and the sublime, to argue against the beautiful. The American Sublime, so important to Harold Bloom in his commanding grasp of our literature and our religious imagination, promotes the breakdown of eighteenth-century measure and balance, largely in the interests of interpretive Gnostic extension of meaning. In such fashion a desire to have what Blake called "sublime allegory" leads back to the Bible, upon which in so many ways our literature is founded.

A quite different aesthetic is always seeking to draw the artwork back to human scale. For this reason James Merrill ended his *Changing Light at Sandover* on a scalar note.[6] He and his friend David are talking about their method of Ouija board communications. The angel reassures them it works, given the "long amazing and unprecedented way from you to us." Then Merrill asks the angels about this distance, which he expresses as follows:

The old one I keep asking, about scale:
Microscopic particles on one hand,
And on the other, Majesties, your Grand
Design outspiralling past all detail—;

When we suppose that history's great worm
Turns and turns as it does because of twin
Forces balanced and alert within
Any least atom, are we getting warm?

The Archangel Gabriel answers Yes to this, and we are assured that a scalar balance persists in the universe at all levels of magnitude. Parity may fail in very special cases, but generally the size of things and beings counts for less than the scale at which they interact with their environment. We too are frightened, as was Pascal, at the infinite spaces of the universe, but we need to recognize these infinities within ourselves, as scalar equivalents of "the long amazing and unprecedented way."

Such cosmic concerns do not usually surface in quotidian realistic literature, though they are common in fantasy and science fiction. They appear necessarily, however, in a poem like Merrill's, which is modeled on Dante's *Divine Comedy,* and they similarly come up for Ashbery, whose attentiveness to his world tracks infinite detail in memory and perception, as *Flow Chart* meanders downstream like the ancient Trojan river. Ashbery's task will have been to locate and dramatize Merrill's "twin forces balanced and alert." For if there is no compensating spring or balance, the flow will go on forever, unchartable. Some device must guide or control the flux, the Heraclitean stream, but that device must not be a demonic diagram—a false discipline. In fact, the device of control, because we are imaging the long poem as a natural being—what the scientist calls a "complex adaptive system"—must arise from the chaotic flux itself. No imposed allegorical summary or *moral* will give the *Flow Chart* meditation its reduced, interpreted meaning. Rather, what gets the flow to an island of vision must come somehow out of a texture or weaving, the poem's uncharted discovery of the chart of its own flowing. For the moment, however, we commence our inquiry by looking for some method of emergent discovery: where is the "chart" to emerge from? In *Hidden Order,* John Holland places what will become our answer to this question in the sixth position, under the heading "Internal Models." In any strictly complex system, he observes, the problem is that the system must "eliminate details so that selected patterns are emphasized. Because the models of interest here are interior to the agent, the agent must select patterns in the torrent of input it received and then must convert those patterns into changes in its internal structure. Finally, the changes in structure, the model, must enable the agent to anticipate the consequences that follow when that pattern (or one like it) is again encountered." If one were to ask how such self-organizing patterns are paralleled in literature, the answer is not far to seek. Throughout his long and distinguished theoretical career, Northrop Frye showed that complex excesses of detail were always controlled through the strategic use of archetypal structures. These structures play a prominent role in the *Anatomy,* and no less clearly in Frye's two major books on the Bible, *The Great Code* and *Words with Power,* where the archetypal frequently appears in what we might call moments of prophetic concentration. These moments balance the scale on which any excessive accumulation of details occurs. Archetypal *strettos* give to Holland's "torrent of input" a place of repose, an eye of the hurricane, before the excess inevitably continues. The internal model takes many shapes, of course, depending on the story or poem in question. In what we are about to consider, the central stabilizing archetype is a function of number.

Sixes and Sestinas

The idea of number is inherently involved in the concept of scale, in that the series of natural numbers always suggests comparisons between sizes or quantities. With number, scale plays a part when we discuss proportioning and factoring. Let me give a basic example. Take the number six. It is the first so-called perfect number. Six is the number of sides to each cell in that perfect housing complex—the bee's honeycomb. Six is the number of points of *all* snowflakes—the "silent syllables" of snow, Longfellow called them. There is an infinite number of snowflakes, each different from every other, and yet *all* have six points. They embody the scalar perfection of six. This is a perfect number because both the sum and the product of its parts yield a six: $1 + 2 + 3 = 6$, or $1 \times 2 \times 3 = 6$. The second perfect number is 28: $1 + 2 + 4 + 7 + 14 = 28$, and the same holds for the factors as divisors. The learned scholar of Indo-Muslim antiquity, Annemarie Schimmel, reminds us not only of powerful religious symbolisms adhering to the lunar 28 (with its internal 7s), but oddly that all the cells of the skin are regenerated and replaced every 28 days![7]

Perfection of number is so elevated that six was for the Ancients the number of the created world. Six Days of Creation—the product of the first "male" number (2) and first "female" (3). To quote Schimmel: six "summarizes all of the plane figures of geometry (point, line, and triangle), and since the cube is composed of six squares, it is the ideal form for any closed construction." Hence that preference of bees for six; or perhaps the sixes in Kekulé's famous dream of the benzine ring C6H6—a parable known to all scientists. Hexagrams and six-pointed stars equally have a long history of mysterious meanings, most of which are well known to historians of numerology, although less well known than the alchemical pentangle, as in Sir Thomas Browne's *Garden of Cyrus,* or a modern case, Charles Palliser's *The Quincunx,* or the very high fives of John Hollander's double *pentina,* "Island Pond," which was dedicated to James Merrill.[8] Six controls the sestet of the sonnet form.

Suppose then we wanted six to be our model of perfection—or rather, suppose number itself could be our domain for searching out harmonious repose, the fullness of the creation. Then we would enhance the role of six even more than in the sonnet, by inventing the sestina. This poetic form, originating among the troubadours, practiced by Dante and Petrarch, has six stanzas, each of which has six lines. But instead of rhyming, the sestina classically takes the final word of each of the six lines from the opening stanza, and then uses one of the six final words to end a different line in every other subsequent stanza. The six final words thus keep changing their position as they pass from stanza to stanza. A further rule requires the last final word of each stanza to become the *first* final word in first line of the stanza following. Not only are these rules required—but when all six stanzas are complete the poet adds a seventh, *three*-line envoi, which includes all six final words within it.

Auden wrote a beautiful sestina, the seventh poem of *On This Island* (1937) which begins:[9]

> Hearing of harvests rotting in the valleys,
> Seeing at end of street the barren mountains,
> Round corners coming suddenly on water, . . .

where the next three lines end: islands, cities, sorrow. These six words rotate and alternate position as follows:

Stanza I:	valleys	(A)
	mountains	(B)
	water	(C)
	islands	(D)
	cities	(E)
	sorrow	(F)
Stanza II:	sorrow	(F)
	valleys	(A)
	cities	(E)
	mountains	(B)
	islands	(D)
	water	(C)
Stanza III:	water	(C)
	sorrow	(F)
	islands	(D)
	valleys	(A)
	mountains	(B)
	cities	(E)

and so on, to the end of the six main stanzas, until we reach the envoi:

> It is the sorrow; shall it melt? Ah, water
> Would gush, flush green these mountains and these valleys
> And we rebuild our cities, not dream of islands.

Auden's sestina recapitulates a famous model, the so-called double sestina of Sir Philip Sidney's "Old Arcadia," where the six final words are: *evening, mountains, morning, valleys, music, forests.* Because Sidney was doubling his sestina form, he has a total of twelve stanzas, with a correspondingly intensified three-line envoi, shared by the two shepherds who divide the twelve stanzas, six each. It takes no oracle to perceive the difficulty of writing such poetry, and the reward when successful. Famous sestinas include Pound's early "Sestina: Altaforte," nor is one surprised that Merrill, a master of such forms, used a double sestina to pivot his *Scripts for the Pageant,* the final volume of *Divine Comedies.*[10] The "Samos" section of the poem recalls *Mirabell: Books of Number* (Volume Two) giving an Auden colloquy, "The Last Word as Number." Such numerological art is, of course, not necessarily arcane. Elizabeth Bishop wrote a deliciously *realistic* sestina, "A Miracle for Breakfast," where the end-words were: *coffee, crumb, balcony, miracle, the sun, the river.* Another Bishop poem, "Sestina," uses *house, grandmother, child, stove, almanac, tears,* and the effect, equally domestic and naturalistic, is no less powerful, although the power of the recurrence is difficult to characterize. It clearly involves the ritual of following a rule, a rule-following that far exceeds the effects of rhyme in even the most complex stanzas, such as those invented by Spenser.

Before turning back to John Ashbery and *Flow Chart,* let us talk about how that ritual effect works. To some degree technical intricacy is, for the poet, its own reward. Only a true craftsman can begin to choose the end-words correctly and then manipulate them without the sestina strangling in its own cords. The sestina design has to work by constraining its degrees of freedom; a parable for this arrangement would be the use of the ropes that tied up Ilse Aichinger's "Bound Man."[11] In her short story Aichinger showed how the bound man was more free to move, the more closely bound he was, since the principle of freedom was made possible through a chosen self-limitation. The sestina form, unlike even the rhyme-schemes of classic English poetry, turns in upon itself in an unusual way, so that every part of the sestina conspires with every other part to spread out in all directions, inside the poem at large, to produce a containing and environing space.

The effect of repeating the six words is that they *rhyme without being individually reshaped,* as in the phonetics of standard rhyme. Each time an end-word is repeated it changes shape, not in itself, but in the immediate changing dramatic context of each succeeding stanza. One of the great principles of poetry, and perhaps even literature in general, is at work here: when Pound said "make it new," and when Sir Philip Sidney spoke of the zodiac of the poet's own wit, they were saying that poetry is the disposition of language into new formal arrays. *Free verse is the most complex and difficult of such dispositions*—a fact frighteningly unknown to most so-called successors to Whitman and the French. Rhymed verse has always been central to our language, as Milton knew, and as, before him, the Elizabethan poet Samuel Daniel wrote in his epochal treatise, "The Defence of Ryme" (1603).[12] Rhyme itself, of course, is not a defining essential of poetry; the ancient Greeks and Romans rarely, if ever, used it. Milton wrote *Paradise Lost* in blank verse (that is, his own special style) so that his technique would permit an "ancient liberty [to be] recovered to heroic poem from the troublesome and modern bondage of rhyming."

What goes unnoticed frequently is that rhyme, which seems to metamorphose language from within, depends entirely on the placement, indeed the collocation and juxtaposition of words, which in turn requires formal structures such as the lines of stanzaic forms. The rhyming words in traditional rhymed verse are different but sound the same, because generally they share a doubling of the vowel structure. With the sestina the method goes almost in the opposite direction. The poetic form takes a radical turn toward an even more basic metamorphosis. Now the *rhymed* words are always the *same* words. Their sameness however is perpetually transmogrified. As we hear or read the poem, the six end-words of each stanza *seem* to be rhyming, *seem* to be changing the shape of their sense and sound. The structured, diagrammed change in their stanzaic positions produces the uncanny effect that each repeated word is no longer what it was in a previous use. In short, with the sestina, the same words are all always different. They exist in a diagrammed formal model of linguistic infinity—which, of course, is the fact of language in general.

Ashbery's *Flow Chart* Sestina

Let us now return to Ashbery's poem and to our initial question: how was he to control the poem's meander? Could there be somehow an island in the stream? The answer was to be expected: Ashbery uses not only a double sestina, but derives it, as if in *homage,* from an exceedingly complex double sestina of Algernon Swinburne, "The Complaint of Lisa." Swinburne, one of the greatest formal virtuosi our language has known, was no stranger to complex poetic forms—here, for example, he allows some of his end-words to rhyme as well as repeat, through the course of his twelve twelve-line stanzas and the (doubled) six-line envoi. The most remarkable of his tricks is the way he builds his numbers around the word *sun,* and its double *sunflower.* Swinburne does something completely modern: he departs stealthily from Sir Philip Sidney's classic form, using slanted off-rhymes, as would many later poets in less demanding forms. This is the virtuoso design that Ashbery acknowledges following, taking his end-words from the Swinburne archetype. Ashbery's sestina comes at page 186 of *Flow*

Chart, close to the end of Part V of the whole poem. It makes a settled peace, before the concluding sixth section of *Flow Chart,* and gives to the whole poem its inner model of reconciliation.

In today's critical atmosphere of cultural studies there is little attention paid, or value accorded, to the technical demands of art. Thus most professional scholars, schooled in what Merrill called "Popthink," will hardly notice the broader significance of Ashbery's experiment with the sestina.[13] But here he seeks a place of perspective, so as to rise above the often despairing critique his *Flow Chart* makes of our society and its hopeless addiction to moneyed mediocrity. Shortly before the sestina begins, a parabasis, where the speaker comes forward and directly addresses his or her audience as "you," occurs much as it would in a comedy by Aristophanes. Ashbery's speaker steps forward from the stage to announce that something wonderful is going to happen in the poem, to delight its readers. This wonder is so confident of its power that the poet can humorously, yet gravely state: "You will be amazed at how touched you will be because of it . . ." and, as things turn out, the claim is justified—as if Pegasus turned to the crowd, calling out: Watch me run this race!

The sestina is technically a marvel. Mostly, it praises the sunflower, the heliotrope of Derrida's "white mythology," where metaphor turns to the sun (as Stevens said it would), affirming "the idea of the poem," its redeemed diagram. Chart and charting a course have, one suspects, always been important to the poet who could write (refining upon Stevens' "A Clear Day and No Memories"[14]): "And then some morning there is a nuance." The line is from the relatively early "Sunrise in Suburbia," as also this description of imaging an amble or just a recognition of a vista:[15]

> A light wilderness of spoken words not
> Unkind for all their aimlessness,
> A blank chart of each day moving into the premise of
> difficult visibility

And which is nowhere, the urge to nowhere,
To retract that statement, sharply, within the next few
    minutes.

The chart is mostly blank when we are merely doing nothing much, when our metaphysic is suburban at heart—maybe in the laurel-fringed grounds of an old Connecticut house now next to another, the same, whose *nature* has been reduced by development. What is left of the older natural scene is "nuance." That being the case, what will be our journey? The chart will be the guide to measuring a progress, mostly inner in its walk and vista. In the context of this poetic guidance the sestina of *Flow Chart* serves at once both to fill and to empty the scene, by transforming memory from linear to circular apprehension. The flow is finally to revolve or, as Whitman would say, to eddy. As noted, Harold Bloom, strong champion of Ashbery's work, found on first reading "The New System" that "it was difficult to see how Ashbery got from point to point, or even to determine if there were points," but the critic eventually discerned "a beautiful and simple design" to the poem.[16] This was based on a pattern Bloom finds throughout Ashbery: (a) "self-acceptance of the minimal anomalies we have become;" and (b) "the wintry reduction of that conferred self," both fine observations. Yet one asks, is the poet awash in a personal pursuit of his own identity, as if an Ashbery got up every morning, read his Emerson, and proceeded to write an endless allegory of the self. That may be an American obsession, as pertaining to a people in exile; but it does not seem to me to address the artist in Ashbery. Questions of identity merely thematize a self, as they thematize Whitman's "Real Me." Instead, Ashbery is concerned with the "real There," and Gertrude Stein would have applauded this choice.

Flow Chart expresses or projects or ruminates the *world* of an identity, nevertheless. Ashbery's "There" is a world divided by diurnal cycles of time, as much as complex and turbulent sequences of temporal flux. Such a world lends itself to the ancient six-fold theory of proportions. The sestina form has the power to intervene in the flux of sequence. It therefore has a sort of gyroscopic power to balance larger forms. Sir Philip Sidney, for example, has used his double sestina to settle the narrative flux of the *Old Arcadia.* He placed the sestina towards the end, as Ashbery does, to anchor the final set of *Eclogues,* which give lyric perspective to the dreamy narrative of the *Arcadia* proper. As with musical compositions, placement is everything, justifying Sidney's word "architectonic." Ashbery uses his double sestina, in fact, *to get away from questions of identity.* The sestina objectifies the surrounding flow, supplying a mysterious chart for the journey. The rotational form of the sestina is of a piece with "the bacchanalian whirl," which Hegel described as the ideal form of vision and belonging *(Preface to the Phenomenology).* Why turn to a poem of absolute, *perfect* rotation, if not to seek a sort of rescue from flux, which, unbalanced, unchecked, uncharted, would be a chaotic ocean-road to death? One of the many learned poetic allusions in *Flow Chart* comes early: to William Cowper's "The Castaway," a poem to the memory of a sailor fallen overboard from the deck of Lord Anson's flagship—a human utterly lost, "wash'd headlong from on board."[17] Cowper's great poem builds toward a recognition that he, the poet, in his mental distress and illness, has also utterly lost balance:

> No voice divine the storm allay'd,
>   No light propitious shone;
> When, snatch'd from all effectual aid,
>   We perish'd each alone;
> But I beneath a rougher sea,
> And whelm'd in deeper gulphs than he.

To rescue the narrator and his narrative is then the purpose of the inleaved lyric. Ashbery takes his twelve end-words *(breath, her, way, death, sunflower, sun, day, bed, thee, dead, done, me)* directly and unchanged from his model, Swinburne's "Complaint of Lisa," which in turn was suggested by Boccaccio's tale in Book Ten, Chapter Seven of the *Decameron.*[18] The "Complaint" weaves round and round a lament for lost unattainable love, honor, and peace, and is finally like nothing so much as Richard Strauss' late contrapuntal composition, the *Metamorphosen,* based on the *liebestod* motif. Both works share a kind of lugubrious excess of internal reference.

The Swinburne sestina uses an oddly ancient Greek metric tone, almost as if it were quantitative verse, achieving the highest virtuosic level—and Ashbery matches this mastery of the complex form, line by line. Like Swinburne, since he follows the end-words of the *Complaint* exactly, Ashbery is able to build four internal rhymes into each stanza: *breath/death; way/day; sun/done; bed/dead.* Twelve divided by four yields the ultimate ternary, as befits a poet deeply familiar with the works of Spenser and Marvell. When Paul Valéry remarked that "the poetic state or emotion seems to me to consist in a dawning perception, a tendency toward perceiving a *world,* or complete system of relations," he was led to say also that with highly wrought poetic forms objects and beings were altered from their normal state, becoming "*musicalized,* somehow commensurable, echoing each other."[19]

Valéry identified this music as a kind of dream in which, in Ashbery's case, the six-fold character of the double sestina allows us to see, finally, that the whole six-part meditation of *Flow Chart* is, in fact, one immense sestina. As with all environment-poems, the relationship between the sestina and the whole poem exemplifies the utterly crucial role of scale in the artistic process. To paraphrase William Empson's celebrated commentary on Sidney's double sestina—the words "are the bones of the situation"—the words in Ashbery circumscribe a world. As Empson observed, the varying repetitions of end-words permit the poet to "extract all the meaning possible" from the materials of the poem. From these considerations emerges a notion of the poet as philosopher, the poet as world-definer, whose forms control the flowing picture of conscious life, yet without seeking to crush variety. No wonder then, to quote Byron a second time: "all convulsions end with me in rhyme; and, to solace my midnights, I have scribbled another Turkish story."

Equally important, though less formal, is the weight given to the terms of diurnal return, of rest, of light, of repose, of heliotropic energy, and finally of death, whose opposite is breath. Throughout the sestina, Ashbery calls for a larger perspective, rejecting or questioning what he names the *culte du moi,* the "me" of the final line. The mysterious beloved of Swinburne's "Complaint" becomes the interior paramour for Ashbery's poem, and *love* here is entwined with poetic inspiration. Finally, one's beloved and one's muse are one, helping each other to be different, and yet ministrant, until we see that poetry provides the true horizon for our inner joy or shipwreck.

An exemplary work of art, Ashbery's sestina is perfectly tuned to reveal the point of the entire description of flow that the poem as a whole provides. The sestina anchors or gives shape to an otherwise exceedingly elusive poem, whose six-fold structure might otherwise stand unrevealed. And we can go even further, to say that such compositions show us that if art is not concerned with things like the perfect number six, with rhythm, rhyme, and form-making powers, it will become an empty vessel of clichés, of the hopelessly prosaic and banal, those very banalities and stupefied appetites that undermine democratic ideals. As experience and theme, Ashbery's double sestina gives the reader an idea of democratic excellence, since the chivalric and elite poetic form of the sestina, so like a great athletic tournament, is embedded in the open, diagnostic, democratic excursion of the rest of *Flow Chart.* The sestina formally transforms the surrounding poem into a celebration of a human life—the private becomes public, entering the larger sphere.

13

Coherence

We live at the end of the long twilight of Romanticism, and this book has presented a theory of the poetry to come. In a strict sense this future is unpredictable, and yet clearly the fundamental conditions of literature will support the invention of new modes, one of which is the environment-poem. The great nineteenth-century Romantics mingled a fascination with natural scenes with a more powerful interest, namely, the "growth of the poet's mind" (as Wordsworth put it), or more generally, imaginative consciousness. This latter topic was the subject of Harold Bloom's 1970 anthology of criticism, *Romanticism and Consciousness.* It is the subject of Geoffrey Hartman's well-known book, *Wordsworth's Poetry: 1787–1814.* While consciousness is never entirely absent from art, the major new condition of our world is so powerful that it perforce changes the role of individual consciousness and clouds the outlines of group consciousness. As we shall see, a new field of force characterizes a world radically different from that of authors coming out of tradition. If Clare's immersion in the Northamptonshire countryside was conditioned by enclosure, that is, by his exclusion from ancient common lands, if Wordsworth retired to the Lake Country in large part because London was for him an impossible place to live, if urban/suburban life mirrors yet another ecosystem for Ashbery, then for all poets to come an environment is emerging whose qualities count for much less than their quantified aspect, "the numbers."

The poets I have dealt with experiment with the borders of an essentially new situation, clearly foreseeing its coming, but holding still with older vistas. The imaginative field they have seen coming calls for its complementary imaginative system, for the literature of numbers needs some principle of order no less than any older literature. This principle will allow the numbers to cohere, by relating the individual, the idiosyncratic, to their complexity of emerging patterns. My chief concern, recalling Coleridge and the *Biographia Literaria,* is that *coherence differs from consistent mechanical conformity,* for with certain basic mathematical orders, following the distinction drawn by Kurt Gödel's famous paper, coherence shares the property of *completeness,* as distinct from *axiomatic consistency.*[1] The new poetry seeks expressions of various kinds of complete orders, as in an ecosystem, quite the opposite of an ideological fiction, which would derive poetic elements from fundamental axioms, obeying laws of consistent logical derivation. That puts the matter in its most extreme form, but there is agreement that for the Coleridgean Romantic, literary forms resembled machines whenever their symbolic mode was mainly allegorical, with ideas corresponding to images on a one for one basis, like a simple lever in a machine matching a simple rotor in the same machine. The machine of allegory is simply too consistent in its movements from axiomatic idea to fanciful image. We might be comfortable enough with such analogies, but the trouble is that literature deals customarily with representations of different kinds of world, and worlds in turn are usually thought to be more real than the fictions, fantasms, images, and stories representing them. From symbol to reality, from fiction to fact, from the poem to the world, the bridges appear to be uncertain as soon as we ask pragmatic or epistemological questions about why we want such artificial doublings in the first place.

If we identify coherence with a loose and notably inconsistent completeness, we reach the artistic representing of environments, a representing pressed so far that the poem actually *is* an environment. This view would assert that there are two external real worlds, the one we daily walk around in (or drive cars through), and the one the environment-poet has invented. Both would have equal shares of the real—equal shares of Being. This view blurs the sharp distinction between fictions of fact and fact itself, but the point is that such poems are not *about* the environment. In some sense they share the same character, the same intrusion, the same coextension in our lives as has the environment. Supposing then that such poems are intended to surround us in exactly the way an actual environment surrounds us, there will occur a breakdown of the old distinction—a classical distinction throughout critical history, no matter how complex its profile at different historical periods—between the world within the poem and the world "out there," outside the poem. The environment-poem seeks symbolic control over the drifting experience of being environed, and it introduces the experience of an outside that is developed for the reader inside the experience of the work. While this outside/inside game closely resembles a stream of consciousness technique intended to reveal elusive states of mind,[2] the environment-poem converts natural surroundings and their common surrogates, like the furnishing of a house, for example, into a surrounding that actually has more presence than any state of mind. It is as if the dream had become real. My sense of the literary history here is that only with proleptic visions like Clare's or distinctly "scientific" visions like those of Whitman and Ashbery will the actual world around us come to have a metaphysical value, but the price of seeing this will be to blur the classic distinction between idea and thing. Oddly, then, the consequence of an interest in science will be a metaphysical blurring and uncanny fragmentation of the unexamined manifold of "things we all know to be the case." Of course, this is like saying that life itself is a mystery, but we are not taken aback if we say such things, as our more meditative moods lead us quietly to wonder why there is something rather than nothing—an ancient question.

For modern literature the logic and history of image/fact relationships has been carefully analyzed in an encyclopedic study by Harry Berger, Jr., where the author shows in particular how Renaissance Neoplatonic thought counterposed its complex idealism against the poet's hypothetical fictions of second worlds (for example, a pastoral world as in Spenser).[3] Berger clarifies the fluctuations of mind that pertain whenever the so-called real world meets its representation (we would say its "reproduction") in a secondary world, and also the fluctuations occurring between this interactive encounter and the communication between the poet and the audience, between reader and author, or even between listening and speaking. Romantic poetry probed further cognitive obscurities occurring when art negotiates between the real and the fictive, and eventually in our time it has been suggested that nature is an immense informational network,[4] such as only the environment-poem could represent by introducing the individual to an awareness of number and numbers (as distinct from numerals). But now, once more, we return to consider the ancient question: what dynamic process confers unity on the work of art? Perhaps unity here means some kind of symbolic vitality, and the dynamic principle we seek is only a normal, natural function of language, when ordered in a poem.

A Very Short History

Poetry and environments have an old affinity, since both are examples of an economy of means. In the modern world transformations of land values are perhaps our most prominent manner of divorce from tradition, from traditional ideas of the purposes of natural order. We are not surprised that although we may be born into such a natural order of life, our quite proper empirical bias always questions any unexamined idea of teleologically driven nature. What is an end, what a beginning, we ask, and these questions appear in literature as much as anywhere else.

Not only since the Renaissance, but from earlier times when Aristotle's *Poetics* laid down the principle of poetic probability, whereby poems had beginnings, middles, and ends linked each to each by chains of probable causes, it came to be a given of Western literature that poems were characterized by a wish to achieve coherence of action. But there is as much uncertainty in literary modes of coherence as there is in modern physics at its most speculative. Especially in the romance forms of literature, the probability principle bends to allow digression, excursion, ornamental and *oriental* amplification, allegorical magic, and a host of persuasive improbabilities, but coherence of action remained foundational for Western poetics right on through into the nineteenth century, when certain poets, following examples usually drawn from prose fiction, found they might question probable causation.[5] Precursor novelists like Cervantes and then Lawrence Sterne anticipated such trends, bringing causality as such under full-scale scrutiny, while in the present era a fiction writer like William Burroughs quite undermines our norms of causality in narrative. In poetry the genre of prose poem extends this liberating perspective, by suggesting that as the metric conventions are relaxed, the degree of prosaic causality increases—but that is not always a clear consequence of the hybrid. Stéphane Mallarmé's "Un coup de dés n'abolira jamais le hazard" used what he called "the simultaneous vision of the Page" to invent modernity for the poems of our time. Analyzing chance and probability, Mallarmé's poem is displayed on its page as a prophetic hypertext.

As soon as the poet discovers or, as it may happen, *rediscovers* new forms, it follows that new methods and modes of causality spring up. One such modality in poetry is what I have been calling "descriptive." Once again, to draw a distinction I have insisted upon, as description forces its grounding shapes and frequent shapelessness upon the poem, especially upon the visionary poem, the poet seeks not so much causal consistency and consequence, as a more widespread sense of coherence among all parts of the poem. "Nature will be reported," says Emerson, and the job of enthused description is to show how "all things are engaged in writing their own history."[6] Modern coherence is an effect of synchronous Mallarméan unity, which possesses its own order revealed over minimal time, as if duration were compressed into an epiphany of complex emergent properties. Such coherence as a source of unity is obviously much looser than any neoclassical rule or Aristotelian norm, and for this reason often seems to us more *real;* the virtually instantaneous has for us the appearance of reality.

The idea of coherence also applies to poetry by opposing any strict conformity to an unchanging fundamentalist rule—"read your Bible," as the bigot said. Whitman certainly thinks it applies to democracy, and when it becomes the main power of the poem, it leads to the strange idea that the poem might be, not a causally determined dramatic plot or *praxis,* but a casually discovered, virtually random or chaotic environment, a double of nature herself in her "untrammel'd play." Ashbery has spoken of his own "doubling impulse," which reveals not only a poem/environment equivalence but reveals this mode as uncanny, which we expect with doublings.

Ecology belongs to a real and exactly experienced surrounding scene, which today might include outer space. An awareness of the degree to which we have sought to control and insulate ourselves from unimproved nature incites our environment-poets to question all unexamined versions of causality. Diurnal knowledge involves complex visions of the moment. These visions in turn lead to a balancing between pleas either to control or to decontrol human uses of natural resources. Dispute and outrage have met studies like Bjørn Lomborg's recent statistical account whose message is mainly that the "litany" of environmental jeremiads has inadequate proof, finally lacks substance, that in fact things are mostly getting better.[7] It does not take much frog watching or turtle searching, or much first- or second-hand knowledge of surrealistically massive clear-cutting by timber companies, and so on, to see that in the context of the numbers Lomborg is somehow mistaken, despite his enormous statistical array—and yet, his desire to balance the balance seems necessary and critically important. Although there is always a danger that we overestimate or misjudge the effects of human predation and human population growth, we would surely all wish to be skeptical environmentalists. Our long-range survival demands critical thinking and a poetry aware of threats to natural balances.

Hesiod: Dynamics in the Environment and Its Poem

Just how resources are to be allocated for human survival is the virtually epic subject of one of our oldest Western masterpieces, the *Works and Days* of Hesiod (ca. 750 B.C.E). A builder friend said to me, "You don't buy a house; you buy land." Hesiod would say the same. His poem is central to an understanding we can now undertake, that is, to determine at least approximately how we are to find a dynamic principle animating the environment-poem. Where land seems to have always had an inherent link with habitation, the mere ownership of land, its mere financial exploitation, seems to obstruct any understanding of the absolute necessity for humans of acquiring some measure of environmental wisdom. Habitation is not exploitation, and yet the two are vulnerable to grave imbalances at the heart of their existence as sources of reasonably benign societies. It is in this latter sense that Hesiod's poem is almost a classic reminder that we humans need the skill to navigate our conflicts over possession.

The important poems all have a certain kind and level of energy, and we may speak generically of their dynamic, their dynamic principles. If natural environments display complex interactions of their participants or particles operating at different levels of energy, so too with their double, the environment-poem. This form, we have seen, rarely or perhaps never presents an Aristotelian plot or *praxis,* with its strong sequential causality, but instead has an encircling, almost spatial character, like that of a good map, which arises from a different mode of action—the discovery of the surround. If often, as with an Ashbery poem, nothing seems to happen, then where, we ask, is the desire or motivation of the work? It seems to hide itself from obvious notice.

Two levels of answer to our question will clarify the place of desire in this poetry. In the first place, as we have continuously stressed, the environment-poem is always developing information, if not in the mode of the newsworthy. It is always looking at the world with uncommon precision of image and perceptual exactitude, as, to give another contemporary case, Helen Vendler has so often found to be true in the poetry of Seamus Heaney; this pursuit of what one might call "natural precision" is issuing from a particular dynamic, the desire to know through attending to the phenomena.[8] If humans desire to know, it is because we are entranced by the wonder of things appearing to us, ambiguously at first, and then, through knowing, with some degree of precision. We desire this exactitude, on one level of our being, with one aspect of our libido. There is hence one modality of desire in the environment-poem, as a vessel of knowing.

But, equally important for the present dynamic requirement, there is the environmental scene itself, along with the form encoding it. This second dynamic level is all important in our appreciation, and it is not surprising that it makes its first great appearance in the oldest of all Western environment-poems, the *Works and Days.* We suppose Hesiod to have flourished in the middle of the eighth century B.C.E. While in the context of English literature it is customary to speak of a profound *Georgic* influence, after Virgil's poems of that title, we should start by retreating in time to Virgil's Greek model, Hesiod. His descriptive poem, drawing on early techniques of formulaic oral poetry, brings Hesiod's other great poem, the *Theogony,* down to earth, with a woven rendering of the life of the land—its values, its cultivation, its economic uses, including sustenance and trade and the disputes inevitably surrounding transactions involved, and so on, through the rendering of a complex ancient environmental vista. Aside from a theme of conflict between the speaker and his brother, there might appear to be nothing happening in the poem, since its main aim is clearly to present a way of life in ancient Boiotia. Labor seems an insufficient drama. Classically and in our common experience, conflict is the clearest sign that energy is seeking expression, whether in physics or in society. Hence labor must be related to the idea of Justice.

This precisely is the question the Hesiod confronts at once and pursues throughout. The poem begins by announcing that there is bound always to be Strife *(eris)* in the world; in the theogony of the Greeks Eris is a goddess of great power. She and her energy stir up trouble, all the way from family quarrels to widespread warfare. Such disorder and conflict will interfere, the poet says, with all the forms of natural fertility and benefit. Now, let us suppose that archetypally this negative force were the only driving energy in the poem; in that case we would be talking about a poetry where one *daimon* of discord would run the show like a dictator, and the poet's efforts (for Hesiod is the chief learner and information purveyor in the poem) would be trapped forever in a circle of natural breakdown. In breakdown, the poem would lose its free energy and would enter a condition of arrested liminality. It would remain on the threshold of imminent freedom, but never achieving an advance into the open.

Yet this is exactly what Hesiod denies, and in his denial provides a genuine dynamic for the environment-poem. He introduces a second avatar of *eris,* which Eric Havelock names the "good strife" and Hesiod's recent translators call "competition."[9] By vigorously opposing the forces of disorder, by opposing the other strife, this second competitive drive works against chaos in nature. The dynamic then creates an agonistic balancing act, so that between the good and the bad strife there is a vital reaching toward the useful distribution of energies within the larger natural and social environment. Hesiod establishes the dynamic for the poetic form, which only becomes more complex with Virgil's *Georgics,* where the issue is no longer the competition, good and bad, between the local farmer and the *basileus*—the strong-arming baron—but now extends to cover the field of a whole people. Virgil, it is well known, writes in the period of partial Octavian recovery from universal civil war. "The *Georgics* is the great poem of united Italy," as L. P. Wilkinson observes, and once again a governing idea of the proper use of the land and a true valuation of environmental wealth leads to a shift from the dominant strife of war to the better strife of peace.[10] Hence the four poems of the *Georgics* end with the elaborate description and praise of the harmonious kingdom of the builder bees. Readers have long wondered why Virgil closed this almost utopian vision with a serious mythological return to the tragic story of Orpheus. For an answer again we turn to Wilkinson, who summarizes the role of the poet in precisely the way we are led by environment-poets to consider. Orpheus "stands for the life of the individual, associated with the bitter-sweet pains and pleasures of love. One side of Virgil's nature could not be satisfied with the impersonal side of the state"—and, we might add, nor could it be satisfed with the impersonality of natural environments when conceived solely as ecological aggregates. There has to be the human integer in this equation, otherwise there will be no animation of the image of life, nor therefore any humanity balancing the impersonal Darwinian struggle to survive. Book Three of the *Georgics* had represented the pains and death of living creatures, but the Orphic presence and the promise of a larger life-force has the final say, here and in its Hesiodic precursor, and equally in the poems I have been chronicling. In this context, once again, Ashbery provides the larger example. He has more than once said to his interlocutors, "My poems are about love." All the tension in his poetry refers to the balancing effects of warring emotions and conflicting perceptions of the complexity of the world we live in.

Without a sense of the double strife, we will surely think such a remark sentimental. But within the Hesiodic frame of reference we discover that the ancient model anticipates the most modern of ecological concerns and prefigures ideas of environmental survival, although without Darwinian science to back up the vision. The dynamic of the double strife remains, however, entirely Darwinian in its import, and we sense its relevance to the present pass in human history. The double strife is of main concern for today's global environmentalist research, but more important in the present context, it remains the source of symbolic energy in the poems we have been discussing. Beyond science and poetry, furthermore, there is the intensely pressing socio-political need to inform ourselves as to the difference between the claims of the good and those of the bad strife, by developing an awareness that the one may masquerade as the other, the bad hoping to gain the benefits of the good.

The Sense of Space

As regards the ultimately Hesiodic vision of land and its use, Edward Soja and other postmodern geographers have argued at length and in detail that as economic beings we inhabit a postmodern geography, which needs to be fundamentally understood as requiring a new spatial ontology.[11] There is no turning back to an indefinitely extended agrarian or more primitive economy, where populations are broadly spread across open land masses, while in our review of the descriptive natural history underlying visionary Romanticism we have seen that space expands and contracts according to the uses to which land is put, by which it is known to poets like Clare and Whitman. The dynamic forces of production and trade actually change the notion of the "extent" of land, for factories concentrate land-use, and cities concentrate and compress their urban populations. Many issues enter upon a new phase in history—how humans occupy space, how they use its natural and artificially enhanced resources, how they come to believe they own it, or it owns them, among several dimensions important to literature. Our own American literature shares in such changes, although we desperately need a renewal of respect for our great poet's *Democratic Vistas,* as in Hesiodic fashion it attacks the uncontrolled social acceptance of voracious greed. Although tears fall when we sing "from sea to shining sea," the phrase suffers from expansion and greed, yet we can give it back to the diurnal moment of more ordinary lives lived in place. If all the initial opportunities were greater in the new land, they were paid for in the blood of others, whether black slaves or Native Americans, and all our finest authors have tried to deal with this fact, if only in the oblique way that Melville's whaling ship, the *Pequod,* refers to the slaughter of the Pequod Indians. But, I would argue, by admitting predatory human motives—attending, as it were, to Aesop's *Fables* and to our own related literature—we will get closer to a coherent sense of living space, a world willing to search for natural principles of coherence. These principles would not be without transcendent values, for we can ask, with Bloom, "In what form the twenty-first century will behold the return of the gods."[12] We then must ask, where and in what difficult terrain, must we search for the good strife, thriving in a field of natural fact, developed with a sense of a world beyond any particular national or other borders. If I then seem often to depart from the intense atmosphere of the art of poetry, reaching for its crudest ground in the soil of the earth, this has been in the interest of indicating how ideas of extension over the space of the earth are most powerfully and energetically affected by certain basic changes in the surrounding environment of art, and I have found certain poetic forms inhabiting that environment.

In the most general sense, the function of space for literature is to provide a limited cosmology, in that the literary and artistic cosmos is a constellation of images and actions we usually call "allegory." We then reach what may seem an unusual conclusion, namely, that the environment-poem is the opposite of or requires opposition to allegory. This genre recognizes what might be called the endemic error of allegory, that "a field of possibilities open into infinity has been mistaken for a closed realm of things existing in themselves."[13] Instead, the environment-poem imagines or discovers a manifold in nature that has no perfect isolationist wall around it, and further lacks any superimposed hierarchic system of images and actions permitted only "from above." This mode also undercuts ritual, dispensing with consciously inscribed or prescribed authority or statute, favoring rather interaction between participants living on this side of some horizon. Its reason for being is merely life itself, needing no higher justifications. This environment-poetic thus resists the common human tendency to allegorize existence, an allegory reducing our strange lives to mainly moral axioms that cannot, without radical inconsistency, lead to any adequate story of the way we get through life. We have seen the environment poets discovering a limited but true knowledge by means of making the rounds in search of the perpetually vanishing traces of our having passed this way. In a scientific sense this poetry is always self-organizing and nonlinear (admitting that these mathematical ideas are here metaphors only), and it awaits the emergence of order amidst a calculated disorder of Wallace Stevens's "mere being." It is owing to this view of the poetic that I find myself needing to agree with Marianne Moore, who wrote Dr. Williams on July 7, 1957, that "[the rhythm is the person] . . . I am, always have been fantastically interested in rhythm," a conviction she particularly experienced in the work of translating La Fontaine's *Fables.*[14] This approach to poetry and literature in general is not any more abstract than is music, and it allows us to get beyond the vice of slavish thematics; it allows us positively to find patterns arising from the complex, seemingly undirected array of elements in the poem, as the poet found these when tracing her walk to the horizon. The environment-poem requires us, in both writing and reading, to practice a casual, unauthorized, but always intensely focused noticing. It must engage in this reception of variety because that is the normal structuring of the environing surround, and today an oppressive sense that new environings are upon us, that the variety is under threat, makes the poetry all the more important for us to value and understand.

The Numbers Game

Ecology shows us that, extending around us, environments are as plural as we find individual humans to be. Despite all this many-sided variety, one incontrovertible shared condition pertains: all poets and artists living and working since the late eighteenth century in the West submit to the increasing authority of a dimension, a condition, an environment we may simply call numerosity, or just "the numbers." To an extreme degree the numbers themselves are the essence of the coming environmental reality.

In 1798 Thomas Malthus published his prophetic text, *Essay on the Principle of Population,* and since about that time populations have exponentially increased in number, especially in recent decades. The ecological fact of our current double geometric rate of increase is scary enough, for those who think beyond suburban backyards and lawns. But a critic of literature might pass over the fact, were it not that poetry is an art practiced on a high level by only a tiny number of individuals; at the top of the heap these are called persons of genius, for good reason. Malthus was thinking about a ratio of food supplies to numbers of people to feed, but the larger significance is that large numbers become the new main issue, as any economist will tell us. For poets these systemic changes are of paramount significance. Take an example Frederick Pottle discussed during the late days of New Critical upheavals.[15] In Book VIII of *The Prelude* Wordsworth announces his intention to show "love of nature leading to love of man," but he finds that he cannot present a vision of social complexities. "Though he had the best of intentions, he could never handle close-packed, present, human crowds in the mode of imagination." Among poets Shelley had a sure grasp of the collective representation. In fiction Defoe could manage it, or Poe, or others as we shall see, but with Wordsworth the inability actually produced a singular strength. Pottle's shrewd comment reveals a gap between the natural numerosity of social groups and the poet's virtually private ecstatic consciousness, for which (for whom?) numbers are memorably reduced to a "host of golden daffodils."

A poetry written within the new environment of human propagation had to discover new integers, exactly the Whitman quest. One might leap to a reasonable compromise, however. What about the novel? Surely its prose narrative and its discursive breadth permit the novel to succeed where even traditional epic poetry could hardly be expected to keep up with standardizing industrial technology and all its consequences. The novel—think once more of *Moby-Dick,* with its tendency toward the literary "anatomy"—can hold and display masses of information.[16] Yet numbers as such clearly trouble Henry James, one of the greatest masters of consciousness, though at the same time a harshly realistic social commentator. Granted that James saw more clearly than most writers that for most people, high and low, the reification of numbers constantly occurs in the field of money and monetary transactions and expectations. Money makes the numbers real, as they say in Las Vegas. Balancing or cooking the books leads to a new definition of the Book, as a learned critic has observed. So numerous indeed were books themselves becoming in Henry James's day that when he wrote his 1899 essay on "The Future of the Novel," he began by commenting on the flood of publications which was "threatening the whole field of letters, as would often seem, with immersion."[17] Like other fiction writers of his time, when Henry James specified the central role of numbers, he perceived that Honoré de Balzac was "an insatiable reporter of the immediate, the material, the current combination." If James appears at times obsessed by the equation between numbers and money, as critic he can still ask how the "poet" in the novelist's soul could manage the Balzacian effect, since there is so much fire and poetry in the *Comédie Humaine.* "One asks one's self as one reads him what concern the poet has with so much arithmetic and so much criticism, so many statistics and documents, what concern the critic and the economist have with so many passions, characters and adventures. The contradiction is always before us; it springs from the inordinate scale of the author's two faces; it explains more than anything else his eccentricities and difficulties."[18] The novelist as Mt. Rushmore!

In a poetic genre he seems almost to have invented by refining upon Robert Browning, the interview-poem, Richard Howard has written "Avarice, 1849: a Distraction."[19] Balzac is to be photographed by the great Nadar, and they are discussing avarice, possession, owning, desire—those potential infinities leading to "exaggerations of our mutual weakness." What then is the true proportion between a striving for peace and a striving to outdo the other fellow? Between quiet and stillness ("My dear Balzac, you must remain quite still") and the restless desire to gain or express always more? But if this question of adjusting character and scale assails Balzac and yet he triumphs, then the case of Emile Zola was for James more troubling and somehow more subtle, since he reckoned that Zola's heroic effort was slowly confining him to the *cage* of his own writing, with no exit. Zola reveals to us on the highest level the problem of the numbers. In his 1903 article James builds the argument that with Zola's vast series of "scientific" novels, all based on accumulated documentation, "it was the fortune, it was in a manner the doom . . . to deal with things almost always in gregarious form, to be a picture of *numbers,* of classes, crowds, confusions, movements, industries."[20] James could illustrate this reading most graphically perhaps in his remarks on

Au bonheur des dames, a colossal department-store novel, but the point applied to Zola across the board. The scientific novel meeting the new demographics had to present a "population," as James calls it, a "labyrinth of mutual relations," while all these webs and networks were man-made environments—the *grand magasin* was an ecosystem for sustaining happiness as *la mode.* Another more ordinary case: with the decline of arcades and of the department store (and their replacement by automotive "shopping malls"), the size of certain *omnium gatherum* fictions and non-fictions seems to have increased, as if to compensate for a disappearing semiotic. (Niche-marketing is a counter-measure against numerosities, as shoppers testify.) Whatever the documented scene, it has derived from the one term James had italicized, *numbers.*

Writing their parallel but much less prose-driven works, the poets after Malthus are all authors working in a new world where the truth is always a song of occupations (as in America we often start conversations with strangers by asking "what do you do?"). Walking through the Louvre with Emerson, Henry James was forcibly struck that his great compatriot, "sparsely constructed as he was," had seemed "so little spoken to by works of art," perceiving each splendor only "in the most general terms."[21] Maybe that proved that Emerson was a philosopher, which James was reluctant to believe. Or perhaps the example had more general force, since Emerson was so powerfully the American, completely involved and distracted by the vast and empty scene of American size. In this quest American poetry was a leader, after Whitman. He called coherence "cohesion" and "adhesion"; environmentalists call it "balance," and all these terms imply ethical responsibility toward the use of natural resources.

In the literary context of balancing large numbers and powerful environmental masses, my chief concern is to distinguish coherence from mechanistic conformity. For poetry and Romantic theory, of course, *organicism* marks a watershed, and eventually the idea of organic form participates in the new formal and scientific study of ecology. The Romantics had rediscovered an ancient truth, much like Lovelock's Gaia Hypothesis:[22] Nature was the vital domain whose "life" was everywhere sensed by lively organs like the human eye or ear, and whose range allowed the widest variety of different physical shapes, sizes, and values to be interactively combined—hence *organically* related to each other, providing a model for the extremely various "confusions" marking the greater Romantic lyric. James's term "confusions" seems at first extreme, and yet it is to be opposed to the controlled articulations of a more classical style, which in learned circles had long held sway as an ideal of Western poetics. Further, the poetics of large numbers leads away from the internalization of the quest-romance, the great intrapsychic drama Harold Bloom has so powerfully illuminated. There is nothing trivial or misleading about this sublime sense of our literary lives. But there is a problem for accounting of the floating temporality in literature, which Americans (North, Central, and South) have experienced as time removed from history. Not incorrectly some have seen this view as time subjected to spatial dominance. If we say that North Americans in particular have perhaps unwittingly moved beyond Romantic vision toward a poetry more democratic and empirical, we are pointing to what the first British settlers had found on stepping or staggering or clambering ashore: a scene of unparalleled newness, whose only signpost pointed to the unknown future. For them and for their immigrant descendants from many countries history was *owned* by someone else, so that in their desire to build an actual future, they at once were forced to leave behind faith in the intricacies of older faiths, including the Christianized versions of nature's laws.

The Americans, we might say, were born into a Darwinian world, no matter how hard ancient creeds fought and have continued to fight against it. Despite post-colonial ideological opposition, American literature always held a different episteme of the main causal relations of highest import. We were forced into a developed empiricism in attitude, if not always in public games of intellectual allegiance. *Whatever works* has always been the American motto, as critical as *e pluribus unum,* although one wonders if they do not amount to the same sentiment, while before these slogans could take root, Americans experienced a long foreground of European natural history, and then the great intellectual divide, the publication in 1859 of *The Origin of Species.* Then at last an ancient poetic wisdom moved into communication with a profound and comprehensive scientific vision. This science continues to advance alongside the poetry we have seen anticipating it and to this day accompanying it. When it is working right, poetry is a kind of knowledge and always anticipates science in a free and imaginative fashion. Poetry has the advantage of being set free from assuming the burden of proof.

Coherence and Emergent Order in Society

For Complexity Theory, which is contributing to the advancement of evolutionary theory, extremely large numbers in nature are subject to principles of emergent coherence, whereby states of initial chaos lead to flowing patterns of unexpected order. When a system coheres, as a democracy might cohere, the process of the cohering is strictly speaking a *complex* one, in which the democracy continues to let its own order emerge, despite all twists and turns, turbulence and rush. This Bertallanfyan idea that "life" is an emergent requires that the whole be greater than the sum of its parts.[23] We may say of engines that they die, because although their parts are all located correctly, some function is down. Metaphorically, machines do indeed have a kind of life, because we identify life with continuously emerging properties of any system. In his great meditation "The System," John Ashbery imagines the play of these balances by exploring the boundaries between our habits of social indifference to others, our obsessive fascination with "intimacy," and, in a page that might serve as gloss to my account of the environment-poem, by imaging the whole range of questions we raise about the "chaos" in which our emotional lives unfold. "There is no cutting corners where the life of the soul is concerned, even if a too modest approximation of the wish that caused it to begin to want to flower be the result—a result that could look like overpruning to the untrained eye. Thus it was that a kind of blight fell on these early forms of going forth and being together, an anarchy of the affections sprung from too much universal cohesion." Ashbery is pointedly speaking to the difference between coherence and the mistaken consistency of an imposed universal cohesion, a failed cohesion. Robots may fascinate us for a while, and what D. H. Lawrence's poems called "robot democracy" is important as a warning.[24] Environing life being our basis, coherence opposes or is opposed by the lock step of the military, for as Lewis Mumford observed long ago, the Spartan army was the first really large machine in the West. If a society ran itself entirely according to a military table of order and chain of command, it would die as a machine may be said to die, and we have seen enough of such incoherence in recent decades, and throughout the twentieth century, to recognize the sad truth of this hazard. Kafka's humorous affirmation of life in the midst of living bureaucratic death, what he saw as his father's life, is the sermon we still need. If Ashbery deliberately drifts in many of his pages of meditation, that is because improvisation fosters coherence, while it is anathema to principles of blank and formal consistency.

Coherence is never a condition of the ideally closed system. By the same token the coherent poem expresses a scene of gradually self-adjusting and expanding coexistence, a *getting along* within a population. For a democratic vista to work, the poet's inherent difficulty—and it is painfully demanding—resides in reaching the individuality of voice, a separateness somehow needing to belong to the mass. This makes for a new artistic condition, since artistic forms had traditionally mirrored hierarchy and top-down structures of society. So strong is the drive toward the democratic gathering of energies, that such poetry allows itself always to contradict itself, in order to subvert that absolute power of which Lord Acton said, it will corrupt absolutely. Our task will be to find a way of concentrating and focusing diversity, as with the glass one uses to light a fire.

14

Precious Idiosyncrasy: An Epilogue

Coherence is never a simple arrangement or purpose. It depends upon ever changing networks whose form is neither too full nor too barren of nodes and internal connections. Kenneth Burke showed how Whitman marshals the magic power of images to build symbolic bridges, by which the poet (and his society) might overcome the tension between the mass and the "precious idiosyncrasy and special nativity and intention that he is, the man's self."[1] A *phrasing* of our democratic existence seeks to preserve such idiosyncrasy, as if in response to Tocqueville's worry that Americans tended paradoxically to conform. Whether we will ever get back to the personal, in Whitman's sense, is a disturbing question that we need always to be asking. Burke ended his article with a medley he composed, made of the first lines of 53 separate Whitman poems, the whole collage producing a set of variations on a theme. The collage worked because all the separate original units were, democratically, brought together to constitute a large variation-system. Every initially isolated phrase, when summed with the others, contributes to a cohering organism alive everywhere in the intransitive and finally infinite present moment, a moment that lacks history because, in this cohering moment, it fundamentally does not need history. Idiosyncrasy of this kind defies time, even when the sad pressure of years weighs heavily upon it. More precisely, poetry intervenes to balance history and the disappearing moment, by restoring the evanescent. Now the transcendent Romantic idea is but catalytic, not controlling.

"Sparkles from the Wheel"

We are never wrong to think of the future yet diurnal implications of wondrous events maintaining an uncertain flow, as when Mary Kinzie's poem on the summer begins with an evocation of the seasons passing:[2]

> Black and white, the flocks of tiny creatures
> Steer their feathered bodies for brief stretches
> From one mock orange to another, or,
> Loose on the ground, lift into the branches
> Of a spruce as if melted upwards
> From the earth.
>   The lines in which they fly
> Weave a weft across the warp of needle
> And foliage the heat will soon make dormant.
>
> At intervals, one of these blessed, blessing,
> And preoccupied bright beings (a chickadee
> Or yellow-throated finch or oddly "vertical"
> Dwarf woodpecker with flecks of bleeding scarlet)
> Will wholly disappear from the design

Or see how a moment rises to the surface of time in Ashbery's genre-painting pastiche, "The Evening of Greuze":[3]

> Examine mirrors in the studio.
> The lizard's glint, the horse's velvet blanket
> Will surprise you into veiled hope one day.

Or hear Ammons, on "Triphammer Bridge," memorialize that most enigmatic and, if one knows it, magnificent crossing:[4]

> *Sanctuary, sanctuary,* I say it over and over and the
> Word's sound is the one place to dwell: that's it, just
> The sound, and the imagination of the sound—a place.

Or, among so many possible excerpts from Marianne Moore's work, this from "He 'Digesteth Harde Yron:'"[5]

> And what could have been more fit
> For the Chinese lawn it
> Grazed on as a gift to an
> emperor who admired strange birds, than this
> one who builds his mud-made
> nest in dust yet will wade
> in lake or sea till only the head shows.

These verses, chosen at random from books on my shelf, are but ones of many that suggest a sense of entering and remaining inside a continuing moment-filled flow, and this flow we might finally exhibit with a famous late Whitman poem, "Sparkles from the Wheel." Finding a "pause aside," the poem catches old New York street life.[6]

> *Sparkles from the Wheel*
>
> Where the city's ceaseless crowd moves on the livelong day,
> Withdrawn I join a group of children watching, I pause
> aside with them.
>
> By the curb toward the edge of the flagging,
> A knife-grinder works at his wheel sharpening a great knife,

Bending over he carefully holds it to the stone, by foot and
knee,
With measur'd tread he turns rapidly, as he presses with
light but firm hand,
Forth issue then in copious golden jets,
Sparkles from the wheel.

The scene and all its belongings, how they seize and
affect me,
The sad sharp-chinn'd old man with worn clothes and
broad shoulder-band of leather,
Myself effusing and fluid, a phantom curiously floating,
now here absorb'd and arrested,
The group, (an unminded point set in a vast surrounding,)
The attentive, quiet children, the loud, proud, restive base
of the streets,
The low hoarse purr of the whirling stone, the light-press'd
blade,
Diffusing, dropping, sideways-darting, in tiny showers
of gold,
Sparkles from the wheel.

This famed lyric perhaps prejudices the case, because the idea of an environment is directly and thematically spelled out in the shape of the poem. If we include its title in its form, which is authorized by the typical Whitman gerundive construction, the full sixteen lines repeat the phrase "sparkles from the wheel" *three times,* enclosing the middle repetition by the phrase used at the beginning and the end, dilating the vast surrounding, while the sparks seem able to fall on and on, diffusing and dropping forever into an invisible Timaean receptacle or space-making *chora.* In line with true description, each spark is a passing appearance, and every spark is like each of us, a "very puny object" answering "the immense form of society at large." Tocqueville had remarked that, faced with "the still more imposing aspect of mankind," democratic man is threatened by a deep emptiness: hence "his ideas are all either extremely minute and clear, or extremely general and vague; what lies between is an open void."[7] For the poet this void has to be somehow filled, either by a liminal *tableau vivant* or by an excited and almost random argument that we humans make progress by participating in each other's lives, an argument of the middle.

The poet cannot imagine a vision fully before composing it in its actual wording, because that actuality is the voice of the world surrounding the poet's eye, the detail of observation within the circle. The individual's perception is the issue, not egotism. Richard Chase was perhaps too much the cool rationalist when he wrote of Whitman's *Drum Taps* that "many of the stirring, martial pieces seem not only stirring but hysterical," and that "the main weakness of the Civil War poems arises from the poet's using them too personally, to work out troubles of his own."[8] The opposite, given our notion of participation in the environment, must be more true. When Whitman says "I will thread through my poems that time and events are compact," like a modern scientist he includes himself in his own experimental threading. He knew through his own involvement that his own "consecutiveness and ensemble" were a deliberate design: "All my parts cohere—there are no loose joints: *Leaves of Grass*—(intact, unbroken, not a comma removed) from first to last—from the very earliest poems to the very latest—from Starting from Paumanok to Sands at Seventy."[9] *All my parts cohere.*

In one of his last letters, Wallace Stevens wrote to Joseph Bennett of some final hasty impressions gained on rereading Whitman for several hours.[10] Stevens's brief comments center on the fact that Whitman at his best wrote "naturally, with an extemporaneousness and irrepressible vehemence of emotion." Three things stand out here: Whitman "seems often to have driven himself to write like himself"—to follow almost obsessively his own theory of poetry. Whitman also manifestly makes collections and "gatherings-together of precious Americana, certain to remain precious but not certain to remain poetry"—that would be, to have written great journalism, if not great poems, and furthermore to have shown always an "opulence" in the gathering, as Stevens names it. And finally, even as Whitman makes "poems in which he collects large numbers of concrete things, particularly things each of which is poetic in itself or as part of the collection," and while these "have a validity which, for many people must be enough and must seem to them all opulence and élan," the main broader effect of the whole of *Leaves of Grass* is to counterbalance its own aggregation. Stevens goes on to say, "It seems to me, then, that Whitman is disintegrating as the world, of which he made himself a part, disintegrates. *Crossing Brooklyn Ferry* exhibits this disintegration."[11] For Stevens "the superbly beautiful and moving things" gather and disperse simultaneously, which, precisely, is what happens in any living landscape or in the disintegrating moment when the tides and the rivers of time and space tell us of the water's meaning. Then, in words of Ashbery's rhapsody on the poem, "A Wave,"

> There are moments like this one
> That are almost silent, so that bird-watchers like us
> Can come, and stay awhile, reflecting on shades of difference
> In past performances, and move on refreshed.

The double strife of nature and our inclusion in that strife will surely seem to disturb these pictures of natural flow, yet we had better consider actual eristic scenes in nature. To think about the environment is neither to endorse the predatory (as in television programs on nature where the main item is one beast devouring another) nor to deny its existence, but rather to examine the reasons for adjustments of natural balance. Darwin expressed no doubts about a cruelty running throughout the whole system of natural evolutionary development. Why should we be pleased at the order of the celestial bodies, when we think of the fury of a single star? John Clare would rather question the sublime, as in one sonnet on his own thoughts—"The Shepherd's Tree," or as it is locally named in another manuscript, "Salter's Tree."[12]

> Huge Elm thy rifted trunk all notched and scarred
> Like to a warriors destiny—I love
> To stretch me often on such shadowed sward
> And hear the sighs of summer leaves above
> Or on thy buttressed roots to sit and lean
> In careless attitude and there reflect
> On times and deeds and darings that have been
> Old castaways now swallowed in neglect
> While thou art towering in thy strength of heart
> Stirring the soul to vain imaginings
> In which life's sordid being hath no part
> The wind in that eternal ditty sings
> Humming of future things that burns the mind
> To leave some fragment of itself behind

La Fontaine would have recognized this poem in his own *Fables*—the central thought is that we exist only by humming with mind and with our capacity to be moved by the passage of time. That humming vision is what a descriptive poetry seems always to convey, and it is a chastening and natural sense of the shortness of life, engaging us to wonder what we may be doing, being here at all, in the first place.

There is a juncture then, as between the claims of cadence and coherence, if in our sense of environment the inconsistently "complete" and the coherent are one. If the poem is to come to an end, it will almost necessarily have to exaggerate the middle section of each development of idea and image. We usually say that to cohere is to come to a conclusion. A coherent sentence is one that at least seems to have a beginning, middle, and end, if not always a clear logical continuity between subject and predicate. But here, as if we were returning to Heraclitus for instruction, conclusion means not *finishing off* the parts. Here coherence implies a permeable containment of all constituents, whether in a natural environment of trees, bugs, birds, animals, waters, winds, and all such creatures, or a human environment of cities and towns and isolated dwellings, and the flexing of the outer edge does not somehow weaken the inclusion. As soon as one has said that, one has said that coherence depends upon man and nature resolving their differences in a healthy way, without iron closure. The double strife of conflict and cohering Whitman discerns is what makes him a great poet, something quite beyond his merely expressive gifts, though dependent upon them. If we take caution from the failed efforts of his imitators, we should not reject their efforts. Many have thought that Whitman's democratic optimism shines too brightly, providing too quick and easy examples for those who have not followed him in laboriously studying the art of poetry. The result has too often been neither strong democratic voice nor powerful poems. Yet Whitman was never the mindless optimist; if anything he was a tragic rhapsode, and his example remains among the most subtle in spite of its grand scope and scale. Rightly, in *Democratic Vistas,* he says that the nation must have "cohesion at all cost," but always, we see, on the basis of the precious idiosyncrasy.[13] He is already an environmentalist of the state, proclaiming that it consists of "*these* United States." As Borges said, "Whitman was already plural,"[14] and because he obeys the ecological principle of the necessary variety of species, he can also provide the model for all subsequent authors of the environment-poem. Here the whole of *Leaves of Grass* instructs its reader in a larger poetic conception, whereby democratic range and acceptance are matched in finesse by an exquisite strength in the art of poetry. In the phrasing of that art we leap beyond ourselves, simply by noticing exactly where we are.

"Looking through Layers of Films of Time"

We return then to our point of departure, the horizon. When John Clare wrote poems protesting the enclosure of ancient common lands, he scanned the boundaries of the natural sight he so much trusted, and he recognized as on so many occasions that "in the blue mist the horizon's edge surrounds."[15] For him and those who write like him, coherence provides the logical and empirical principle of such environing horizons, whose power draws the poem simultaneously into its exact moment while imagining beyond that moment. A mechanical consistency appears to be an obsessive ritual of self-defense. Dubious estimates of short-term gains, attempts to defraud the slow ticking of the clock, cheating on the numbers, always amount to a guarantee of long-term incoherence, because they refuse acceptance of the ever receding horizon line whose edge, if only we could imagine its recession, would save us from the deluded idea that we control whatever finds a home beyond the line of sight. The truth is massive in character, but subtle in expression. We never know what lies beyond the horizon, and because all is finally flux, we can only guess and hence should let that limitation anchor us to our contracting and expanding, narrowing and dilating present moment. Technology today promises the actual use of immensely large and immensely small numbers, as computing devices become ever smaller and more powerful. The danger is that icons will become the empty categories of an unreal real world. The great poetry of natural limits, such as Turgenev's magical story, "Bezhin Meadow," or Whitman's "Crossing Brooklyn Ferry," or Ashbery's "A Wave," will pass unheeded.

There is a diurnal truth we may so easily lose. "The Huntsmen are up in *America,* and they are already past their first sleep in Persia,"[16] wrote Sir Thomas Browne in an essay on the magical numbers devising the Garden of Cyrus.

Knowing we are surrounded, we must yet think beyond the receding circle, which, as our exploring scout, is also advancing. The humming fragments of our thoughts leave strange traces on the ground, or momentarily in the air. "Like air, almost" is the right title for one of our poems. In a world where the spatial ontology is rapidly changing, our poets would teach us an evolving knowledge, imagining for us the main fact of our experiencing and almost understanding time. Acknowledging the frailties of our control over nature, yet succeeding so powerfully in the realization and promise of control, we late moderns readily come to imagine that we can raise the ordinary to a higher plane. With disciplines of thought we hardly grasp, we would transfigure sleeping and waking, sitting still and walking abroad. Who then will set the upper limits of our quest for common wisdom, if we are discontented with diurnal knowledge? Despite all our most active efforts to gain control over time, it remains only an infinitely fine film of apperception, "like gold to airy thinness beat," and all we possess of it is the layering it leaves, the minute encrustations of an allusive drift.

Notes

Index

Notes

Introduction

1. Walt Whitman, "A Backward Glance O'er Travel'd Roads," appeared as introduction to the 1888 *November Boughs.* My text is Sculley Bradley and Harold W. Blodgett, eds., *Leaves of Grass* (New York, 1973), 566–67. This Norton Critical Text is hereafter cited as *NTN.*

2. See Eric Robinson, ed., *John Clare's Autobiographical Writings* (Oxford, 1983), 33–34. My work on Clare goes back many years, an early stage being represented in "Writing and the Extreme Situation," a chapter in my book entitled *Colors of the Mind: Conjectures on Thinking in Literature* (Cambridge, Mass., 1991). Clare, who knows great natural scenes, is also the master of the natural miniature. Commenting on Thoreau's journals, Loren Eiseley once noted exactly the point of correspondence between Thoreau's naturalist notations and the miscellaneous minutiae of Ashbery's verse: "Reading in Thoreau's Journals today. It strikes me that Thoreau's writing is like his own landscape—a vast expanse of weeds, brush, thickets, and just occasionally a singing bird with a soft note hidden in some unexceptionable underbrush. Thoreau, in other words, is as chaotic as the world of nature and just as full of trivia with here and there some remarkable observational nugget." Kenneth Heuer, ed., *The Lost Notebooks of Loren Eiseley* (Lincoln, Nebr., 1987), 98. My involvement with Whitman also goes back many years, and I eventually linked him with John Ashbery, on whom I had lectured at the

Dactyl Foundation of New York and at the University of Arizona. In the 1950s, with my friend and undergraduate co-editor, the late Leo Raditsa, I had published, besides John Ashbery, a number of his contemporaries and seniors, such as Kenneth Koch, Gregory Corso, Paul Goodman, Paul de Man (we were the first to publish him in English), Herbert Marcuse, James Agee, Walker Evans, Jackson Pollock, and others in our magazine, *i.e., The Cambridge Review.* It would be useful, no doubt, to discuss other contemporaries in the ensuing pages, but my reader will have to fill in some of those missing reports.

3. Lawrence Buell, cited below, epitomizes Max Oelschlager, *The Idea of Wildness: From Prehistory to the Age of Ideology* (New Haven, 1991), as a "neo-primitive reading." The epithet indicates a tension apparent throughout the history of ecology, since the overuse and/or artificial control of environment—an old human activity—seems to some to be inevitable and hence reasonable, while to others it clearly threatens the heart (and soul) of our natural existence. Is "sustainability" natural, desirable, impossible, or quite foredoomed? Imagine the gap between the comfortably enclosed terrain of Selborne for Gilbert White and the global perspective of a major activist, say Bill McKibben, in *The End of Nature* (New York, 1990) or among historians Alfred W. Crosby, *Ecological Imperialism: The Biological Expansion of Europe, 900–1900* (Cambridge, 1986), both of whom write in the tragic shadow of Rachel Carson and other earlier ecological heroes. Buell provides extensive references in *The Environmental Imagination: Thoreau, Nature Writing, and the Formulation of American Culture* (Cambridge, Mass., 1995) and more recently in *Writing for an Endangered World: Literature, Culture, and Environment in the U.S. and Beyond* (Cambridge, Mass., 2001).

4. On coherence theory versus correspondence (representational) theory, see Roger Scruton, *Modern Philosophy: An Introduction and Survey* (New York, 1994), 99–104, and John McDowell, *Mind and World* (Cambridge, Mass., 1996), *passim;* see also Donald Davidson, "A Coherence Theory of Truth and Knowledge," reprinted in Ernest LePore, ed., *Truth and Interpretation: Perspectives on the Philosophy of Donald Davidson* (Oxford, 1986).

5. See Edward O. Wilson, *The Diversity of Life* (Cambridge, Mass., 1992), with Wilson's other books on biodiversity, for example *The Future*

of Life (New York, 2002). Broadly, nature's complexity links to its diversity of living species. The refrain of all traditional "natural history," from Pliny down to the present, has been that the creatures of the earth are virtually infinite in diversity of kinds. But we now seek the science this implies. On the teaching of the great ecologist, G. Evelyn Hutchinson, and his influence upon Wilson and Robert MacArthur, see Donald Worster, *Nature's Economy: A History of Ecological Ideas,* 2nd ed. (Cambridge, 1998), 375–379.

6. See Bill McKibben, *The End of Nature,* 2nd ed. (New York, 1999), new introduction, xv–xvi.

1. Clare's Horizon

1. See Edmund Husserl, *Cartesian Meditations: An Introduction to Phenomenology,* tr. Dorian Cairns (The Hague, 1960), 110. Relations in consciousness sensed to be "perceptual" often appear for Husserl to be connected to the musical succession of tones, heard as flux, yet connected "in sequence." See his *Phenomenology of Internal Time-Consciousness,* tr. James S. Churchill, ed. Martin Heidegger (Bloomington, 1966), 23, 30, 33, where tones are correlated with visual stimuli. Poetry always seeks a synaesthetic combination of the tonal and the visual.

2. Ralph Waldo Emerson, "Circles," in *Essays and Lectures,* ed. Joel Porte (New York, 1983), Essay X, First Series, 403. Emerson reaches for the uncertain horizon, calling us "to do something without knowing how or why; in short, to draw a new circle" (414).

3. "The Flood," in *John Clare,* ed. Eric Robinson and David Powell (New York, 1984), 194. The three sonnets are placed in the Robinson-Powell "Helpston" group, i.e., written sometime between 1812 and 1831.

4. John Clare, *Autobiographical Writings*, ed. Eric Robinson (New York, 1983), 33–34. Throughout this and other Clare citations I keep his original spelling except in cases where emendation is needed, to avoid utter confusion, as with the sonnet quoted in Ch. XIV.

5. D. M. Thomas, *Alexander Solzhenitsyn: A Century in His Life* (New York, 1998), 48. Clare was delighted by Hazlitt's account of trying to jump over his own shadow—see *The Natural History Prose Writings of John Clare,* ed. Margaret Grainger (Oxford, 1983), 194.

6. Joseph Conrad, *The Mirror of the Sea,* Ch. I, "Landfalls and Departures." I cite the Marlboro Press edition (Marlboro, Vt., 1988), 2.

2. The Argument of Form

1. Aubin's volume was published in 1936 by Modern Language Association, then reprinted by Kraus Reprint (New York, 1966). On the *Monthly Review,* see Aubin, *Topographical Poetry,* 255. Aubin always reflects his period and is not much of a theorist in our sense, but he is splendidly ironic about the way most of these descriptive "cultural constructions" are uninspired—how can such "construction" and "work" be otherwise? Without meaning to, Aubin exposes the folly of our times, the neglect of literary excellence. He persistently shows how morals and enthusiasm mate, awkwardly in the Augustans, but in many ways more subtly with the Romantics. See *Topographical Poetry,* 118–19, 213–15 (on the mannered "display of rural felicity"), 242–57 (on journey-poems). There is, Aubin shows, much useful knowledge seeking expression here, and the genre seems to mirror a rising belief in the value of secular knowledge—"enlightenment learning"—and in this the poetry parallels the ascension of the novel. Simultaneously, the drama has to decline, since dramatic economy of plot, action, and thought necessarily inhibit the miscellaneous widening of scope required to render a "real world," i.e., render the social environment the nineteenth-century novel always evokes.

2. Oliver Goldsmith, in "The Traveler, or a Prospect of Society," line 386: "Laws grind the poor and rich men rule the law," a line recalling Pope, but more broadly a view found in Juvenalian satires on the proper use of wealth. Goldsmith's own financial troubles led him to views like those of Clare, who wrote: "Enclosure came and trampled on the grave / Of labour's rights, and left the poor a slave," or "The Parish hind, oppression's humble slave, / Whose only hope of freedom is the grave." See J. W. and Anne Tibble, *John Clare: A Life* (London, 1932), 329; essential, and very detailed, is John Barrell, *The Idea of Landscape and the Sense of Place: 1730–1840: An Approach to the Poetry of John Clare* (Cambridge, 1972); with this and other works of Barrell, see the *Journal of the John Clare Society;* Christiana Payne, *Toil and Plenty: Images of the Agricultural Landscape in England: 1780–1890* (New Haven, 1993); Tom

Williamson and Liz Bellamy, *Property and Landscape: A Social History of Land Ownership and the English Countryside* (London, 1987).

3. "Learn to exaggerate": I heard Berlin say this in a lecture on Herder.

4. Robert Sattelmeyer, *The Natural History Essays* (Salt Lake City, 1980), "Walking," 93–136. See also herein, "Autumnal Hints," 173.

5. Lawrence Stapleton, ed., *H. D. Thoreau: A Writer's Journal* (New York, 1960), 66.

6. The learned generation of Panofsky and Saxl assumed the centrality of these concerns. See Robert Klein, *La Forme et l'intelligible: Ecrits sur la Renaissance et l'art moderne* (Paris, 1970).

7. See especially Book X of *The Republic;* suspicion of art runs all through the *Dialogues,* as noted in S. H. Butcher, *Aristotle's Theory of Poetry and Fine Art* (New York, 1951).

8. Immanent form, an ultimately protoromantic notion, is implicit when Aristotle refers to the drama as a "living creature," possessed of a "certain definite magnitude" (*Poetics,* 1450b). See Alexander Nehamas, "Plato on Imitation and Poetry in Republic 10," in *Plato on Beauty, Wisdom and the Arts,* ed. J. Moravcsik and P. Temko (Totowa, 1982), 47–78; Aryeh Kosman, "Acting: Drama as the Mimesis of Praxis," in *Essays on Aristotle's Poetics,* ed. Amelie G. Rorty (Princeton, 1992), 51–72.

9. See John Hollander, review of Stanley Cavell's *The Claim of Reason, Critical Inquiry,* 6, no. 4 (1980), 587.

10. Thomas Sprat, *History of the Royal Society:* cited in Joel E. Spingarn, *Critical Essays of the Seventeenth Century* (Oxford, 1908), vol. II, 118.

11. Ralph Cohen: *The Art of Discrimination: Thomson's The Seasons and the Languages of Criticism* (Berkeley, 1964). Hybrid of body and spirit—see Thomson's *Castle of Indolence,* Canto II, where the Knight Selvaggio (descended from Spenser's Sir Satyrane?) hunts and rides in the wild, "But more he searched the mind, and roused from sleep / Those moral seeds whence we heroic actions reap."

12. "The circle of hermeneutic enclosure": for an illuminating and, as always, a readable account of interpreting texts like the Bible, see Frank Kermode, *The Classic: Literary Images of Permanence and Change* (New York, 1975). Ch. II deals with Schleiermacher and Dilthey, citing Fredric Jameson's translation of Dilthey's "The Rise of Hermeneutics" in *New Literary History,* III (1972), 229–44. The issue raised in the present context

(not Kermode's) is whether hermeneutics had to wait for a Romantic (and German) sense of a natural *Umwelt* in order to see how to construct a parallel interpretive *Umwelt.* See also my *Colors of the Mind* (Cambridge, Mass., 1991), 246–48; the important collection of essays in *Hermeneutics: Questions and Prospects,* ed. Gary Shapiro and Alan Sica (Amherst, Mass., 1984); Friedrich Schleiermacher, *Hermeneutics: The Handwritten Manuscripts,* ed. H. Kimmerle, tr. J. Duke and J. Forstmann (Missoula, 1977); Scheiermacher, "The Hermeneutics: Outline of the 1819 Lectures," *New Literary History* 10 (Autumn 1978), 1–16.

13. See the essays on Goethe and Hölderlin in Wilhelm Dilthey, *Poetry and Experience,* ed. R. A. Makkreel and Frithjof Rodi (Princeton, 1985), 3–5, 287–93.

14. Montaigne describes his library in *Essays,* Book III, "Of Three Kinds of Society," which Florio in 1603 translated as "Of Three Commerces or Societies." That is, the library, which perforce recalls Borges (and Eco), creates a panopticon of universal symbolic transaction—the connection to Bentham's panopticon as prison hovers in the background of our latter-day interpretation. The library is a prison allowing the prisoners to go anywhere, unlike Plato's Cave, where they are chained in front of the movie showing on a back wall.

15. Samuel Johnson, "The Vanity of Human Wishes. In Imitation of the Tenth Satire of Juvenal," ll.1–2.

16. Robert Frost, "Snow Dust," *The Yale Review* (January 1921).

17. See David Newsome, *Two Classes of Men: Platonism and English Romantic Thought* (New York, 1974), 13. Coleridge, weaving webs of pantheist, Spinozist, Platonic, and Schellingian ideas of The Idea, is not to be seen in rigorous conceptual terms, unless his criticism is also allowed to link with his poetic works (on which see Thomas MacFarland, John Beer, A. D. Nuttall).

18. See Stephen Halliwell, *The Aesthetics of Mimesis: Ancient Texts and Modern Problems* (Princeton, 2002), 318. See ch. 11 *passim,* and especially pages 360–61 on A. W. Schlegel.

3. Description

1. Gérard Genette, *Narrative Discourse: An Essay in Method.* Tr. Jane Lewin (Ithaca, 1980), 86–112, where description is a subset of "duration" (*durée*); also, *Figures of Literary Discourse,* tr. Alan Sheridan, introd. Marie-Rose Logan (New York, 1982), 134–35, where Genette argues that description is the indispensable "slave" of narrative. The most intrusive device of prose narrative is the use of represented dialogue, the He said/She said method of advancing the action, and the descriptive in narration is mainly what the dialogue intrudes upon, less so in German fictions, more so in English "dramatic" fictions like those of Dickens. Generally speaking, description makes it possible to create "atmosphere," although in novels like *Vanity Fair* the dialogue creates an atmosphere of gossip, that is, of its own Bakhtinian use; dialogue itself becomes an atmosphere or general environment in which the action is advanced under the control of rumor. That had been Bunyan's aim in the originating scene in *The Pilgrim's Progress.*

2. See Bertrand Russell, *The Problems of Philosophy* (1912), new introd. John Perry (New York, 1997), ch. V, 46–59; also, Russell, *The Philosophy of Logical Atomism* (1918), ed. David Pears (La Salle, Ill., 1985), ch. VI, 109–23. Ray Monk's recent biography describes the rift between Russell and Wittgenstein, which among other deep problems involved the movement toward claims for language-in-use, and later turned into the theory of the language-game, as given in Wittgenstein's *Philosophical Investigations.* Wittgenstein leaves the role of logic in a most peculiar state. I have heard a mature professional philosopher recall that when he first studied the unpublished Blue and Brown Notebooks, he thought and felt that "philosophy was over." There is no need to give a trivial professional reading of the rift, but we can see, in our context, that any deep theory of the language-game will make it worthless, or frankly impossible, to separate acquaintance from description.

My use of the terms here is intended to suggest that if unmediated acquaintance exists, it will of itself demand that the poet express an ineffable aspect of the environment. Then, if the acquaintance is what escapes our descriptions, the poet will need methods for preventing this escape from happening altogether, or as a final effect. This could be seen as the defining task of the Romantic poets in general, to prevent the disappearance of acquaintance while maintaining the extension of descriptions into the domain of the idea.

3. W. K. C. Guthrie, *A History of Greek Philosophy. Vol. I. The Earlier Presocratics and the Pythagoreans* (Cambridge, 1971), 2, and ch. I, passim. With an abiding concern for *arche* as originating state or moment, there arises a regression to the source of things, and hence regression to mythology, on which topic see Marcel Detienne and Paul Veyne, *Did the Greeks Believe Their Myths?* Tr. Paula Wissing (Chicago, 1988); Marcel Detienne, *The Masters of Truth in Archaic Greece,* tr. Janet Lloyd. Foreword by Pierre Vidal-Naquet (New York, 1996), esp. ch. V, "The Process of Secularization." See also Glenn W. Most, "The Poetics of Early Greek Philosophy," in *The Cambridge Companion to Early Greek Philosophy,* ed. A. A. Long (Cambridge, 1999), 332–63. Among general studies of Greek epistemology and ontology, see Bruno Snell's (1948) *Discovery of the Mind in Greek Philosophy and Literature,* tr. T. G. Rosenmeyer (New York, 1982) and the classic earlier work, Eduard Zeller, *Outlines of the History of Greek Philosophy,* 13th ed., tr. L. R. Palmer (New York, 1980).

4. John Clare, "Childhood," in *The Midsummer Cushion,* ed. Kelsey Thornton and Anne Tibble (Carcanet Press, 1990), 102.

5. See Harry Berger, Jr., *Fictions of the Pose: Rembrandt Against the Italian Renaissance* (Stanford, 2000), esp. pages 171–96, on "the fiction of objectivity." For environment-poems representing the landscape (even the urban landscape), Berger raises the question: to what degree is it a mere fiction that we can "describe" such manifolds, a question the present book seeks to answer. Clearly the history of the picturesque is a history of nature taking a pose. Yet "seeing as" permits humans to see the natural surround as a form of some kind. Owing to the ancient Greek notion that music is the most mimetic of all the arts, we may perceive that the posing of nature is more like the shaping and harmonizing of melodies, using certain scales and modes.

6. John Donne, "Elegy XVI. On His Mistress," lines 50–56. On the walking tour of Jones and the poet, see Donald E. Hayden, *Wordsworth's Walking Tour of 1790* (Tulsa, 1983); Kenneth R. Johnston, *The Hidden Wordsworth: Poet. Lover. Rebel. Spy* (New York, 1998), 203–34; Stephen Gill, *William Wordsworth: A Life* (Oxford, 1989), 44–67. Walking with

sublime or "educational" aims is to be distinguished from the Clare/Whitman/Ashbery perambulation, as exemplified in John Clare, "A Morning Walk," in *The Midsummer Cushion,* ed. Thornton and Tibble, 153–58: "The walks that sweetest pleasure yields / When things appear so fresh and fair / Are when we wander round the fields / To breathe the morning air . . ." Clare is as curious as anyone, but he needs to go slow, so that he can observe without any prearranged educational scheme. In his diurnal knowledge there is no "lesson plan."

7. Herman Hesse, *Peter Camenzind,* tr. Michael Roloff (New York, 1969), 90. The converse of Hesse's procedure characterizes the unique, anti-Romantic, fantastic and obsessive works of Raymond Roussel, the subject of Ashbery's third Norton Lecture and perhaps more important for the poet, the subject of his 1961 essay, "On Raymond Roussel." There Ashbery draws attention to the "rhymed, photographic descriptions of people and objects," a technique later modulating into the bizarre, yet exact, where "the things described are fantastic scenes or inventions." See Ashbery, "On Raymond Roussel," reprinted as Introduction to Michel Foucault, *Death and the Labyrinth: The World of Raymond Roussel,* tr. Charles Ruas (New York, 1986). Description becomes *descriptionism,* as Borges labeled one comic version of its excess, as when the *nouveau roman* of Robbe-Grillet enhances the "photographic."

8. See Sir Walter Scott, *The Antiquary,* ed. David Hewitt (New York, 1995), epigraph to ch. VII. The George Crabbe lines:

> ——Pleased awhile to view
> The Watery waste, the prospect wild and new;
> The now receding waters gave them space
> On either side, the growing shores to trace,
> And then, returning, they contract the scene,
> Till small and smaller grows the walk between.

Here classic descriptive technique in Claudian fashion defines the "view," the "prospect," and the "scene," in their changing perspectival relations to scale, so that the waters work like a painting to achieve a contraction of the vista.

9. I am grateful to the distinguished American landscape painter,

James Crosby, for alerting me to an important study by Abraham A. Davidson, *The Eccentrics and Other American Visionary Painters* (New York, 1978). The American painters' mix of mimetic precision and mysterious haze, while not without origins in the work of Turner and others, is peculiarly appropriate for the sense that in physical fact our landscape is at times so "out of scale" that it calls for a visionary technique, which can be found in artists as controlled as Inness, though more obviously in the Hudson River artists, or Ryder.

10. Note the transliteration in Jacques Derrida's important article, "Khora," in *On the Name,* tr. Ian Mcleod (Stanford, 1995), 89–127. In the *Timaeus* Plato uses *chora* to mean a kind of spatiality or possibility of place in the world. In *Timaeus* 52a–b Plato says that this fundamental *chora* provides a seat or fixed place in which we can locate all things that come into being. The dialogue could not be more "Pythagorean" (in Sir Thomas Browne's sense), if not technically in its massive use of number symbolism and harmonic theory. From the poetic point of view the dialogue is interesting, however, because it anticipates in mythic fashion the modern notion that our world consists of various environing spaces, full or empty, all of which betray signs of life, if only on the level of the atom. Plato's universe is in fact a living creature, an idea he inherits from the Presocratics. Such a thought gives a special value, then, to the *chora* as space, for this becomes the scene or even the mere medium of things coming into being and passing away, which is what we call an environment. Donald Zeyl, editor and translator of the *Timaeus,* notes in his introduction that Plato's account of the Receptacle, the womb of creation we might say, or as he says, the "wet-nurse" of all creation, "is at best obscure" (as he admits, 49a3–4) and at worst incoherent. The obscurity has been picked up in the arguments of Gilles Deleuze and Félix Guattari, in *A Thousand Plateaus,* tr. Brian Massumi (London, 1987), but curiously it seems necessary that it recur, since, if nature is an idea, it is also a contradiction: its life-process has too much becoming in it for it to have the ideal stability of a true Platonic Form. The analogy I am drawing implies that when (52a) Plato says space "always exists and cannot be destroyed," providing the fixed site or place for all becoming things, this environing space can only be "apprehended by a kind of bastard reasoning that does not involve sense perception, and it is hardly even an object of convic-

tion [*pistis*]. We look at it as in a dream when we say that everything that exists must of necessity be somewhere, in some place and occupying some space, and that that which doesn't exist somewhere, whether on earth or in heaven, doesn't exist at all." Plato, *Timaeus,* ed. Donald Zeyl (Indianapolis, 2000), 42. When we think of environments, too, we are victims of the same "bastard reasoning," because try as we may, it is natural or at least easy to think of site and place, whereas space is a weird sort of nonconstruction, part thing and part idea. On Plato's cosmology, see F. M. Cornford, "Translation and Commentary on the *Timaeus,*" and John Dillon, "The Question of Being," in *Greek Thought: A Guide to Classical Knowledge,* ed. J. Brunschwig and G. E. R. Lloyd (Cambridge, Mass., 2000), 62: the Timaean receptacle and spatial extension *(chora)* is "a sort of field of forces, consisting of empty three-dimensionality, which nonetheless has a distorting and disruptive effect on the geometrical emanations of the Forms that are projected onto it." *Chora,* and also the chorographic poetry that a poet like Clare derives from such an intuition—had he known Thomas Taylor's accounts of Neoplatonism?—thus names the turbulent surface of the living ground on which or in which every thing is placed, even imprinted, while this siting or placement remains always shaken and oscillating in the changes of the becoming. We might say then that a truly descriptive poetry would always need to undermine the comfort of place, or the nostalgia for home that place humanly implies. Chorographic vision questions topos or *place,* by showing turbulent movements within *space.*

This is nowhere more obvious than in Tocqueville's account of the American scene. He persistently comments on the paramount role of sheer scale in the American land mass. This scale is set against an emptiness of all; the few Native Americans were discounted as "filling" the space. Of the Ohioans he says: "These men left their first country to improve their condition; they quit their second [the Eastern seaboard] to ameliorate it still more; fortune awaits them everywhere, but not happiness. The desire of prosperity has become an ardent and restless passion in their minds, which grows by what it feeds on. They early broke the ties that bound them to their natal earth [*terre natale*], and they have contracted no fresh ones on their way. Emigration was at first necessary for them; and it soon becomes a sort of game of chance, which they pursue for the emotions it excites as much as for the gain it procures" (Chapter XVII). *Democracy in America,* Vol. I, ed. Phillips Bradley, rev. tr. Henry Reeve (New York, 1954), 305. See the same passage in the new H. C. Mansfield and D. Winthrop translation (Chicago, 2000), 270–71.

11. Lee Rust Brown, *The Emerson Museum: Practical Romanticism and the Pursuit of the Whole* (Cambridge, Mass., 1997), 50: "Emerson's source for the natural 'plenum' is Parmenides."

12. On John Taylor, see J. W. and Anne Tibble, *John Clare: A Life* (London, 1972), 120, and more extensively the important study of Tim Chilcott, *A Publisher and His Circle: The Life and Work of John Taylor, Keats's Publisher* (London, 1972).

13. John Clare, *Northborough Sonnets,* ed. Eric Robinson, David Powell, and P. M. S. Dawson (Carcanet Press, 1995). Carcanet, working with the Mid Northumberland Arts Group, is an important publisher of modern Clare editions.

4. Ashbery's Clare

1. John Ashbery, *Other Traditions* (Cambridge, Mass., 2000), 5, 8.

2. The need for a new biography to update and refine the Tibble's 1932 volume and other, briefer biographical summaries will soon be met a new biography from Jonathan Bate, whose *Romantic Ecology: Wordsworth and the Environmental Tradition* (London, 1999) deals at some length with Clare's unusual position.

3. John Clare, "The Village Minstrel": Ashbery's comment, *Other Traditions,* 8. "The Village Minstrel" is in the authoritative Clarendon Press volume: *The Early Poems of John Clare: 1804–1822* Vol. II, ed. Eric Robinson and David Powell (Oxford, 1989), 123–79.

4. *Other Traditions,* 11. The fragment cited on page 14 is to be found in *The Later Poems of John Clare: 1837–1864,* Vol. II. ed. Robinson, Powell, and Margaret Grainger (Oxford, 1984), 1090. The lines would have been written down or copied out by Knight during Clare's long stay at the Northampton Asylum. The lines appear in the Oxford Authors paperback volume, *John Clare* (New York, 1984), 427, where no doubt Ashbery read them.

5. Arthur Symons wrote an Introduction to his exquisite volume, *Po-*

ems by John Clare (London, 1908), page 19 cited ("begins anywhere"). For essays, early reviews, and so on, see Mark Storey, ed., *Clare: The Critical Tradition* (London, 1973), from which the Norton Lectures drew a number of citations.

6. John Clare, "Mouse's Nest," in Oxford Authors, *John Clare,* 263.

7. On this vagueness effect, see Paul de Man, *The Rhetoric of Romanticism* (New York, 1984), 132. The poet wants "just enough light to perceive shapes and contours but not so much that the brilliance of the surfaces would prevent the eye from penetrating beyond them"—i.e., a cloudy Northern sky versus a bright cloudless Mediterranean light.

8. On this "indistinctness," see Adrian Stokes, *The Image in Form: Selected Writings,* ed. Richard Wollheim (New York, 1972), 211–35. Stokes inspires thoughts on the materiality of media in painting, architecture, etc., and the materiality of the written word, which is more powerfully present as an aesthetic "value" in self-taught poets like Clare and Whitman than with highly educated poets like Wordsworth and Shelley.

9. William Wordsworth, "Composed after a Journey": see Oxford Authors, *William Wordsworth,* ed. Stephen Gill (New York, 1990), 287 and 711n.

10. John Ashbery, *The Double Dream of Spring* (New York, 1976), 35–36. *Dream* is included in *The Mooring of Starting Out: the First Five Books* (New York, 1997), 225–307.

11. The Parmenidean principle is given in Fragment 6 of the main Parmenidean source. See Kirk and Raven, *The Presocratic Philosophers,* 2nd ed. (Cambridge, 1983), 247. This translation is close to Kathleen Freeman's, in her *Ancilla to the Pre-Socratic Philosophers* (Cambridge, Mass., 1983), 42: "For it is the same thing to think and to be," which equally resembles Kirk and Raven, 247: "What is there to be said and thought must needs be," these and others rendering the Greek. See also Jonathan Barnes, *The Presocratic Philosophers* (London, 1982), 157: "The same thing is both for thinking of, and for being." W. K. C. Guthrie, *History of Greek Philosophy,* Vol. II, *The Presocratic Tradition from Parmenides to Democritus,* 14: "For it is the same thing that can be thought and can be." Guthrie gives a literal reading of the Greek, as follows: "The same thing is for thinking *(noiein)* and for being *(esti),*" and he quotes Mansfeld's German reading, "The object of thought is at the same time the subject

of being." For another perspective, see Gregory Vlastos, *Studies in Greek Philosophy:* Vol. I, *The Presocratics* (Princeton, 1993), ch. 7.

Perhaps the clearest and most immediately perspicuous rendering is David Krell, Introduction to Martin Heidegger, *Early Greek Philosophy: The Dawn of Western Philosophy,* tr. D. R. Krell and F. A. Capuzzi (San Francisco, 1984), 5: "Thinking and the thought 'it is' are the same." On the other hand, one senses that Parmenides was making an ontological rather than epistemological statement, which would mean roughly that Being is dependent upon Thinking, and equally, if one is to Think, it is of something that has Being—yet the debates among expert scholars revolve around the extreme difficulty of knowing what the philosopher had in mind, not least because he has written his "thought" in a hexameter poem, not at all the discourse of modern philosophy. As one ponders this relationship between poem and discourse, one is led to Karl Popper, *The World of Parmenides,* ed. Arne F. Peterson (New York, 1998), where Parmenides is understood to be a natural philosopher, a cosmologist, for whom Being and Presence are functions of there existing a world around us, which we have no choice but to register as our foundation of knowledge. This cosmological presence of Being occurs with poets like Clare and Ashbery, since they allow their poems to mirror an arriving at a mimesis, by letting the reader experience the way one thinks one's way toward such an arrival, along Heidegger's "path," as it were. The poems dramatize the continuous liminal process of arriving and approaching and approximating—not as guesswork, but as footwork. Geoffrey Hartman writes of a generalized liminality, from Arnold van Gennep and Victor Turner, in "History-Writing as Answerable Style." See *New Directions in Literary History,* ed. Ralph Cohen (Baltimore, 1974), 101–04. In the English Institute sessions (1974–75), published as *The Literature of Fact,* ed. with introduction by Angus Fletcher (New York, 1976), I invited Victor Turner to address the Institute; his paper is included in the volume. My own work on liminality dates to the late 1960s, with its hippie climate, so important for Turner's later anthropological research. As applied to Renaissance literature, these liminal studies had formed one critical basis in my essay on Spenser's Fifth Book, *The Prophetic Moment* (Chicago, 1971).

12. Edward Thomas, "Women, Nature, and Poetry," *Feminine Influ-*

ence on the English Poets (1910), 80–87, cited in Storey, 314. "For such a writer the usual obstacles and limits are temporary or do not exist at all, and as with children the dividing between the real and the unreal either shifts or has not been made." In *A Language Not to Be Betrayed: Selected Prose of Edward Thomas,* ed. Edna Longley (Carcanet Press, 1981), 29.

13. Seamus Heaney, "John Clare: A Bi-centenary Lecture," in *John Clare in Context,* ed. Hugh Haughton, Adam Phillips, Geoffrey Summerfield (Cambridge, 1994), 130–47. In this important collection, see especially "Clare's Politics," by John Lucas; "Progress and Rhyme," by Hugh Haughton; "John Clare: the Trespasser," by John Goodridge and Kelsey Thornton. Adam Phillips treats Clare's "complex and contradictory set of identifications," and Nicholas Birns discovers crossings between the facts of Clare's environment at Helpston and the difficulty of defining "nature" in that context.

14. Kenneth Johnston, *The Hidden Wordsworth: Poet, Lover, Rebel, Spy* (New York, 1998), 192.

15. I owe this anecdote of early rising to my colleague, Prof. Jackie DiSalvo. Graves remarked in a 1953 *Hudson Review* essay, besides the comment Ashbery quotes, that Clare's "obsession with Nature made him think of a poem as a living thing, rather than an artifact, or a slice cut from the cake of literature." Storey, ed., *Clare: The Critical Heritage,* 414. This belief parallels James Lovelock's, *Gaia: A New Look at Life on Earth* (Oxford, 1987)—a Timaean ecology.

16. It is by no means clear whether tourism was not always in part a mode of what we now call ecotourism, given the degree of early travelers' interest in natural as well as social history. Ecotourism is by now a business. Will renewed fears among tourists not change this fashion? For a cultural view, among many books, see Andrea Loselle, *History's Double: Cultural Tourism in Twentieth-Century French Writing* (New York, 1997).

17. "School Boys" in *The Early Poems of John Clare: 1804–1822,* Vol. II, ed. Robinson and Powell, 586; "Autumn," 589.

18. Keats to Taylor: see Tim Chilcott, *A Publisher and His Circle: The Life and Work of John Taylor, Keats's Publisher* (London, 1972), 119–21.

19. John Barrell, besides the detailed ecological and art-historical account in *The Idea of Landscape,* gives further pictorial background in *The Dark Side of the Landscape: The Rural Poor in English Painting*

1730–1840 (Cambridge, 1980); see esp. 155–56, and the subsequent discussion of Constable.

20. George Deacon, *John Clare and the Folk Tradition* (London, 1983); now available in paperback, this is a key work for "reading" Clare, in that Deacon has discovered the actual music of songs known to the poet, as herein reproduced. Deacon has in fact recorded some of these songs on CD. The musicology here alerts us to the song aspect of many, if not most of the poems. A ballad like "The Maid of Ocram or Lord Gregory" (Deacon, 112–20) has the old ballad language ("the wind disturbs my yellow locks / the snow falls on my skin") that gives to Clare his uncanny directness and perceptual acuity. Ashbery shares these qualities in his own peculiar wavering poetic forms—meanders fully under control.

21. See, in a postmodern perspective, Marjorie Perloff, *Wittgenstein's Ladder: Poetic Language and the Strangeness of the Ordinary* (Chicago, 1996); Henry Staten, *Wittgenstein and Derrida* (Lincoln, Neb., 1984); and above all the philosophical writings of Stanley Cavell, especially: *Must We Mean What We Say?: A Book of Essays* (Cambridge, 1976) and *The Claim of Reason: Wittgenstein, Skepticism, Morality, and Tragedy* (New York, 1979).

22. Margaret Grainger, ed., *The Natural History Prose Writings of John Clare* (Oxford, 1983). Who but Clare [Grainger, 35] could have described the sound of a nocturnal bird as "its creeping and danger-haunting cry"?

5. Diurnal Knowledge

1. A. C. Bradley, *Oxford Lectures on Poetry,* introduction by M. R. Ridley (Oxford, 1965), "The Long Poem in the Age of Wordsworth," 201.

2. John Ashbery, *Reported Sightings* (Cambridge, Mass., 1991), xi.

3. Jonathan Bate, *Romantic Ecology,* 19. On Sidney's *Arcadia,* 18. My sense is that our understandable interest in the pastoral and its tradition, from Theocritus to the present, has a way of skewing our sense of city versus country, court versus country, not so much because pastoral omits its laboring "swinkers," as because the tradition was always an intensely literary activity, even in its hardest forms. The literarity interferes with our reaching the question: but what then can be, might be, an intelligent and humane grasp of the natural in its environmental truth? The tradi-

tion of pastoral tends, despite moments of extension, to place the natural too far outside these social concerns. Spenser is wondrous, in that he allows the natural to subsist as a persistent wave of truth throughout his stories as well as in the *Calender.* He more than most poets accepts that man is a social animal. By and large, with him as with other poets, pastoral remains an essential exercise in social perspective (on the class struggle, as Empson kept insisting).

4. David Wiggens, "Nature, Respect for Nature, and the Human Scale of Values," *Proceedings of the Aristotelian Society:* The Presidential Address (1999), 1–32. Wiggens connects issues of "our own welfare or contentment" to a useful response we humans may take toward the sublimity of Nature (11), and he has no hesitation in his invocation of the beauty of Nature, since, as a philosopher, he finds that such beauty tells us central things about our own need for "collective deliberation" (19). Wiggens sees Nature "as some sort of limitation upon our will," (26) and while this thought would have been self-evident to everyone living before the age of modern technology, it has the function in the argument of telling us something which is still true, but only masked by technology—since technology is always and only a prosthetic help, and we humans adapt to it quickly enough, like a person who adapts to his dentures if their technology is handled well by the dentist. A pacemaker is prosthetic, even when it works perfectly and seems to disappear from our consciousness. Our job then, extrapolating from Wiggens, would seem to be that his idea of our needing a sharper and more intelligent grasp of *religio* than the ones that blind us to the limiting place of nature will inevitably lead to a new form of philosophic and pragmatic "engagement not only with ecological questions themselves but with the frightening insufficiency of the ideas that now do duty for respect for Nature" (28). My own view is that this prescription, while right and necessary, will not and cannot get anywhere until there is open disclosure of the "big lie" about the raw and ruthless imbalances perpetrated in the interests of the ignorantly super-rich, to put it mildly, interests exemplified by the frequently grotesque present administration in the United States. The *environment of ideas* is hence critical and depends entirely on a more courageous and intelligent resistance to monopoly power, which is but another name for the "absolute" power of which Lord Acton said (and he

was in religion a Catholic) that it "corrupts absolutely." Monopoly in itself is violently anti-environmentalist, and in the light of this claim it is critical that we understand the distinction between a totalitarian state and what Whitman called "cohesion at all costs."

5. Crane used his own phrase, "adagios of islands" *(Voyages II),* to illustrate this "poetic logic" or movement of thought through which images in a poem possess a logic. See Allen Grossman, "Hart Crane's Intense Poetics," in *Hart Crane,* ed. Harold Bloom (New York, 1986), 221–54.

6. Bertrand Russell, *Problems of Philosophy,* 51.

7. Ibid., 48.

8. Scott's diary (March 1826) was quoted by J. G. Lockhart in his *Memoirs of the Life of Sir Walter Scott, Bart.* I quote Lockhart from my copy of the Cadell 2nd ed. (Edinburgh, 1839), vol. VIII, 292. See Claire Thomalin, *Jane Austen: A Life* (New York, 1997), 257.

9. Michel Foucault, *The Order of Things* (New York, 1970), 346. Besides numerous texts of Paul Valéry on the precision of poetic expression, see Gérard Genette, *Mimologics,* tr. Thais E. Morgan (Lincoln, Neb., 1995), esp. ch. 12, "Failing Natural Languages," 226–29.

10. David Reynolds, *Walt Whitman's America,* (New York, 1995), esp. chs. 3, 4, 5. Bryant, a more reliable editor than Whitman, one must admit, occupied the chief editor's desk for about 50 years at the *New York Evening Post;* we should also recall Poe's journalistic career.

11. William Kovach and Thomas Rosensteil, *Elements of Journalism: What Newspeople Should Know and the Public Should Expect* (New York, 2001). Since the authors assume that "the primary purpose of journalism is to provide citizens with the information they need to be free and self-governing" (17), one must ask: what is the value of unmeasured, unpondered stories when, as logic dictates, the news dies as soon as it is no longer new? In short, the idea of information needs to be scrutinized for the life span of the newspaper story, or worse, the TV story. It is as if, in a serious traditional sense, these are not really stories at all, but opinion dressed up in narrative clothing. Or, to push further, the role of opinion is so great that the required neutrality of true or false information cannot be retained, given the desperate need to pretend that the news is not instantly dying. Nor is this the fault of readers or viewers. The mortality of

information is built into any mode of future-leaning discourse; future shock is already dead.

12. Alexis de Tocqueville, *Democracy in America,* vol. I, tr. Reeve, rev. Francis Bowen (New York, 1954), ch. XI, "Liberty of the Press in the United States." He sees there is nothing sacrosanct about claims for this liberty, albeit required by the First Amendment. The press, he says, has "a singular power, so strangely composed of mingled good and evil that liberty could hardly live without it, and public order can hardly be maintained against it" (191).

13. Chuck Anderson, *The Big Lie: The Truth about Advertising* (London, 2000). Anderson's inside view, while mostly involving British businesses, derives authority in part from his own considerable success as an advertising executive—it takes one, to know one!—and his expositions apply most seriously to advertising as a mode of gaining political power.

14. Tocqueville, *Democracy in America,* vol. I, 194.

15. Jorge Luis Borges, *Collected Fictions,* tr. Andrew Hurley (New York, 1998), 135. Throughout Borges there runs a paradox of the denumerable infinity of signs and objects, as in the stories "The Library of Babel" and "Tlön, Uqbar, Orbis Tertius."

16. Erich Auerbach, *Mimesis: The Representation of Reality in Western Literature,* tr. Willard R. Trask (Princeton, 1953), ch. 18, "The Interrupted Supper."

17. "Iter Boreale," in *The Poems of Richard Corbett,* ed. J. A. W. Bennett, and H. R. Trevor-Roper (Oxford, 1955), 31–48. We might suppose that this modest and light-toned poem is the origin of such great works as "The Prelude"! In Corbett and other Cavalier poets and Royalists one sees the beginning of a major poetic nostalgia (cf. Corbett's once famous lyric, the ballad "Farewell, Rewards and Faeries"). The journey in some sense recurs to the myth of the Golden Age, but slowly accretes a more naturalistic manner. Herrick, a Royalist, shares this Horatian dream.

18. See M. A. Screech, *Montaigne and Melancholy: The Wisdom of the Essays* (London, 2000), 80–81, on Heraclitus in Montaigne.

19. Roy Porter, *The Creation of the Modern World: The Untold Story of the Enlightenment* (New York, 2000), 205 and n3, p. 539. The late Professor Porter's story may not have been quite "untold," but it certainly was never recounted in more lively and significant style. As discourses of

measured and psychological time, we might contrast Roy Porter's clocks with the "early modern" colloquy between Falstaff and Prince Hal on that very subject. By the eighteenth century the clock had become the chronometer, and in every way a scientific instrument. Mechanized time has been with us ever since, so that one interest of the environment-poem is to find a place for unmeasured, but diurnally experienced time. For an excellent introduction to time-experience, etc., see D. H. Mellor, *Real Time* (Cambridge, 1981), esp. ch. 3, "The Presence of Experience." At issue are some of the most profound questions of the "action" of consciousness, whose character is perhaps most familiar to us from the famed words of St. Augustine (*Confessions, X*) on his trouble with defining time—the original *je ne sais quoi* of Western philosophy.

20. Alexander William Kinglake, *Eothen* (London, 1908), 62.

21. Dylan Thomas, stanza 2 of "Altarwise by Owl-Light," in *The Poems of Dylan Thomas,* ed. Daniel Jones (New York, 1971), 171.

22. David Herd, *John Ashbery and American Poetry* (New York, 2000), 130.

6. The Whitman Phrase

1. From *The Life and Letters of John Burroughs.* The naturalist wrote two books about Whitman, and knew him well. My citation comes from Burroughs' notebook used in compiling *Notes on Walt Whitman as Poet and Person* (1867)—from *Whitman in His Own Time,* ed. Joel Myerson (Iowa City, 1991), 311–12.

2. John Donne: *Sermons,* ed. Evelyn M. Simpson and George R. Potter (Berkeley, 1956), vol. VIII, 221. This Easter sermon of 1628 was preached on the text of *I Corinthians* 13.12, "For now we see through a glass darkly, but then face to face." "Then" is a day of resurrection.

3. I have generally used, for Whitman prose texts, *Walt Whitman,* ed. Justin Kaplan (New York: *Library of America,* 1982) (henceforth *LA*). As here, 662. For the verse I have mainly used the *Norton Critical Edition* (henceforth *NTN*) of *Leaves of Grass,* ed. Sculley Bradley and Harold W. Blodgett (New York, 1973). This edition uses the editors' 1965 *New York University Edition.*

4. Whitman, "Salut au Monde," *NTN*, 137. The order counts: in line forty-one Whitman asks, "What do you see Walt Whitman?" and in line forty-three answers, proceeding for another fifteen consecutive anaphoric lines, with "I see." His method is established subtly in Section One, but directly in Section Two, which begins, "What do you hear Walt Whitman," and builds eighteen subsequent lines, all beginning, "I hear." The question for poetic history is simple-seeming in theory: how does the Whitman line, based on his phrase, lead as model to the loosened line-shapes of later poets such as Ashbery (and he belongs in a virtual galaxy of American poets.)? My view, as detailed in later chapters, is that by metonymic détente such later poets substitute their merely accumulated, i.e., not anaphorically linked, image-clusters in sequent lines and paragraphs. E.g., in "Grand Galop," in John Ashbery, *Self-Portrait in a Convex Mirror* (New York, 1975), the poem opens by announcing a potential catalogue, which it then loosely, but not anaphorically, provides: "All things seem mention of themselves / And the names which stem from them branch out to other referents."

5. See Robert Faner, *Walt Whitman and the Opera* (Carbondale, 1951), esp. ch. 5. On the Galilei and opera, see Fred Kersten, *Galileo and the 'Invention' of Opera: A Study in the Phenomenology of Consciousness* (Dordrecht, 1997). Kersten is writing in difficult Husserlian terms, but his book is important because it gives a formal basis for understanding opera as *Gesamtkunstwerk*—the composite of many dimensions of aesthetic effect—and hence a formal basis of explaining Whitman's feeling for the operatic aggregate form. I am grateful to Christine Skarda for drawing my attention to Kersten. One could easily show that opera is the most experimental of all Western art forms.

6. Walt Whitman, "Italian Music in Dakota," *Autumn Rivulets, NTN*, 400. Composers here are Bellini (*Somnambula* and *Norma*) and Donizetti *(Poliuto)*, masters of bel canto, notable for its fioritura style, from which Whitman gets some of his ideas about his poetic of the aria and the recitative.

7. A central passage in *The New Science of Giambattista Vico*, tr. Thomas Bergin and Max Fisch, 3rd ed. (Ithaca, 1968), book two. Numerous articles in *New Vico Studies*, ed. by Donald Verene, and formerly

by the late, much beloved, now greatly missed Giorgio Tagliacozzo, will indicate the scope of application for Vico's concept of a general poetics. My own contribution is "*Dipintura:* The Visual Icon of Historicism in Vico," in *Colors of the Mind: Conjectures on Thinking in Literature* (Cambridge, Mass., 1991), 147–65.

8. I owe this point to my learned friend Mitchell Meltzer, who is generally interested in more theoretical or visionary matters.

9. Whitman, *A Backward Glance, LA,* 662. Pragmatism is here too broad a reading of "science," since Whitman clearly explored the latter in what for him were the available avenues of "popular science." The topic calls for further research as to the paradox of any modern science becoming a "popular" interest, for this means much to American expansion as a function of engineering skills. The United States is the only country to have literally grown up along with the development of modern technology—Britain, by contrast, was already full grown by the seventeenth century, despite all sorts of internal political strife. Imperialism plays a central role in the resourcing of this technological development, but the United States is unusual in that technology has molded our whole way of life, from the beginning—just consider Mark Twain's riverboats, or the new agricultural machinery and its relation to very large plowed and harvested lands, or the cotton gin, not to mention the engineered machines of electronic power. The main point is the coterminous character of these advances. In American history they are not overlays; they are the armatures, to use Ashbery's word.

10. Whitman, *Democratic Vistas, LA,* 942.

11. Ibid., *LA,* 952.

12. Ibid., *LA,* 958.

13. Whitman (ibid., *LA,* 990–91) castigates "the blind fury of parties, infidelity, entire lack of first-class captains and leaders, added to the meanness and vulgarity of the ostensible masses." Alluding here to *Lycidas,* he is yet entirely modern, aligning the vulgarity of the new masses with their industrial condition—this is 1871—"the labor question, beginning to open like a yawning gulf, rapidly widening every year." What would he say today, thinking of what he calls "scrofulous wealth?" Not to mention the "wily person in office?" This is a dubious time, and he would have hated the moneyed hypocrisy of it, as subversive and treasonous.

14. Ibid., *LA,* 956 ff.; he also says that the machinery of modern society "can no more be stopp'd than the tides, or the earth in its orbit."

15. Ibid., *LA,* 988.

16. Ibid., *LA,* 991.

17. Ibid., *LA,* 992.

18. Charles Eliot Norton, review of *Leaves,* Sept. 1855, in *A Century of Whitman Criticism,* ed E. H. Miller (Bloomington, 1969), 2.

19. William Dean Howells, review of *Leaves,* Nov. 1855, in ibid., 7.

20. See *A Century,* 13–18, for Henry James's review of *Drum Taps,* Nov. 1865. The review reveals more about its author than about its subject, as contrasted with the Howells piece, which is a remarkable evocation of Whitman's art. Fred Kaplan, *Henry James: The Imagination of Genius* (New York, 1992), 498–99, tells the moving story of James in later years reading Whitman's poems aloud to the company at Edith Wharton's house: "his voice filled the room like an organ adagio," she said. He crooned "Out of the Cradle" "in a mood of subdued ecstasy." Hearing James read aloud "from his soul," Wharton was less surprised to hear him also say that he considered Whitman "the greatest of American poets."

21. Edward Pessen, *Jacksonian America,* rev. ed. (Urbana, Il., 1985), 194. An essential condition of historical understanding is thus stated by Pessen: "The complexity of truth suggests that at times in history, personality prevails over ideology, petty and subjective motives account for the behavior of mighty men, entire nations are turned this way or that by actions more accidental than designed. Significant issues *were* touched on by every act of the Jackson administration. But they are not exclusively the great issues of class, property, distribution of wealth, or social status" (290). The remarks immediately following in my own text are taken from another expert work on the Jacksonian era, by Robert V. Remini. See his lectures, *The Legacy of Andrew Jackson: Essays on Democracy, Indian Removal, and Slavery* (Baton Rouge, 1988), 24. Few presidents have aroused more heated opinions, and I focus deliberately on Jackson's part in the legacy of universal suffrage. An equal voting right is more often an ideal than a fact, but as I develop the grammar of the Whitman phrase, I insist that the idea of universal suffrage makes all the difference to the way Whitman wrote.

22. *Letters of George Gissing to Eduard Bertz,* ed. A. C. Young (London, 1961), 163.

23. Sean Wilentz, *Chants Democratic: New York City and the Rise of the American Working Class, 1788–1850* (New York, 1984), 115–16.

24. By altering "parcel" to "particle," Emerson gives to his *Nature,* ch. I the note of science, all the brighter since this belongs to a nature "uplifted into infinite space." At this moment Emerson is an astronomer, but as scientist, despite his enthusiasm over the modern Jardin des Plantes, he rather resembles a Presocratic cosmologist.

25. See Marcel Proust, *A la recherche du temps perdu,* vol. I, *A l'ombre des jeunes filles en fleurs* (Paris, Pléiade ed.), 529, 531, 536; vol. II, 47, 584; vol. III, passim, as indexed under "Noms de Personnes," 1279. In C. K. Scott Moncrieff, *Remembrance of Things Past,* tr., ed., and retranslated by Terence Kilmartin and Andreas Mayor (New York, 1981), vol. III, 242, 256, 260, 262–63, 380–82, and throughout *Time Regained,* e.g., 899–903, where the power of the musical phrase (and its visual equivalents in painting and the novel) is explored as the stimulus to memory.

26. Whitman, "A Broadway Pageant," sec. 2., lines 61–65, *NTN,* 245.

27. Leo Spitzer, "*Explication de Texte* Applied to Walt Whitman's Poem 'Out of the Cradle Endlessly Rocking'" (1949), *in A Century of Whitman Criticism,* ed. E. H. Miller (Bloomington, 1969), 273–84. Paul Claudel's method of "chaotic enumeration" accords with Spitzer's study of environing context in *Classical and Christian Ideas of World Harmony: Prolegomena to an Interpretation of the Word "Stimmung,"* ed. Anna G. Hatcher (Baltimore, 1963), and is specified in "Interpretation of an Ode by Paul Claudel," in *Linguistics and Literary History* (Princeton, 1948), 193–236; reptd. in Leo Spitzer: *Representative Essays,* ed. A. K. Forcione et al. (Stanford, 1988), 273–326.

28. "Sea Surface Full of Clouds" in Wallace Stevens, *Collected Poems* (New York, 1964), 100. "The macabre of the water glooms / In an enormous undulation fled," comes at the end of sec. II.

29. I link environmental thought with a paradox of *Walden,* discovered there by Stanley Cavell, *The Senses of Walden* (San Francisco, 1981), 54: "that what is most intimate is furthest away." See Cavell, *The Claim of Reason,* parts II and IV. Also, *In Quest of the Ordinary: Lines of Skepticism and Romanticism* (Chicago, 1988), especially the Tanner Lecture

(1986) on "The Uncanniness of the Ordinary," 153–80, and "Postscript A. Skepticism and a Word Concerning Deconstruction," 130–36, with Postscripts B and C also concerning metaphoric usage in relation to the "unnatural" (146–47). Emerson's essay on Montaigne is subtitled, "Or, Skeptic."

30. Whitman, "A Thought," *NTN,* 704.

31. Ezra Greenspan, ed., *The Cambridge Companion to Walt Whitman* (Cambridge, 1995), "Some Remarks on the Poetics of 'Participle-loving Whitman,'" 92–109. See the sensitive reading of "When lilacs last," by Helen Vendler, in *Textual Analysis: Some Readers Reading,* ed. Mary Ann Caws (New York, 1986), 132–43, especially 142: "The rhythm of the death carol is not periodic. Rather, like the waves of the ocean or the verses of poetry, it is recursive, recurrent, undulant, self-reflexive, self-perpetuating." See above in my Chapter 12, "Waves and the Troping of Poetic Form."

32. Proust, *The Guermantes Way,* tr. Moncrieff and Kilmartin, 472.

33. Emerson, *Essays: First Series,* "Circles," in *Ralph Waldo Emerson: Essays and Lectures,* ed. Joel Porte (LA, 1983), 410. See Eric Wilson, *Emerson's Sublime Science* (London, 1999), 76–98 ("Electric Cosmos"), and 70–75, on "Emerson's Hermeticism." Wilson shows that the influence of Goethe's nature philosophy upon Emerson had a strong hermetic tinge, which of course marks all Romantic literature insofar as it dwells, in the tradition of Renaissance alchemy, upon "affinities" between elements and different levels of natural being. Such is very much the general tenor of Emerson's Oration for the Society of the Adelphi (1841), "The Method of Nature," where he speaks of "elective attractions" (*LA,* 118), but the Goethean notion of elective affinities runs all through the *Essays.* Electricity in this discourse is always elective; there is a general fascination, as evidenced by the popular lectures of Faraday, with the mutual attraction of positive and negative charges, a fascination that rewrites the dialectic notions of logical polarities and their interaction in Hegelian terms. The North and South Poles are now electrified.

34. Whitman, *Specimen Days, LA,* 850–68, under the title "An Egotistical 'Find,'" 855–56. See W. C. Harris on Whitman and the stress of Union: *Arizona Quarterly,* 56, no. 1 (2000), 29–61.

35. The reader should consult Bloom's essay, "Whitman's Image of Voice: To the Tally of My Soul," in *Walt Whitman,* ed. Harold Bloom

(New York, 1985), 127–42; also, Bloom, "Freud and the Poetic Sublime," in *Poetics of Influence,* ed. John Hollander ((New Haven, 1988), for background to the Longinean tradition as it relates to Bloom's Freudian, Kabbalistic, and Gnostic theory of the American Sublime.

36. Harold Rosenberg, *The Tradition of the New* (New York, 1961), part 4, "The Herd of Independent Minds." (A parallel work would be J. L. Borges' satire, *The Chronicles of Bustos Domecq.*) Rosenberg's 1969 *Artworks and Packages* (Chicago, 1982), "Lights! Lights!" discusses the shift from Happenings to Environments in modern art. See also the notice (133) of Louise Nevelson's work, "Atmosphere and Environment I."

37. Abraham Davidson, *The Eccentrics and Other American Visionary Painters* (New York, 1978), 134. In this important passage Davidson distinguishes between the "normal" visionaries among his painters and those sharing Whitman's "cosmic" vision as it establishes an American scale of "vista," the sense of extending *chora* shared by painters like Ryder and especially Blakelock, who go out into the study of light itself, thus avoiding the "spookiness" of the normalizing of vision.

38. "Our Real Culmination," in Whitman, *Complete Prose Works, LA,* 1074.

39. Edwin Markham, *The Man with the Hoe and Other Poems* (New York, 1899). The eloquence of this ekphrastic poem is unexpected, but then we encounter a similar expressive power in other poems, such as "The Whirlwind Road,"—"I felt the Mystery the Muses fear" (line 8). In the 1899 Doubleday and McClure edition, Markham shared copyright with his original publisher and employer/distributor; the co-holder was the *San Francisco Examiner.* The volume's frontispiece was an engraving of its original, and the title poem was "Written after Seeing Millet's World-Famous Painting." "World-Famous" is P. T. Barnum talk, and it fits Markham's generally middle-brow sublimity.

40. *Artist as Critic: The Critical Writings of Oscar Wilde,* ed. Richard Ellmann (New York, 1969), 125.

7. The Environment-Poem

1. *The Poems of Emily Dickinson,* ed. Ralph W. Franklin (Cambridge, Mass., 1998), poem no. F610/J354.

2. When Emerson writes "The world is a plenum or solid; and if we saw all things that really surround us, we should be imprisoned and unable to move," Lee Rust Brown, *The Emerson Museum* (Cambridge, Mass., 1997), 49–50, states that the source is Parmenides. Brown believes that by "tricking or troping our way through the suffocating solidity of the natural sphere," we manage to escape. On *chora* see Ch. 3, n10 above, and Plato, *Timaeus,* tr. and commentary by F. M. Cornford (London, 1908). *Chora* implies spatial extension, space extended around, as opposed to the more sharply pointed, narrowly localized dimensionality of the term "place" or "placement." The latter is traditional in English poetry, from Marvell's "Upon Appleton House" to Wordsworth's poems "on the naming of places." Yet even here, place drifts outward into *chora.* The difference of space and place is subtle and at times elusive; how would one describe the *Four Quartets* or Eliot's miniature *Landscapes?* If one thinks of a poem like Basil Bunting's *Briggflatts* and then, in the Whitman tradition, the various "places" in Hart Crane's *The Bridge,* one despairs of any neat separation, beyond saying that by perceiving the *daimon* of place rather than the "nature" of space or *chora,* one creates an emphasis. Perhaps our guide should come from the title of a lyric of Seamus Heaney, "Field of Vision." What kind of place, or space, is the Pequod, in *Moby Dick—a scene that moves from day to day?* Signatures, *daimons, lares and penates* (a word Walt Whitman wrote in his word-list notebook), and all such pinpointing figures are to a degree opposed to the extension of the "field of vision" that occurs when one perceives the genre of the environment-poem, as a distinctly different operation, perhaps a truly modern one in the sense that "environment," while an ancient intuitive and philosophical experience, is observationally modernized under the influence of science. See the essay *"Khora"* in Jacques Derrida, *On the Name,* tr. Ian McLeod, ed. Thomas Dutoit (Stanford, 1995).

3. A. R. Ammons, *Garbage* (New York, 1993), 101.

4. J. L. Austin, "Performative Utterances," in *Philosophical Papers,* ed. J. O. Urmson and G. J. Warnock (Oxford, 1961), 231.

5. Tenney Nathanson, *Whitman's Presence: Body, Voice and Writing in Leaves of Grass* (New York, 1992).

6. "The Uncanny," in Sigmund Freud, *Collected Papers,* authorized translation under the supervision of Joan Rivière et al. (New York, 1959),

vol. IV: "Papers on Metapsychology," 368–408, esp. 377: "Thus *Heimlich* is a word the meaning of which develops toward an ambivalence, until it finally coincides with its opposite, *Unheimlich. Unheimlich* is in some way or other a sub-species of *Heimlich.*"

7. "Journey to the Interior," in Theodore Roethke, *Collected Poems* (New York, 1975), 187–89. All journeys in poetry, even the *Odyssey* or Joyce's equally "poetic" *Ulysses,* move in some sense "to the interior," owing to the equation between life and pilgrimage of body *and* soul.

8. Sermon 9 (Easter, 1628), in *Sermons of John Donne,* ed. E. M. Simpson and G. R. Potter (Berkeley, 1956), vol. VIII, 219–36. Vision, seeing, and prophecy are diverted in modern literature from the Christian field of Revelation, to be situated rather in the field of the psychic. See Tzvetan Todorov, *The Fantastic: A Structural Approach to a Literary Genre,* tr. Richard Howard (Ithaca, 1975), esp. Ch. 3.

9. Walt Whitman, *Leaves of Grass,* ed. Malcolm Cowley, the 1855 "Song of Myself," lines 403–05. In *NTN,* 47, where the 1892 lineation is identical.

10. Ibid., line 487.

11. Ibid., line 998.

12. At least two issues arise from this sense of an existing or lasting world. (a) How can we be sure it does exist? (b) How far and in what mode does our knowledge of the world extend? The first question, while involving the second, points to fundamental questions of knowledge, of epistemology. The second question, presupposing the first, points to the physics and the observation of knowable things, and it leads eventually to questions such as is space infinite? Both questions finally lead to environmental concerns, given the definition of ecology as "the scientific study of the relationships that exist among organisms and all aspects, living and non-living, of their environments," John Cloudsley-Thompson, *Ecology* (London, 1998), 1.

13. Marc Bloch, quoted in Jacques le Goff, *The Medieval Imagination,* tr. Arthur Goldhammer (Chicago, 1988), 53.

14. Roland Omnès, *Quantum Philosophy: Understanding and Interpreting Comtemporary Science,* tr. Arturo Sangalli (Princeton, 1999), xv.

15. As in Bryant's Wordsworthian exercise, "Inscription for the En-

trance to a Wood," or his common equation of "youth in life's green spring" *(Thanatopsis)* with the guiltless, unchanging garden of the *locus amoenus.* The traditional topos leads, however, to Bryant's "Night Journey of a River," with its ecological sentiment: "Oh, glide away from those abodes, that bring / Pollution to thy channel and make foul / Thy once clear current." This poem may here be looking back to original purity of the Thames River of John Denham's *Cooper's Hill* or "To the River Isca" of the mystical Henry Vaughan—see *The Words of Henry Vaughan,* ed. L. C. Martin (Oxford, 1937), 39–41. Again, the river is among the most ancient elemental scenes of passage, nourishment, purification, and indeed life, and not just for Baptists. Rivers are the purifying terrestrial blood stream of England in Michael Drayton's monumental 1613 rhapsody, the *Poly-Olbion: or a Chorographicall Description of Tracts, Rivers, Mountaines, Forests, etc.*

16. See George Saintsbury's 1874 article on *Leaves of Grass,* in *NTN,* 786.

17. John Cowper Powys, *A Glastonbury Romance* (Woodstock, NY, 1996), 666.

18. Whitman, *NTN,* 840.

19. See my article on James Russell Lowell, *in Garland Companion to American Nineteenth-Century Verse* (New York, 1998).

20. Gilles Deleuze, *Proust and Signs,* tr. Richard Howard (New York, 1972), 96. On the role of momentary reminiscence and its relation to the Idea in Proust, see Deleuze, 96–104: questioning "the antecedent unity of the Search," Proust moves toward an ideal environment, in my sense, "a figure of encasing, of envelopment, of implication." (103)

21. Ibid., 97.

22. André Malraux, *The Conquerors,* tr. Stephen Becker (London, 1983), 184.

23. Jorge Luis Borges, *Selected Poems,* ed. Alexander Coleman (New York, 1999), 213. Alastair Reid's translation: ". . . He mutters to himself: I am almost dead, but still my poems retain / life and its wonders. I was once Walt Whitman." Early Borges, Pablo Neruda, Aimé Césaire, and many other American poets of the twentieth century borrow and learn from Whitman as their chief master. His influence, bad as well as good,

is of course immense. But Whitman's early appeal to Hopkins or Swinburne is perhaps more revealing, since they both extravagantly marked their own literary independence from British tradition.

24. Julian Green, *Diary: 1928–1957,* tr. Anne Green (New York, 1964), 201.

25. Ibid., 137.

26. Bonnie Costello, "John Ashbery's Landscapes," in *The Tribe of John: Ashbery in Contemporary Poetry* (Tuscaloosa, 1995), 60–80.

27. Percy Bysshe Shelley, *A Defence of Poetry,* in Donald H. Reiman, ed., *Shelley's Poetry and Prose* (New York, 2002), 531.

28. Montaigne, *Selected Essays,* tr. Charles Cotton, ed. Blanchard Bates (New York, 1949), 602.

29. The English version of *La Fabrique du Pré* by Lee Fahnestock, *The Making of the Pré* (Colombia, Mo., 1979) presents both English and French texts, including facsimiles of the holograph manuscripts. Fahnestock's arrangement of the volume is an almost perfect rendering of the environment-poem created as an image of diurnal knowledge.

30. "The Groundlark": *John Clare* (Oxford Authors: Oxford, 1974), 273.

31. "The Marten": ibid., 244.

32. The final line of the song, "I wish I was where I would be," in ibid., 411.

8. Waves and the Troping of Poetic Forms

1. Eric Wilson, *Romantic Turbulence: Chaos, Ecology, and American Space* (New York, 2000), 127. Wilson quotes a Whitman squib on the way all molecules of matter "swing too and fro" and fill the space of the universe with a "jelly-like vibration." Scholars familiar with the metaphysics of light in *Paradise Lost* and *The Divine Comedy* will notice how far from these works extends the Whitman plasma, with its unpredictable and highly material wave-like perturbations. In *Walden,* as Sharon Cameron notes in *Writing Nature: Henry Thoreau's Journal* (New York, 1985), 133, the wave motion appears in the flight of hawks "high in the sky, alternately soaring and descending, approaching and leaving one another, as if they were the embodiment of my own thoughts." Thoreau,

as so often, harks back to the Anglican seventeenth century, here to the famed "Digression of Air" in Burton's *Anatomy of Melancholy.*

2. Richard Feynman, *QED: The Strange Theory of Light and Matter* (Princeton, 1985), 23, n3.

3. Ibid., 83–84.

4. Whitman to Traubel, as quoted in John Hollander, *The Work of Poetry* (New York, 1997), 183. Here Hollander is analyzing the internal structure of the Whitman "list." He notes it goes back to the Shield of Achilles in the *Iliad,* a poem of Whitman's earliest reading. See also W. H. Auden, *The Enchafèd Flood: Or the Romantic Iconography of the Sea* (Charlottesville, Va., 1950) and the learned commentary of L. G. Pocock, *Odyssean Essays* (Oxford, 1965), ch. VII, "The Nature of Ocean in the Early Epic." Besides the poems of Hart Crane, especially *Voyages,* the typology of ocean in *Moby Dick* reaches its archetypal horizon when in ch. 132, "The Symphony," Ahab drops a single tear into the ocean—that "one drop" of mercy Doctor Faustus imagined in his desperate last hope for salvation, at the last scene of Marlowe's tragedy.

5. P. Erik Gunderson, *The Handy Physics Answer Book* (Visible Ink Press, 1999), 173. For another definition of the wave, see Edward P. Clancy, *The Tides: Pulse of the Earth* (New York, 1969), 61–69. For those who can do the math, the famed Feynman Cal Tech physics lecture-course, three volumes, edited by Professor Leighton, is recommended. Clancy gives us the basic phenomena: wave length (distance in which the shape of the wave repeats itself), yielding the phase of the wave; directional versus standing waves, some progressing forward while others stand still in one spot or region; amplitudes of waves (their height or depth from trough to crest), their frequency, and so on. Without flow and wave motion it is doubtful that water would have seemed so powerful in human imagination. See Gaston Bachelard, *Water and Dreams: An Essay on the Imagination of Matter,* tr. Edith R. Farrell (Dallas, 1983), esp. 19–70, chs. 1 and 2. Bachelard always takes us back in thought to the Presocratics.

6. Desmond King-Hele, *Erasmus Darwin: Grandfather of Charles Darwin* (New York, 1963). Erasmus Darwin shared in what I have called "the temporalizing of the Great Chain of Being," which underlies the actual historical development of the Sublime in the arts, after the seven-

teenth century. The static traditional world picture had to permit change into its constitution, even to include ruin and decline, as in Gibbon and in many artists, before the Sublime could achieve its relevance to any world the West was trying to imagine. This temporality has still not been sufficiently noticed.

7. A parallel discourse has been explored by Hayden White in his studies of the theory of history. See his *Tropics of Discourse: Essays in Cultural Criticism* (Baltimore, 1978).

8. Given his unusual autodidactic studies of language, and his active use of these studies through the employment of words he carefully listed, defined, and gave pronunciations for, it is impossible to think of Whitman in any other way. The notion belongs to the large historical question as to what made for a new "American language." See James P. Warren, *Walt Whitman's Language Experiment* (University Park, Pa., 1990).

9. Ernst Cassirer, *The Myth of the State* (New Haven, 1961), 250.

10. Ibid., 184.

11. Isaiah Berlin, "Vico's Concept of Knowledge," in *Against the Grain: Essays in the History of Ideas* (Princeton, 2001), 112.

12. John Hollander, *Work of Poetry,* 182.

13. John Hollander, "A Theory of Waves," in *A Crackling of Thorns* (1958), as reprinted in *Selected Poetry* (New York, 1993), 328. I read Racine's poem in *Anthologie de la Poésie Baroque Française,* vol. I, ed. Jean Rousset (Paris, 1968), 246–48. Baroque, among many things, explores the early ideas of modern physics, when its poetry studies reflected surfaces, bubbles, clouds, waves, and various elemental phenomena. A favorite subject is the undulant surfaces of architectural facade, and the metamorphic treatment of scene through lighting-effects—with an accent on the word "effect"—on which see Roland Barthes, *On Racine,* tr. Richard Howard (New York, 1964), 21–24, "The Racinian *tenebroso.*" Chiaroscuro also divides zones of light in paintings into the partials of waves.

14. Hollander, *Work of Poetry,* 184.

15. See "Science and the Poets," in *The Writings of John Burroughs,* vol. VIII, "Indoor Studies" (New York, 1968 reprint), 80. Burroughs describes how Emerson is "aroused" by science with all its surprises and its

"mysteries, its metamorphoses, its perceptions of the unity, of the oneness of nature. . . . In his laboratory you shall witness wonderful combinations, surprising affinities, unexpected relations of opposites, threads and ties unthought of." This recalls Thoreau's *Journal* entry, Sept. 2, 1851: "There are flowers of thought and there are leaves of thought——most of our thoughts are merely leaves—to which the thread of thought is the stem."

16. *Cape Cod,* in *Henry David Thoreau* (*LA,* 1985), 979.

17. Hans Blumenberg, *Shipwreck with Spectator: Paradigm of a Metaphor for Existence,* tr. Steven Rendall (Cambridge, Mass., 1997). Cf. Leopardi's great poem, "L'Infinito." See also George P. Landow, *Images of Crisis: Literary Iconology, 1750 to the Present* (London, 1982), especially ch. 2, "Shipwrecks and Castaways," 35–130.

18. "The Ocean to Cynthia," in *The Poems of Sir Walter Ralegh,* ed. Agnes M. C. Latham (Cambridge, Mass., 1951), lines 426–35.

19. Edmund Spenser, *Shorter Poems,* ed. W. A. Orem et al. (New Haven, 1989), 703, lines 259–65.

20. G. Wilson Allen, *A Reader's Guide to Whitman* (New York, 1970), 166.

21. Jean-Georges Noverre, *Lettres sur la Danse et sur les Ballets (lettre XIV),* quoted by Suzanne Langer, *Feeling and Form: A Theory of Art* (New York, 1953), 172.

22. On William D. O'Connor, see *A Century of Whitman Criticism,* ed. E. H. Miller (Bloomington, 1969), 22–23.

23. Edward Dowden, "The Poetry of Democracy: Walt Whitman," in *A Century,* 40.

24. Randall Jarrell's famous article, "Some Lines from Whitman" appeared in 1953. Quoted here from *A Century,* 228.

25. Ezra Greenspan, in his collection of commentaries, *The Cambridge Companion to Walt Whitman* (Cambridge, 1995), 92–109, "Some Remarks on the Poetics of 'Participle-Loving Whitman'."

26. John Cowper Powys, "Walt Whitman," in *NTN,* 840.

27. The examples above are drawn from Whitman, *NTN,* 34; 109; 100.

28. Benjamin Lee Whorf, "Thinking in Primitive Communities," in *Language, Thought and Reality* (Cambridge, Mass., 1956), 72. Gerald

Holton, in his *Thematic Origins of Scientific Thought* (Cambridge, Mass., 1973), 105, suggests that, in connection with the views of Niels Bohr, the Sapir-Whorf hypothesis applies to "the scientific area of a culture."

29. Ed Folsom, "Appearing in Print: Illustrations of the Self," in *The Cambridge Companion to Walt Whitman,* ed. Ezra Greenspan (Cambridge, 1999), 135–165, esp. 141–42.

30. On Whitman's Macpherson, see David Reynolds, *Walt Whitman's America* (New York, 1995), 314–15. Whitman owned *the Fragments of Ancient Poetry (1760)* in a Philadelphia edition of 1839, titled *The Poems of Ossian.* He both emulated and questioned the inflated style of Macpherson's frequent apostrophes ("O Thou that rollest above," etc.), warning himself on one occasion, "Don't fall into the Ossianic, by any chance." Reynolds and others have observed that the Ossianic model served the development of the prose-poem.

31. The Marquis de Chastellux, *Travels in North America in the Years 1780, 1781, and 1782,* tr. H. C. Rice (Chapel Hill, 1963), vol. II, 392.

32. Whitman, *Specimen Days,* in *LA,* 15–16.

33. Gérard Genette, *Figures of Literary Discourse,* 96. The obscurity of Whitman's stylistic origins in part arises from our not seeing that for him Sir Walter Scott's poems, which he knew early, along with Ossian and the ancient epics, would have had the effect of rhapsodic roll-calling, would lead into his own anaphoric techniques. Furthermore, European travelers, including such fine-tuned listeners as Charles Dickens, would hear at once that Americans had a passion for fustian which, some have thought, is the basis for the over-the-top grandeur of Marlowe's plays, particularly the two Parts of *Tamburlaine.* Of course, Marlowe was so popular that he was himself partly responsible for the fustian fashion. He certainly knew how to exploit it. On the mirth caused by the American language, see the John S. Whitley and Arnold Goldman introduction to Charles Dickens, *American Notes for General Circulation* (1842), in the Penguin Edition (1985), 23–25. Dickens was delighted by the Choctaw chief, Pitchlynn, who was a great reader and who had been greatly impressed by the battle scenes in *Marmion* ("'On, Stanley! On,' were the last words of Marmion," as my own father would quote, with a chuckle). As for the Indian chief, "Scott's poetry appeared to have left a strong impression on his mind," says Dickens (*Notes,* 210).

9. Middle Voice

1. Emile Benveniste, *Problems in General Linguistics,* tr. Mary Elizabeth Meek (Coral Gables, 1997), ch. 14, "Active and Middle Voice in the Verb," 145–52.

2. Herbert W. Smythe, *Greek Grammar* (Cambridge, Mass., 1978).

3. Whitman, "What can the future bring," *NTN,* 631.

4. Whitman, "Native Moments," *NTN,* 109.

5. Eric Charles White, *Kaironomia: On the Will-to-Invent* (Ithaca, 1987), 53n.

6. Whitman, "Song of the Answerer," *NTN,* 166.

7. A. N. Whitehead, *Modes of Thought* (New York, 1968), 66.

8. These lines were eventually excluded from *Leaves,* but had appeared in 1860. See Whitman, *NTN,* 635.

9. Whitehead, *Modes of Thought,* 74. Whitehead's Fourth lecture, "Perspective," relates to vagueness and detail in the construction of aggregates, as with an environmental manifold. In *Process and Reality: An Essay in Cosmology* (1928), ed. D. R. Griffin and D. W. Sherburne (New York, 1978), 204, Whitehead is concerned to hold that society is plausibly a human "environment" for humans, since humans are "social animals" (Aristotle) in every sense.

10. See R. M. Sainsbury, *Paradoxes* (Cambridge, 1988), "Vagueness: The Paradox of the Heap," 25–49. Sainsbury is concerned with vague objects as he calls them, "mountains are part of reality, but they are vague. They have no sharp boundaries: It is vague where the mountain ends and the plain begins. So it is easy to see that vagueness is a feature of reality, and not just of our thought and talk." For Ashbery's poetics it is clear that vagueness is a defining issue, as for Whitman it is the heap.

11. For anecdotes from Helen Price see *Whitman in His Own Time,* ed. Joel Myerson (Iowa City, 2000), 26.

12. See Whitehead, *Modes of Thought,* 111, 164.

13. Whitman, *NTN,* 642.

14. John Ashbery, "The System," in *Three Poems* (New York, 1986), 59. While Ashbery has written lyric poems, both long and short, "The System" with its poetic prose remains the most important descendent of the

Preface to the 1855 *Leaves of Grass,* and it virtually defines the conditions of the environment-poem of the future.

15. Charles Feidelson, *Symbolism and American Literature* (Chicago, 1965), 17–19.

16. Coleridge quoted in Richard Holmes, *Coleridge: Early Visions* (New York, 1990), 230, from *The Friend,* II, Dec. 1809.

17. Betsy Erkkila, *Walt Whitman among the French* (Princeton, 1950). See especially ch. II, sec. V, on Stuart Merrill and Francis Vielé-Griffin. On the latter see Valéry's memorial tribute, "The Necessity of Poetry," in *The Art of Poetry,* tr. Denise Folliot (New York, 1961), 216–30. T. S. Eliot's Introduction to this volume makes the useful comment: "No one should write 'free verse'—or at least offer it for publication—until he has discovered for himself that free verse allows him no more freedom than any other verse" (xiii).

10. Ashbery and the Becoming of the Poem

1. I have here used Kathleen Freeman's translation of Fragment 9, from her *Ancilla to the Pre-Socratic Philosophers,* 93.

2. See Martin Heidegger, "On the Essence of Ground," in *Pathmarks* (Cambridge, 1998), 97–135. I am aware of all the political overtones of "ground"—as in the present Homeland Security legislation, nothing could be more obviously incorrect for American democracy than to emphasize the Germanic *Heimat.* At issue always is the environmental question; what, in practice if not in principle, is the method of properly harmonizing the many (individuals) with the singular (one idea, one nation, etc.). It was to understand some of the pragmatics of these questions on the American scene that Kenneth Burke developed his ideas of political "mystification" as a device for "courtship" or political seduction. Underlying the pragmatics of our national motto, *e pluribus unum,* there are deeper questions which were long ago confronted in ancient Athens; see Jean-Pierre Vernant, *Origins of Greek Thought* (Ithaca, 1982), ch. 6, "The Structure of the Human Cosmos."

3. See Arthur Rimbaud: the poems "Départ," "Les Ponts," and "Génie," and on these Yves Bonnefoy, *Rimbaud,* tr. Paul Schmidt (New York, 1961), for a sense of the link in Rimbaud between the discontinuous im-

age, the idea of departure *en voyage,* and the role of hallucination in these disarticulations. One asks: does Whitman hallucinate his imagery? Is he, although grounded in journalistic and diurnal fact, a literary cousin of Henri Michaux, who took fantastic voyages and provided all their names? He would belong then in Ashbery's "other tradition," with Raymond Roussel of *Impressions d'Afrique.*

4. Ezra Pound, "Papyrus": *Personae* (New York, 1926), 112.

5. Heidegger, *Early Greek Thinking,* 79.

6. Recalling Derrida, this question points to the crossover between alchemical symbolism (signatures) of the letter, the status of the self and identity (the person), negative theology, Kabbalah, and the "ownership" of real property that concerns Derrida, especially as regards intellectual property.

7. Many Ammons poems, including his distinctly environment-poems like the late *Garbage,* also infiltrate philosophical diction in order to question the "existences" he mentioned—examples would be "Abscission," "Putting on Airs," "Saying saying away," in A. R. Ammons, *Brink Road* (New York, 1996).

8. Charles Kahn, "Why Existence Does Not Emerge as a Distinct Concept in Greek Philosophy," in *Philosophies of Existence,* ed. Parviz Morewedge (New York, 1982), 8, 15–16. See also the editor's "Greek Sources of Some Near Eastern Philosophies of Being and Existence," in the same volume, 285–336.

9. Freud, "The Relation of the Poet and Day-dreaming" (1908), in the *Collected Papers* (New York, 1951), vol. 4, 177: "From there it wanders back [from a current stimulus] to the memory of an early experience . . . then it creates for itself . . . in the future, representing the fulfillment of the wish." Wandering here gives the poet the fluency and digressive play that amounts to imaginative exploration. This is much like Wordsworth's poetic theory of emotion recollected. In Clare and Ashbery the wandering is not entirely intrapsychic, especially with Clare making his rounds; they assemble Nature's chaotic report card.

10. John Shoptaw, *On the Outside Looking Out: John Ashbery's Poetry* (Cambridge., Mass., 1994). On flux, see the concentrated discussion of Ashbery's *Flow Chart* (pp. 301–41), a remarkable exegesis by any standard.

11. *Philosophy and Truth: Selections from Nietzsche's Notebooks of the Early 1870's,* ed. and tr. Daniel Breazeale (Amherst, NY, 1999), 53.

12. Joyce, *Critical Writings,* ed. Richard Ellmann (Ithaca, 1989), 81.

13. See Shoptaw, *On the Outside Looking Out,* 139, on Ashbery's finding it "easy to move from one person in the sense of a pronoun to another," as the poet expressed his lability of personhood in his poems.

14. Roman Jakobson, *Language in Literature,* ed. Krystina Pomorska and Stephen Rudy (Cambridge, Mass., 1987), "Two Aspects of Language and Two Types of Aphasic Disturbances" (95–120) and "Marginal Notes on the Prose of the Poet Pasternak" (301–17). On Ashbery and Pasternak, see David Herd, *John Ashbery and American Poetry* (New York, 2000), 10–13, 35–38, 44–49.

15. See Jakobson, "Marginal Notes," 307. Here, to fill the environment, "it is association by contiguity that predominates." The play of distances in Pasternak's *Safe Conduct* "transforms inanimate objects into a distant, motionless horizon" (311), a metonymic play, as in Ashbery, allowing the poem to "dislocate familiar relationships."

16. See Jakobson, "Marginal Notes, 311–13.

17. Jakobson, "Two Aspects," 111.

18. Donald Davidson, "On the Very Idea of a Conceptual Scheme," in *Post-Analytical Philosophy,* ed. John Rajchman and Cornell West (New York, 1985), 129–44. In regard to Quine, Feyerabend, and Kuhn, Davidson questions the use of "paradigm." He writes: "And the criterion of a conceptual scheme different from our own now becomes largely true but not translatable." *Traduttore, traditore.*

19. Jakobson, "Marginal Notes," 314.

11. Meditating Chaos and Complexity

1. Edward Lorenz, *The Essence of Chaos* (Seattle, 1995), 21–22, 118–19, 126–27.

2. Harold Bloom, "The Charity of Hard Moments," in *Figures of Capable Imagination* (New York, 1976), 169–208. On Ashbery as poet of process, see Merle Brown, "Poetic Listening," *New Literary History* 10, 1 (Autumn 1978), 137.

3. *Notebooks of Joseph Joubert: A Selection,* tr. and ed. Paul Auster, af-

terword by Maurice Blanchot (San Francisco, 1983), 156; this selection available in Paul Auster, *Translations* (Marsilio Publishers, 1997), which also includes Mallarmé, Du Bouchet, and Philippe Petit.

4. Eric Partridge, *Origins: A Short Etymological Dictionary of Modern English* (New York, 1958), 393b.

5. Sir Philip Sidney, *Astrophil and Stella,* Sonnet I. More than one sonnet in the sequence delivers a sense of the problem of originality for Sidney (see Hollander, *Work of Poetry,* "Originality"). For example, Sonnet XV, "You that do search for every purling spring," where the term "denizen'd" connotes native-born and hence leads to the question: how can love be a natural rather than simply artificial "construction" controlled for us by a prior society? Should love not be artificial, for many reasons? Hence, where are the "purling springs" to come from—the garden or the wild?

6. Marie-Rose Logan, "Writing the Self: Guillaume Budé's Poetics of Scholarship," in *Contending Kingdoms: Historical, Psychological, and Feminist Approaches to the Literature of Sixteenth-Century England and France,* ed. Marie-Rose Logan and Peter L. Rudnytsky (Detroit, 1991), 134.

7. Marc Fumaroli, quoted by Logan from his article, "Genèse de l'épistolographie classique: Rhétorique humaniste de la lettre de Pétrarche à Juste Lipse," *Revue d'Histoire Littéraire de la France* 78, 5 (1978), 888. Epistolary verse by the same token has a long and fascinating history, going back to Horace, enriched in the English Renaissance by the *Verse Letters* of Donne, then later the neoclassic *Epistles* of Pope, and shifting into free forms after, say, Dickinson's lyric, "This is my letter to the world." The "informal letter" provides a conventionally complex model for the dazzling miscellany that in the correspondence of Lord Byron draws us into a world which at any moment Byron discovered all around him; his aim, we might say, is to surround and conquer.

8. John Ashbery, "Young Man with Letter," in *The Double Dream of Spring* (New York, 1976), 66. We need to invoke a new imagination, if we are to understand the paramount cultural role of the personal letter, or indeed the diplomatic and commercial letters of earlier times. Our use of telephones and email has changed the basic situation, which was "waiting for the letters to come" and "have you seen the mailman?" and indeed all the changes De Quincey had earlier described in his "English

Mail Coach." Epistolary correspondence alters the size, the scale, and the scope of any social environment, as we see every day with our newly "enabled" society, as it tries to deal not only with the almost unavoidable frauds, but also with the material advantages conferred by the telecommunications industry.

9. John Ashbery, *Flow Chart* (New York, 1991), 3. On these lines see John Shoptaw, *On the Outside Looking Out* (Cambridge, Mass., 1994), 312–15.

10. John Ashbery, "Crossroads in the Past," in *Your Name Here* (New York, 2000), 76.

11. Ashbery, *Flow Chart,* 132.

12. John Ashbery, "Proust's Questionnaire," in *A Wave* (New York, 1984), 50.

13. Ashbery, "Cups with Broken Handles," in *A Wave,* 51.

14. John Ashbery, "The System," the second of the *Three Poems* (New York, 1977), 58.

15. Ibid., 87–88.

16. See Martin Gardner, *The Ambidextrous Universe* (New York, 1964), vii, 209–19. This "fall of parity" occurred in 1957; particles of a rare sort were found to exist which did not display parity—the universal assumption of post-Newtonian physics—when their property of spin failed to display an equally even-handed left-right symmetry. If the universe is not fundamentally symmetrical, then events will drift forward or sidewise in such fashion that no basic classic order of oppositions will hold all the forces in check. Without a certain systemic parity, for example, the U.S. Constitution cannot operate. Ashbery's poetry is always concerned with such sidewise drifting, and his best known poem, "Self-Portrait in a Convex Mirror," shows one way in which parity is prevented in the actual world of our conscious self-awareness. Mirrors are the basic issue for Gardner's ambidextrous universe. Reflection and the reflexive are a lot more puzzling than casual conversation might suggest, starting with the fact that we do not turn upside down when we look at ourselves in a mirror.

17. Ashbery, *Flow Chart,* 199. To the rich psychological senses of "metal," think of Shakespeare's "mettle" usage, and add the fact that metal is the material from which is made "the armature / that supports all these varied and indeed desperate initiatives," as the poem says. But if

metal belongs to mind, it must be mental also and must provide the armature of "the best model anyone has thought up / so far . . ." The sense of metal can by transumption be sexual, as in Byron's "sword wears out its sheath," but in any case brings up the idea of tempering one's understanding and discourse.

18. Ashbery, *Flow Chart,* 194.

19. John Holland, *Emergence: From Chaos to Order* (Cambridge, Mass., 1998), 225; Holland, *Hidden Order: How Adaptation Builds Complexity* (Reading, Mass., 1995), 5–36,—an outline of the seven basics. For a direct application of Holland's account see my article (forthcoming in *Literary Imagination*), "Complexity and the Spenserian Myth of Mutability." My particular reasons for treating *The Mutabilitie Cantos* include these: (a) they treat chaos and complexity directly, through an epochal narrative of cosmological debate, and (b) they belong with *The Faerie Queene,* which is the founding text or poem for the full-blown English Romantic tradition, and hence for Romanticism itself, and not just in Britain.

20. Holland, *Hidden Order,* 37.

21. James P. Crutchfield, "Is Anything Ever New? Considering Emergence," in *Complexity: Metaphors, Models, and Reality,* ed. George Cowan et al. Vol. XIX *of Santa Fe Institute Studies in the Sciences of Complexity* (Reading, Mass., 1994), 479–97. See also Crutchfield, "When Evolution Is Revolution—Origins of Innovation," in *Evolutionary Dynamics* (Santa Fe, 2001), 1–33. The development of interlinked computer networks has permitted researchers like Crutchfield to model evolutionary changes, with their unexpected emergent patterns arising from initial states, moving through chaos to cosmos and back again, so that the computer program effectively is a growing or evolving organism of mathematical properties. General introductions to the field: M. Mitchell Waldrop, *Complexity: The Emerging Science at the Edge of Order and Chaos* (New York, 1992); David Ruelle, *Chance and Chaos* (Princeton, 1991); Stuart Kauffman, *At Home in the Universe: The Search for the Laws of Self-Organization and Complexity* (New York, 1995); *Chaos and Order: Complex Dynamics in Literature and Science,* ed. N. Katherine Hayles (1991); Hayles herself has written extensively on the literary implications of the new science, e.g., *Chaos Bound: Orderly Disorder in Contemporary Literature and Science* (Ithaca, 1990).

12. "The Long Amazing and Unprecedented Way"

1. Byron, not unlike Dryden, is explicit about what I call, in honor of my friend Harold Bloom, "the anxiety of inspiration." In another letter (see *Byron's Letters and Journals,* ed. Leslie Marchand [Cambridge, Mass., 1976], vol. 5, 165) he writes to Moore: "I was half mad during the time of its composition [it was *Childe Harold,* Canto III], between metaphysics, mountains, lakes, love inextinguishable, thoughts unutterable, and the nightmare of my own delinquencies." He would have blown his brains out, he says, except it would have pleased his mother-in-law.

2. John Ashbery, "Not only / But also," in *As We Know* (New York, 1979), 86.

3. On *Flow Chart,* besides the chapter about it in Shoptaw, *On the Outside,* see David Herd, *John Ashbery and American Poetry* (New York, 2000), 209–15. See, in general, the nuanced comments of Richard Howard, "You never know how much is pushed back into the night" (1980), reprinted in *The Chelsea House Library of Literary Criticism,* ed. Harold Bloom (New York, 1989), under "Ashbery," 207–16.

4. Jorge Luis Borges, "A New Refutation of Time," in *Labyrinths,* ed. D. A. Yates and J. E. Irby (New York, 1964), 217–34. The story is included in the *Selected Non-Fictions,* ed. Eliot Weinberger (New York, 1999), 316–32.

5. Erwin Panofsky, "The History of the Theory of Human Proportions as a Reflection of the History of Styles," in *Meaning in the Visual Arts* (New York, 1970), 82–138.

6. James Merrill, *Scripts for the Pageant* (New York, 1980), 196. "Samos," which opens the middle phase of *Scripts,* is a complex double sestina, reflecting (for its midpoint function) the Sidneyan use of the form to balance other materials at a fulcrum, to permit an oscillation around a point. The aim is silence, the state of things inhabiting the center, such that in deconstruction one attacks the primacy of the center, in order to promulgate endless nonsymmetrical discourse, which some have called a "dilation" and Derrida called a "deferral."

7. Annemarie Schimmel, *The Mystery of Numbers* (New York, 1993).

8. John Hollander, "Island Pond," in *Harp Lake* (New York, 1989). Here the form is cross-cut, since its five revolving stanzas are each com-

posed of twelve lines, with complex internal rhymes. In theory these numbers produce what in music are called polyrhythms, which appear throughout modern music. Six provides maximal crossover, as the first "perfect number." Charles Palliser's *The Quincunx* (New York, 1989) derives from Browne. Chapter 75 begins: "It came to me that I was indeed insane. To find coincidences and connexions everywhere was proof of it." One might say that Palliser's narrator and the form of the sestina amount to formal devices for representing what conspiracies actually require in social terms; sixes are optimal numbers for networking.

9. W. H. Auden, "Hearing of Harvests," in *On This Island* (1937).

10. Ezra Pound, "Sestina Altaforte," in *Personae* (1926), 28–29. The Elizabeth Bishop sestina appears in *The Complete Poems: 1927–1979* (New York, 1979), 18–19.

11. "The Bound Man," in *Ilse Aichinger,* ed. J. C. Allridge (London, 1969), 48–64.

12. Samuel Daniel, *Poems and A Defence of Ryme* (Chicago, 1965), ed. Arthur D. Sprague. The *Defence* draws a strong analogy between the idea of the State and the development of poetic forms, as Shelley's *Defence* and *Democratic Vistas* were later to do.

13. Merrill's interviews with Vendler and Bornhauser give his thoughts on sci-fi for poetry—"The simplest science book is over my head." See *Recitatives: Prose by James Merrill,* ed. J. D. McClatchy (San Francisco, 1986).

14. Wallace Stevens, "A Clear Day and No Memories," in *Opus Posthumus: Poems/Plays/Prose,* ed. Milton J. Bates (New York, 1989), 138–39.

15. John Ashbery, "Sunrise in Suburbia," in *The Double Dream of Spring,* reprinted in *The Mooring of Starting Out* (New York, 1997), 262.

16. Harold Bloom, *Figures of Capable Imagination* (New York, 1976), 202–03.

17. William Cowper, "The Castaway," in *Poems,* ed. Hugh I'Anson Fausset (London, 1966), 175–77.

18. Algernon Swinburne's "Complaint of Lisa," *The Complete Works,* ed. Sir Edmund Gosse and Thomas Wise (London, 1925), vol. 3, 37. Shoptaw tells us that Ashbery had not consulted the *Decameron* for the original of the story.

19. Paul Valéry: "Poetry and Abstract Thought," in *The Art of Poetry*, tr. Denise Folliot (New York, 1961), 59–62. Valéry regarded this musical component as an absolute essential for poetry. The prime, egregious, even disastrous aspect of most prosified American "free verse," of "confessional" or "social" realism in American poetry today, is that they are oblivious to the musical principles and origin of verse. Tin ears abound. This no doubt arises partly from the low-grade orthodox view that "anyone can be President," which disgracefully may be true of the presidency, where dubious chicanery at the ballot box allows "the numbers" to confer status, but was never true for a serious art-form, where despite all short-term uncertainties in taste there is a critique of judgment at work, and quality is recognized as superior to quantity. On the other hand, there is something important about so many wishing to "express themselves."

13. Coherence

1. The allusion here is to Kurt Gödel's Incompleteness Theorem, which proved that a system may be either complete (with all its derivations actually or potentially worked out and proven) or consistent, all steps in its proof being consistently derived from logically consistent axioms, but in principle no system such as the *Principia Mathematica* can be *both complete and consistent at once.* For a clear and not unduly technical account, see Ernest Nagel and James R. Newman, *Gödel's Proof* (New York, 1958), 94: "the axioms of a deductive system are 'complete' if every true statement that can be expressed in the system is formally deducible from the axioms. If this is not the case, that is, if not every true statement expressible in the system is deducible, the axioms are 'incomplete.'" The critical point, for me as for Gödel, is that this proof is true only on the condition that the axioms of our paradigm case, arithmetic, are incomplete *only so long as they are consistent.* Completeness and consistency are reciprocals of each other, in this light. Nagel and Newman's most readily available example of this opposed relationship comes from Euclid's geometry, where every theorem is *apparently* consistent in its derivation from first principles, the axioms. But, as Nagel and Newman observe, "Euclid showed remarkable insight in treating his famous paral-

lel axiom [in effect that parallel lines never meet] as an assumption logically independent of his other axioms. For, as was subsequently proved, this axiom cannot be derived from his remaining assumptions, so that without it the set of axioms is incomplete" (56, n. 9). Plane geometry—"Euclid"—as I learned to my distress in school, was to be treated as fully consistent throughout its derivations. But no one ever told me that the axiomatic edifice was necessarily subject to a Gödelian incompleteness. That natural fact, as I think of it, would perhaps have reassured me. For a brilliant and justly admired "popular" exposition of Gödel's Proof, see Douglas Hofstader's *Gödel/Escher/Bach,* which has been reissued by Basic Books (New York, 2002). My own take on Gödel is literary.

In poetics we back away from the logician's and mathematician's analysis of abstracted system. We have nothing that is expressed in ordinary, natural languages that approaches the purity of symbolism available to mathematics, where science constructs questions of concrete mathematical centrality, such as the one already given: is Euclid's geometry complete and also consistent? Instead, we may say that Nature shows many empirical signs of systems being more or less complete, more or less consistent, and then we find ourselves agreeing with Gödel; we pragmatically pit comprehension and coherence against analysis and consistency, and this distinction serves our real-world existence. Poetry treats our experience as living with more loosely paradoxical terms, a vague preference forced upon us by realistic physical limitations, often expressible only in terms of probabilities. The Incompleteness Theorem seems to be, for literature, another way of saying that such imaginative arts live inside the limits of logical paradox, especially paradoxes of self-reference. Metaphor defines the ordinary language equivalent of the Theorem, since metaphor earns a kind of completeness at the price of manifest inconsistency, while the obverse of this statement will also be true. On the uses of paradox in Gödel, see Hermann Weyl, *Philosophy of Mathematics and Natural Science* (New York, 1963), "The Structure of Mathematics," 219–36. Our poetry has to be at home with lived contradictions, such as, for example, the one that shapes the mapmaker's paradox that we cannot simultaneously and exactly represent *both* the shape of our world and its area. We can geometrically project the spherical shape, or we can project the "flat" area, but we cannot accurately have both at once. In a real-world sense, then, we live in a world whose natural shape and natural size are always at odds, a fact well understood by the old English metaphysical poets, who belonged to the age of Mercator. Hence the interest of Donne's compasses and "flat mappe" and Marvell's "world enough and time." Donne's "Good Friday: Riding Westward" seems particularly Riemannian. On a similar case of early modern English knowledge of these matters, see Elbert N. S. Thompson, "Milton's Knowledge of Geography," in *Studies in Philology* 16, 2 (1910), 148–71, especially 165, on Mercator's 1633 atlas, published in Amsterdam. Common knowledge was not unacquainted with one major fact: at sea, when sailors climbed to the masthead, they saw what many laborers working flat areas of land (like Clare's) might never see, Earth's curvature. So much for the idea that it was hard for *everyone* to believe that the Earth was round!

2. Auerbach, *Mimesis,* 540, 549, especially, where insignificant exterior occurrences in a Virginia Woolf narrative are shown to "release" ideas and chains of ideas, permitting her to interpret and extract meanings from "the onrush of new experience . . . in the random moment." Woolf's play of consciousness seems to accord mental states a different process than that projected by the great Romantic poets, a consciousness released by external things rather than preconditioned "great" ideas of things. In this sense *A Room of One's Own,* although discursive, is the archetype of an environment-poem, not to mention the novels where characters engage in elusive searching for the horizon. On these works, see Patricia Ondek Lawrence, *The Reading of Silence: Virginia Woolf in the English Tradition* (Stanford, 1991).

3. Harry Berger, Jr., *Second World and Green World: Studies in Renaissance Fiction-Making* (Berkeley, 1988), especially on the "ecology of mind" and period concepts, 41–62.

4. George Johnson, *Fire in the Mind: Science, Faith and the Search for Order* (New York, 1995), draws an environmental picture of the science of complexity, as developing at the Santa Fe Institute, by showing contexts from Northern New Mexico. Johnson's expertise as general science writer enables him to convey the reading of ecosystems as complex informational transfers, and allows one to imagine that the Gaia Hypothesis, while admittedly "poetic," can lead to a quantifiable sense of

meaning for the Timaean term "global." For the latter, see J. E. Lovelock, "A Numerical Model for Biodiversity," *Philosophical Transactions of the Royal Society,* London, 338/383 (1992). Of course, all mathematical treatment of macro-ecological data, as gathered for example by James Brown and his University of New Mexico colleagues, and indeed almost all ecological data assembled today, the world over, will be put into service in ever larger frames of reference, as "the scale of life" becomes more available for computerized analysis and display.

5. One reason we call something prosaic is that its causes are familiar. One asks: is poetry less causal in form than prose? The prosaic seems to imply that, although we may not reflect on the fact, our sense of a given action is that it is causally familiar ("he cheated on her, so she took revenge"). There is something about poetry that interferes with such a sense of causal efficiency, probably the turning implied by "verse." Prose is a *prorsus, pro-versus,* a pro-verting or forward-turning of language. Traditionally the *prosa oratio* is speech going straight ahead without turns of the kind poetry always employs, even if subtle in its manifestation, as in free verse. Clearly this latter mode or genre makes it easier to let probability "just happen" in the utterance, and yet we find no more "causality" in free verse than in any other kind, perhaps for modern historical reasons. Our exemplars, Clare, Whitman, and Ashbery, all diminish the strictures of regular recurrence to the point that they can move always forward, without having to fit any rhymes, rhythms, figures of recurrence into a sequence of probable predications. Ironically, the *prorsus* that implies at first a steady forward movement does not imply direction, and in environment-poems it resists the strong Western habit: "We must find the end, get to the bottom, of this."

6. Emerson, in *Representative Men,* ch. VII, "Goethe; or the Writer," *LA,* 746.

7. Bjørn Lomborg, *The Skeptical Environmentalist: Measuring the Real State of the World* (Cambridge, 2001). Responding to a 2001 interview with Lomborg, BBC viewers came down on both sides of the question, although there seems to be a passionate directness of expression among those who claim to see environments degraded before their very eyes. Activism is direct, special interests are indirect, it seems (see for this archive: *news.bbc.co.uk/1/hi/talking point*). Seeking balanced views, the

reader should consult Lawrence Buell, *Writing for an Endangered World: Literature, Culture, and Environment in the U.S. and Beyond* (Cambridge, Mass., 2001). Matching concern with caution, Buell gives a variety of central literary perspectives.

8. Helen Vendler, *Seamus Heaney* (Cambridge, Mass., 1998).

9. See Eric A. Havelock, "Thoughtful Hesiod," in *Yale Classical Studies,* 20 (1966), 61–72.

For a detailed ecological account of the poem, see *Hesiod's Works and Days,* tr. and ed. David W. Tandy and Walter C. Neale (Berkeley, 1996), and specifically 42–48 and n. 9, on "the good strife" as "economic competition." For a much larger background to Hesiod's environmental-poem, see Mitchell H. Miller, Jr., "The Implicit Logic of Hesiod's Cosmogony: An Examination of *Theogony,* 116–133," in *Independent Journal of Philosophy,* 4 (Paris, 1983), 131–42.

10. Virgil, *Georgics,* tr. and ed. L. P. Wilkinson (New York, 1982), 21, 42 (on the Orpheus story).

11. Edward W. Soja, *Postmodern Geographies: The Reassertion of Space in Critical Social Theory* (London, 1990), 118–37.

12. Harold Bloom, *Genius: A Mosaic of One Hundred Exemplary Creative Minds* (New York, 2002), 512, in his introduction to Luis de Camoëns.

13. Hermann Weyl, *Philosophy of Mathematical and Natural Science* (New York, 1963), 234. What might be called the formal character of a natural environment is described by Weyl in this way: "In a phenomenology of nature one will have to deal not only with categories of objects, as 'bodies' or 'events,' but also with whole categories that are prior to all construction, e.g., with the continuum of color qualities" (233). This difference occurs always in experimental psychology, as when measuring visual perception of perceptual constancies, for example, size or color constancy. What "units" of measurement, we ask, are going to fit the uninterrupted continuum of the appearance of colors? In the history of art, literature, and music Impressionism arises along with a new awareness of these difficulties.

14. Marianne Moore, *Selected Letters,* ed. Bonnie Costello (London, 1998), 528. Costello extends Moore's notion of poetic rhythm: "John Ashbery's Landscapes,' in *The Tribe of John: Ashbery and Contemporary*

Poetry (Tuscaloosa, 1995), 60–80, where she maps the weaving lines of his poetic reverie.

15. Frederick Pottle, "Eye and the Object in the Poetry of Wordsworth," in *Romanticism and Consciousness,* ed. Harold Bloom (New York, 1970), 278.

16. *Moby Dick* perfectly suggests the stresses of rendering an environment; in 1851 a Scotch reviewer wrote: "The information thus afforded is the only redeeming part in the work, for assuredly both the story and style are sufficiently absurd," as if the information were not what caused the "story and style" to fall out of balance. But then in 1899 a certain Archibald MacMechan (an Ontario Scot, it would seem) wrote that there was in the novel "more than a hint of bombast . . . it is full of reading and is full of thought and allusion; but its chief charm is its freedom from all scholastic rules and conventions. Melville is a Walt Whitman of prose." See Parker and Harrison's Norton edition (New York, 2002). In 1907 Joseph Conrad wrote Sir Humphrey Milford, declining to write an introduction for a World's Classics reprint of *Moby Dick,* saying that "Lately I had in my hand *Moby Dick.* It struck me as a rather strained rhapsody with whaling for a subject and not a single sincere line in the 3 volumes of it." Conrad also told Sir Humphrey that he thought nothing of *Typee* and *Omoo.*

17. *Selected Literary Criticism: Henry James,* ed. Morris Shapira (New York, 1964), 180.

18. Ibid., "Honoré de Balzac" (1902), 193.

19. Richard Howard, *Trappings: New Poems* (New York, 1999), 67–69.

20. *Selected Literary Criticism,* "Emile Zola," 245–46, and 251.

21. Ibid., "Emerson" (1887), 84. This essay catches all the Emersonian conflicts, poised or stretched between the "the moral world" and the yearning for natural science.

22. James Lovelock's Gaia vision, though he is a practical and theoretically sophisticated physical scientist, has been attacked on grounds of its antihumanism, as if he advocated that humans matter less than a well-adjusted natural planet of nonhuman living things—see Luc Ferry, *The New Ecological Order,* tr. Carol Volk (Chicago, 1995), 71. I prefer to think of Gaia as suggesting a Timaean ecological model, where interactions among species would inevitably include humans at the highest level of

importance. But it is also true that ecological concerns may be masking atavistic, anti-enlightenment points of view.

23. Ludwig von Bertalanffy, *Problems of Life: An Evaluation of Modern Biological and Scientific Thought* (New York, 1960), ch. 5, 147–73.

24. For the Lawrence poems, see V. De Sola Pinto and F. W. Roberts, eds., *The Complete Poems of D. H. Lawrence* (New York, 1971), 645, 648. Note that ecofictions like Karel Capek's *R. U. R.* (origin of the robot) and *The Insect Play* both belong to the early 1920s; in Capek's brilliant science fiction novel, *The War with the Newts* (1936), the robotic is again tied to commerce and in setting is given an almost Conradian twist.

14. Precious Idiosyncrasy

1. "Policy Made Personal: Whitman's Verse and Prose—Salient Traits," in *Leaves of Grass: One Hundred Years After,* ed. Milton Hindus (Stanford, 1955), 74–108. Reprinted, Harold Bloom, ed., *Walt Whitman* (New York, 1985), 55–65. It has always been a fundamental of political thought in the West as to whether and how the individual is to participate in a fully democratic polity, and we know how questionable the democratic ideal would have to be for the ancient Greeks, but there is no lack of extant basic thinking and deliberation on this vexed topic. On the radical psychological source of democratic participation, see *Plato's Sophist: Part II of the Being of the Beautiful,* tr. with commentary by Seth Benardete (Chicago, 1986), 141–42. For Whitman, we ask: how can one thing be joined to another? Benardete observes the fluid and imprecise Platonic terminology—a "sharing," a "participating, *(metechein),*" a "taking part," a "commingling," a "receiving," a "fitting together," along with several variant terms in the Greek.

2. "L'Estate": in *Autumn Eros and Other Poems* (New York, 1991), 58.

3. "The Evening of Greuze": in *Chinese Whispers: Poems* (New York, 2002), 53.

4. "Triphammer Bridge": in *Selected Poems: Expanded Edition* (New York, 1986), 88.

5. "He 'Digesteth Harde Yron'": in *The Complete Poems of Marianne Moore* (New York, 1967), 100.

6. "Sparkles from the wheel": *NTN,* 389.

7. Perhaps Tocqueville questioned the uncritical "ideas" of the Americans because he had observed (Ch. XVII, 431) that "General Jackson is a slave of the majority; he yields to its wishes, its propensities, and its demands—say, rather, anticipates and forestalls them." And he perceived the conflict between a highly "informed" people who were not much given to thinking things through, especially for themselves as individuals. This seemingly odd combination had often been noticed by European visitors.

8. Richard Chase, *Walt Whitman Reconsidered* (New York, 1955), 137.

9. "You will see that all my parts cohere": *NTN,* 769.

10. "In one of his last letters": See *The Letters of Wallace Stevens,* ed. Holly Stevens (New York, 1966), 870–71.

11. "This disintegration": See Harry Berger, Jr. *Fictions of the Pose,* 255–57, 259, 271, and 557 n. 20. Berger and Norman Bryson use the French *désaggrégation* to mean, for example, "the breaking or fracturing of domestic space" in Dutch painting. See also Norman Bryson, *Looking at the Overlooked: Four Essays on Still Life Painting* (Cambridge, Mass., 1990), 96–135. The general question is this, and it includes poetry in the modern period: to what extent must an array of scenes and the like be subjected to a prearranged ordering, a posing; was the Hudson river a "posed" landscape at that time, if no longer? Posing a landscape had already occurred in the art of the picturesque. Can a scene "pose" as if coming apart into separate elements?

12. Clare, "The Shepherd's Tree," in *The Midsummer Cushion,* eds. Kelsey Thornton and Anne Tibble (Carcanet Press, 1990), 387; titled as "Salter's Tree," in *Selected Poetry and Prose of John Clare,* eds. Eric Robinson and Geoffrey Summerfield (Oxford, 1979), 163.

13. *Democratic Vistas,* in *LA,* 942. Emerson's guiding idea for democracy was that each citizen "become a law, or *series of laws,* unto himself." The serial character of this discovered law is part of a biophysical set of metaphors that controls all of Emerson's thinking. "Cohesion at all cost" is a phrase from *Democratic Vistas,* in *LA,* 941, where Whitman is discussing "savage, reactionary, clamors and demands." As always, he is balancing the opposed claims of "the origin-idea of the singleness of man," from "the mass, or lump character," of the aggregate. He knew that a failure to adjust this balance would leave the country "stain'd with much blood."

14. "Whitman was already plural": See the beautiful Prologue to *Leaves of Grass,* reprinted in *Selected Non-Fictions,* ed. Eliot Weinberger (New York, 1999), 447. No poet was more important to Borges, ever since he had first read *Leaves of Grass* in 1915 or 1916, apparently having first read him in German translation, and then shortly, in an English edition. Borges seems to have resonated with Whitman's voice throughout his life, perhaps because he too was always "plural." The same connections occur with Neruda and other Central and South American poets.

15. "Enclosure," in John Clare, *Selected Poems,* eds. J. W. Tibble and Anne Tibble (London, 1965), 114.

16. Thomas Browne, "The Huntsmen": in *The Garden of Cyrus. OR, The Quincunciall, Lozenge, or Net-work Plantations of the Ancients, Artificially, Naturally, Mystically Considered* (1658). Opposite this title page Browne placed an illustration of rhomboidal patterning. The treatise is included in *Religio Medici and Other Works,* ed. L. C. Martin (Oxford, 1964), where the quotation appears on pages 174–75.

Index